# BLUE STAR LINE

## Fleet List & History

## IAN COLLARD

AMBERLEY

*Above: Costa Rican Star.* (Chris Brooks/ShipFoto)

First published 2014

Amberley Publishing
The Hill, Stroud
Gloucestershire, GL5 4EP

www.amberley-books.com

Copyright © Ian Collard 2014

The right of Ian Collard to be identified as the Author
of this work has been asserted in accordance with the
Copyrights, Designs and Patents Act 1988.

ISBN 978 1 4456 4557 5 (print)
ISBN 978 1 4456 4566 7 (ebook)

All rights reserved. No part of this book may be reprinted
or reproduced or utilised in any form or by any electronic,
mechanical or other means, now known or hereafter invented,
including photocopying and recording, or in any information
storage or retrieval system, without the permission in writing
from the Publishers.

British Library Cataloguing in Publication Data.
A catalogue record for this book is available from the British Library.

Typeset in 10pt on 12pt Sabon.
Typesetting and Origination by Amberley Publishing.
Printed in the UK.

# BLUE STAR LINE: A HISTORY

William Vestey, 1st Baron Vestey, was an industrialist and food importer with his business partner, Sir Edmund Hoyle Vestey. He was born on 21 January 1859 to Samuel Vestey, a Yorkshireman, Liverpool store owner and merchant. Samuel operated a business in Liverpool, buying and selling provisions which he imported from North America. William and Edmund were both educated at the Liverpool Institute and after leaving school at twelve years of age they were employed in the family business.

At seventeen years of age William travelled to the United States to purchase goods for his father's business and established a canning factory in Chicago, where he made corned beef, which was shipped back to Liverpool. The management of the cannery was later given to Edmund. Vestey Brothers was a partnership formed by William and Edmund in 1879 to consolidate their interests in the meat trade with retail shops and cold stores. They acted as wholesale merchants by purchasing from existing meat importers and the business prospered with the expansion of the population during the Industrial Revolution.

In February 1882, the *Dunedin* sailed from Port Chalmers to London with a cargo of frozen meat. She arrived in Britain in May and had been chartered by the New Zealand & Australian Land Company to carry a cargo of 4,311 carcasses of mutton and 598 of lamb, which totalled 130 tons. Another cargo of 150 tons of frozen meat was shipped on the New Zealand Shipping Company's *Mataura* a couple of months later.

The Australian John Harrison had attempted to develop a refrigeration system using a vapour compression system in 1879 but this failed due to leakage of the ammonia refrigerant. In the same year a successful system was installed in Anchor Line's *Circassia*, and another in the *Strathleven* in 1880. At the time it was imperative that a system was devised to transport meat by sea as demand was increasing in Europe and meat producers in Australia and New Zealand were left with surplus capacity they could not export. The ability to export meat and dairy products from countries in the Southern Hemisphere enabled them to earn capital to purchase goods and supplies from the industrial countries in the north.

William travelled to Argentina in 1890 and shipped frozen partridges, beef and mutton back to Britain. In 1897 they established the Union Cold Storage & Ice Company in Liverpool, which provided refrigerated stores at home and abroad and was also a vital part of the distribution network for their products. The company became the Union Cold Storage Company Limited in 1903 and the brothers began to diversify into different types of perishable goods such as eggs, chicken and other products from China. However, the main source of meat was Argentina, from where they shipped back to Britain by the Royal Mail Steam Packet Company. The Vestey brothers were unhappy with the rates charged by the shipping company and chartered ships on single voyages to bring the refrigerated meat back to the United Kingdom. It was clear to the brothers that their profits could be increased if they were able to reduce the amount paid to transport the meat back to the United Kingdom.

In 1909 the Vesteys purchased two refrigerated ships from Shaw, Savill & Albion. However, after only one voyage both ships were chartered to the Russian government to work out of Vladivostok as mother ships to the Siberian salmon fishing industry. Thomas B. Royden's *Indraghiri* was purchased in 1910 and was renamed *Brodstone*. The Union Cold Storage Company Limited formed the Blue Star Line in 1911, with offices at Holland House, Bury Street, London EC3 and a branch in Liverpool. The company was registered on 28 July 1911, with a capital of £100,000. The two ships that had been owned since 1909 were transferred from Vestey Brothers' ownership to that of single companies named after the ships. These companies were managed by the Blue Star Line.

The company began operations with *Brodstone*, *Broderick*, *Brodmore*, *Brodland* and *Brodvale*. In November 1912, *Brodvale* carried a cargo of coal from Barry Docks to Shanghai, bringing back frozen pork to Britain. She was then transferred to the South American service. *Brodland* was wrecked when she went aground on Aberavon beach in South Wales in 1913 and William Vestey became Sir William Vestey, Bart in the same year. Over the following years the Vesteys acquired a butchery business, a chain of retail shops in Britain and freezing works in Australia and New Zealand. From cattle raising farms in Brazil, Venezuela and Australia and meat processing factories in Argentina, Uruguay, New Zealand and Australia to shipping, cold storage and retail outlets in the United Kingdom, the Vestey empire controlled every link in the chain of supply in the meat trade.

The company owned five vessels at the beginning of the First World War. *Brodhurst* was purchased on the stocks and became the first new ship for Blue Star, although she was originally ordered for W. H. Stott (Baltic) Steamers Limited. *Broderick* was requisitioned by the government to transport frozen meat to British troops abroad but she was torpedoed and sunk off Hastings on 29 April 1918 on a voyage from London to Puerto Cabello.

Demand for meat during the war meant that the company needed to acquire additional tonnage and *Morayshire*, *Banffshire* and *Nairnshire* were purchased from the Scottish Shire Line, becoming *Brodliffe*, *Brodness* and *Brodholme* respectively. The Federal Steam Navigation Company's *Surrey* was purchased and renamed *Brodfield*, and *Kent* became *Brodlea*. *Rakaia* was purchased from the New Zealand Shipping Company and renamed *Brodmead*, increasing the size of the fleet to eleven ships. *Brodliffe* was used as a meat carrier for the armed forces and served as a collier until 1917. She was built for the New Zealand meat trade and had a refrigerated capacity of 278,000 cubic feet. *Nairnshire* and *Banffshire* were built for the Elderslie Steamship Company, a subsidiary of Turnbull, Martin & Company. *Nairnshire* had a capacity of 309,674 cubic feet and *Banffshire* was capable of carrying 100,000 carcasses of mutton in her completely insulated foreholds.

In Madagascar they set up a French subsidiary, Compagnie Generale Frigorifique, and with two coastal vessels they transported live and tinned meat from coastal ports to the abattoirs of Majunga, where it was processed. The two lighters were named *General Pau* and *General Foch* and were designed to tow the *General Jarvoni* and *General Marcus* around the coast of Madagascar. This operation lasted until the end of the First World War.

*Montilla* and *Rubiera* were delivered in 1917 and cost £100,000 each. *Brodness* was sunk by a submarine off the Italian coast in March 1917, *Brodstone* was lost on 15 August and *Brodmore* was torpedoed north-west of Marsa Susa on 27 December that year. At the end of the First World War, the company had lost five ships and had seen the delivery of three new vessels to give it a fleet of nine ships. However, the majority of the fleet were over twenty years of age and a replacement programme was discussed by the company. The G-type vessels *War Hecuba* and *War Sharon* were acquired from the Shipping Controller and became *Albionstar* and *Royalstar* respectively. *Empirestar* and *Normanstar* were delivered by Dunlop, Bremner & Company Limited at Port Glasgow. However, *Normanstar* as *Almeda* went aground on a sandbank following her launching on 19 April 1919 and remained there until 30 April, when she was finally towed to the fitting out basin. *Canonesa* was purchased from Furness-Houlder Argentine Lines in 1919 and renamed *Magicstar*.

The Blue Star Line (1920) Limited was formed on 31 March 1920 to manage or bare-boat charter the fleet of sixteen vessels. These were:

| Vessel | Built | grt | cu. ft refr. | Speed (kts) |
| --- | --- | --- | --- | --- |
| *Albionstar* | 1919 | 7,946 | 368,590 | 12 |
| *Celticstar* | 1918 | 5,575 | 286,699 | 12 |
| *Empirestar* | 1919 | 7,199 | 388,168 | 12 |
| *Gaelicstar* | 1917 | 5,595 | 289,457 | 12 |
| *Gothicstar* | 1899 | 5,713 | 324,318 | 11 |
| *Ionicstar* | 1917 | 5,602 | 289,457 | 12 |
| *Magicstar* | 1893 | 5,534 | 315,234 | 12 |
| *Miltonstar* | 1914 | 3,071 | 152,080 | 9 |
| *Normanstar* | 1919 | 6,817 | 347,408 | 11 |
| *Romanstar* | 1895 | 5,617 | 323,696 | 10 |
| *Royalstar* | 1919 | 7,900 | 431,417 | 12 |
| *Saxonstar* | 1899 | 5,527 | 332,850 | 10 |
| *Stuartstar* | 1899 | 5,736 | 221,280 | 10½ |
| *Tudorstar* | 1899 | 6,837 | 224,786 | 10½ |
| *Tuscanstar* | 1898 | 6,900 | 278,814 | 10 |
| *Vikingstar* | 1920 | 6,445 | 323,697 | 10 |

However, the Union Cold Storage Company Limited became the registered owner of many of the ships mainly for tax purposes. Black and white bands were added to the bottom of the black top on the funnel and the darker pillar-box red was changed to bright orange. The company was not a member of the South American Freight Conference and consequently were forced to voyage out in ballast. Edmund was created a baronet in 1921 and the following year his brother became Lord Kingswood for his role in making food more widely available.

*Doricstar* was introduced in 1921 and was a specialised ship designed for the expanding trade with South America. She was the largest vessel in the fleet, with twin turbines giving her a service speed of 14 knots. She had a cargo capacity of 461,000 cu. ft and was registered as owned by Eastman's Limited, a butchers' shop chain within the group of businesses. Commercial Properties Limited was formed in 1922, with offices at 14 West Smithfield, London EC1, and took over all the retail outlets, including Eastman's, together with all the non-maritime interests. The Union Cold Storage Company Limited took over all the vessels, with Blue Star Line (1920) as managers. The British & Argentine Meat Company Limited was acquired in 1923.

The French-registered refrigerated cargo vessel *La Perouse* was acquired from Société Générale d'Armements Maritimes in 1924 and was renamed *Trojanstar*. She was one of six sister ships, of which *Cumberland*, *Westmoreland* and *Devon* were British and three were French. Union Cold Storage purchased *Kaolack* and *Britanica*, which was used at Buenos Aires for local feeder services in the River Plate. Although the company owned the Argentine subsidiary Soc. Anon. Frigorifico 'Anglo', *Britanica* did not join their fleet of *Anglo No. 1* and *Anglo No. 2*.

In 1925 the company expanded their services to the Pacific coast of North America and this was maintained as an all-year-round service. An order for nine new ships was announced in May, with a total cost of £3,500,000. Vestey claimed that giving the orders for the ships to British shipyards would cost the company around £300,000, against taking the lower tenders from foreign yards. He said, 'We do this willingly, because we believe that it is in the best interests of the company that we should make this sacrifice.' It was claimed that foreign shipyards were able to quote a price of £18,000 per 12,000 tons deadweight less than the lowest British price.

The first contract was for the building of two cargo passenger vessels and this was placed with Lithgow's Limited at Port Glasgow in June 1925. This was followed by an order for two passenger liners, costing £610,000, and this was placed with John Brown & Company Limited on the Clyde. Palmers at Jarrow received an order for two cargo vessels with accommodation for twelve passengers, and three passenger cargo ships were ordered from Cammell Laird & Company Limited at Birkenhead. It is interesting to note that the cost of the refrigeration plants for the vessels ordered from Palmers was not included in the construction and delivery price. Separate orders were later placed for this equipment.

*Stuartstar* was launched in March 1926, followed by *Rodneystar*, *Africstar* and *Napierstar*. Four of the five passenger liners were also launched in 1926: *Almeda* in June; *Andalucia* and *Avila* in September; and *Avelona* in December that year. *Arandora* was launched on 14 January 1927; and the following month the company opened a new passenger service from London to Lisbon, the Canary Islands, Rio de Janeiro, Santos, Montevideo and Buenos Aires. The service became fortnightly by the end of the year. The accommodation on *Avila* was described as equal to

anything afloat and included a large proportion of singles and double cabins and rooms with private bathrooms.

*Stuartstar* sailed from the Tyne on 12 July 1928, following the fitting of pulverised fuel burners of the short flame type to one of her single-ended boilers by Clark, Chapman & Company Limited. This was an experiment that proved successful and following this all boilers were similarly treated.

The Admiralty tops on the 'A' class vessels' funnels were removed in 1928 and Commonwealth & Dominion Line's *Port Albany* was purchased the following year and renamed *Oregonstar*. *Magicstar* was then sold and broken up. Two 'G' type vessels, *Wangaratta* and *Woodarra*, were acquired from the British India Steam Navigation Company and renamed *Tacoma Star* and *Fresno Star* for service on the north Pacific routes. *Sultan Star* was ordered from Cammell Laird & Company Limited at Birkenhead and *Tuscan Star* from Palmer's at Jarrow. She was the first motorship to be owned by the company. *Sultan Star* and *Tuscan Star* were the first new vessels to be launched with the new style of naming. The 'A' class vessels' names were similar to some of those of the 'A' class liners owned by the Royal Mail Line and the new scheme helped to clarify the situation when they received their 'Star' names.

In 1929 *Arandora* was converted into a first class cruise liner by Fairfield's at Glasgow. She was built to carry 164 passengers and the conversion increased this number to 400. Three compartments were fitted on the main deck and two on the bridge deck, extending forward over the saloon, and aft over the filled-in after well. The forward well was also filled in and the cargo space was taken. An electric lift was installed, as were a swimming pool and a ballroom with 15,000 square feet of dancing space. The conversion cost around £200,000. On 15 April 1930 the name of the company was changed to the Blue Star Line Limited and the 'Star' was added to the five 'A' class passenger vessels. It was also decided to split the names of the other ships into two words.

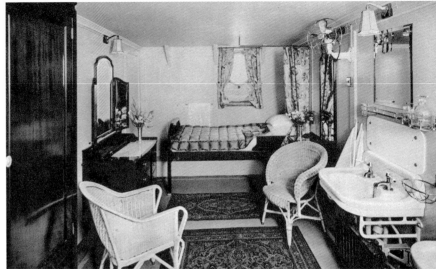

*Above left: Arandora Star* Smoke Room.

*Above right: Arandora Star* two-berth stateroom.

*Below: Arandora Star* at Balholm.

*Arandora Star* anchored at Malta.

Each cruise passenger received a booklet describing *Arandora Star* which said that it was intended for:

Visitors who are interested in their historical associations and ancient buildings, others in the scenery, while others take pleasure in observing the manners and customs of different people. There are also these – generally younger passengers – whose main object is to participate in the pleasures of life which a new place offers.

The booklet described *Arandora Star* as follows:

The *Arandora Star* is solely a Cruising Liner and spends the whole year round taking happy people to beautiful places in the sunshine. She is known in practically every port in the Mediterranean; in summer months she goes beyond the Arctic Circle, and while Great Britain is enduring the fogs and frosts of winter she is far away in the West Indies or the Pacific. Wherever she goes she excites admiration. The graceful lines of her spotless white hull and her bright red funnels with a blue star in a white circle make an unsurpassable picture of ship beauty.

She is 16,000 tons gross – the ideal size for a cruising liner, as her draught enables her to get into ports impossible for larger ships. Her full complement is 400 passengers, who have ample room for exercise and sport on her spacious decks. Overcrowding is unknown. Her engines are oil-driven and her average speed is 15 knots. Above all, the *Arandora Star* is a splendid sea-boat, being equipped with the latest devices to ensure steadiness at sea. Internally, the *Arandora Star* is sumptuously appointed. There is no more beautiful cruising liner afloat. Every room is decorated and furnished in good taste and passenger's comforts are provided for in the most minute degree. The cuisine is of the highest order. Sport and pastimes of every kind can be enjoyed. The energetic can exercise themselves to the top of their bent and those who are cruising for quiet restfulness can find sunny corners where they are undisturbed by the noise of games.

There are six decks on the *Arandora Star*. They are distinguished by letters, as follows – The Main Deck is 'A', the Upper Deck 'B', the Bridge Deck 'C', the Promenade Deck 'D', the Upper Promenade Deck 'E', and over 'E' is the Observation Deck. The numbering of the staterooms commences on 'A' deck. No. 1 is situated on the Port (left) side forward, No. 2 on the Starboard (right) side. Odd numbers are always on the Port side and even numbers on the Starboard. The highest number (275) is on 'E' deck. The entire forward portion of 'B' deck is taken up by the beautiful Louis XIV Dining Saloon, which accommodates all the passengers in one sitting. The Chief Steward's office is near the Dining

Saloon door. Towards the other end of the deck is the Shore Excursion Office, where information regarding the attractions of the various ports of call is obtained. Near it is the Photographic dark room.

Ascending to 'C' Deck we find the Purser's Office, the Doctor's Surgery and the Ladies' and Gentlemen's Hairdressing Rooms. Forward of these is the splendid Entrance Hall, from which wide stairs go down to the Dining Saloon and up to the Lounge. The ship's Shop, in which is stocked a large assortment of articles which experience has proved are in constant demand by passengers, is facing the Entrance Hall. On 'D' Deck are the main Public Rooms – the Ball Room, the Smoking Room and the Lounge. The beauty of these rooms evokes the admiration of every one who sees them. On this deck are also the quiet Card and Writing Rooms. In the Lounge is a Library of books, kept up to date from cruise to cruise. Mounting to 'E' Deck, we come to the wide spaces where Games are played. Aft is the tiled swimming pool, surrounded by the Lido deck provided with lounges for sun-bathers. Forward is the Sun Deck where those who desire quietness can recline or stroll about in the sunshine. There is also the Gymnasium fitted with horses, cycles and every modern device for keeping fit.

On the Observation Deck is a Gallery for watching the Sports on 'E' Deck. Here also are the Paddler Tennis Court and the Quoit Pitches. An orchestra of expert musicians is carried. There are also frequent Cinema Shows with the most up-to-date apparatus. A fully qualified doctor is available on board if required. Medicines are supplied free but professional attendances are charged for. No charge is made for the use of deck-chairs but rugs and deck-chair cushions may be hired on board at fixed charges. A complete and up-to-date laundry and valet service is provided on board. The *Arandora Star* carries four powerful launches which maintain a free 'ferry service' between the ship and the shore. Watches should be set by *Arandora Star* time, which is consistently maintained throughout the cruise.

Sud Americano was launched by Deutsche-Werke Kiel AG at Kiel in February 1929 for the management of Ivar A. Christensen & Company of Oslo and registered to A/S Linea Sud Americano as owners. Following her delivery, the owners disputed whether she was capable of achieving the speed stipulated in the contract and sought compensation from the builders. Following several breakdowns, the owners announced that they would be returning her to the builders as the contract had not been fulfilled. An arbitration court ruled for the shipowners, and the vessel was returned to Deutsche-Werke. The ship was laid up and given the name *Schleswig*.

In July 1931 the Blue Star Line signed a contract with the builders under which they would take the vessel and her sister ship *Holstein*. *Schleswig* was renamed *Yakima Star* and *Holstein* became *Wenatchee Star* for the North American service from the United Kingdom and Europe. Both vessels retained German registration but it was soon found that they were unsuitable for the service and the contract was terminated after one voyage of each vessel. In 1934 both vessels were sold to Hanseatische Schiffs und Betriebs GmbH, Norddeutscher Lloyd, and were rebuilt by having one funnel removed, the hull lengthened, and new engines.

The Ottawa Conference in 1932 guaranteed free entry for Dominion imports into the United Kingdom in return for preference to British imports into Dominion markets. The decision caused problems with Blue Star Lines' old established South American trade and forced them to enter Australian and New Zealand markets, which commenced in 1934.

Several of the older ships were laid up during the Great Depression. *Magicstar* was sold and broken up by Thos. W. Ward at Inverkeithing and many of the ships were forced to operate under ballast on their outward voyages to New Zealand and Australia. *Avelona Star* had one funnel and all of her accommodation removed at Greenock in 1931 and her refrigerated capacity was increased. *Almeda Star*, *Andalusia Star* and *Avila Star* were fitted with Maierform bows and lengthened during 1934–35.

"ARANDORA STAR"
CRUISES

MEDITERRANEAN

SPECIAL WHITSUN CRUISE
May 23rd — 16 days. Fare from
25 gns. Visiting Lisbon, Tangier,
Casablanca, Las Palmas, Teneriffe,
Madeira, Arosa Bay (for Santiago).
TO THE NORWEGIAN FJORDS
June 13th—13 days. Fare from
20 gns. To Ulvik, Eidfjord,
Trondhjem, Aandalsnaes, Molde,
Oie, Hellesylt, Merok, Olden,
Loen, Balholm, Gudvangen, Bergen.
TO THE NORWEGIAN FJORDS
& NORTHERN CAPITALS
To Balholm, Gudvangen, Bergen,
Eidfjord, Ulvik, Oslo, Arendal,
Christiansand, Copenhagen,
Gothenburg. June 27. From 20 gns.

& NORWAY

THE world's most bracing,
most enchanting Holiday is a
Blue Star Cruise, with the highest
standard of comfort and service
ever set in the proud traditions
of the sea. No vessel afloat can
approach the "Arandora Star" for
sheer charm, luxury and comfort.

For full particulars of these and other cruises apply to

THE BLUE STAR LINE

A new Maierform section was fitted to *Doric Star*'s bow at Jarrow in 1933 and a new liner service to Australia and New Zealand was inaugurated by *Sultan Star* and *Tuscan Star* that year. It was also decided that a second major building programme would begin and eight fully refrigerated vessels of between 11,000 and 13,000 tons were ordered from Cammell Laird & Company Limited at Birkenhead and Harland & Wolff & Company at Belfast. The Cammell Laird-built ships had a narrower funnel and all of them were oil burners, with a speed of 16 knots.

The tug *Brodstone* was built for service on the Thames by Alexander Hall & Company Limited and delivered to the Blue Star Line in 1934. *Roman Star*, *Saxon Star* and *Tudor Star* were sold in 1934 to Societa Anonima Ricuperi Metallici, Savona, and broken up following being laid up for several months. *Saxon Star* and *Roman Star* arrived at Savona within two weeks of each other, followed by *Tudor Star*. In November 1934, *Celtic Star* became the largest vessel to pass under Tower Bridge, berthing at New Fresh Wharf in the Pool of London.

*Trojan Star* had her machinery re-arranged in 1935, which enabled her to develop 50 per cent more power. An exhaust steam turbine was added to each reciprocating engine; they had already been arranged to fit superheaters to the boilers. This combination of the additional exhaust steam turbines and superheat enabled the machinery to develop increased power from the steam of the existing boiler plant. The work was carried out by North Eastern Marine Engineering Company Limited of Wallsend and the Bauer Wach exhaust turbines came from Swan Hunter & Wigham Richardson. New fuel bunkers were fitted by Smith's Dock Company, North Shields, and a new propeller came from Manganese Bronze & Brass Company Limited. The work increased the speed of *Trojan Star* to 12 knots.

1931 advertisement.

Work to enable them to operate to Australia and New Zealand was also carried out on *Stuart Star* and *Napier Star*. *Stuart Star* was built as a three-island vessel and the well decks were built up to the level of the bride deck. *Napier Star* was lengthened forward and the well decks were also built up, with a new topgallant forecastle and a Maierform bow installed. Similar modernisation was carried out on *Rodney Star*, *Afric Star* and *Trojan Star*. *Imperial Star* was delivered in January 1935 and was the first of a group of four new motorships designed to operate to Australia and New Zealand. *New Zealand Star* was followed by *Australia Star* and *Empire Star*.

Following the launch of *Dunedin Star* (1) on 29 October 1935 by Cammell Laird at Birkenhead, the Blue Star Line placed an order with the builders for another cargo liner. It was claimed that the enterprise of the Blue Star Line had been responsible for helping British shipping and the shipbuilding industry to a degree that was unequalled, probably, by any other British shipping company. In a period of under ten years they had placed or completed orders for no fewer than nineteen ships, which averaged two new ships a year.

It was estimated that 30,000 people were engaged in the business of the Union Cold Storage Company and the Blue Star Line and they had nearly £20 million of public money and nearly 40,000 small British investors. In proposing the health of Cammell Laird & Company Limited, Sir Edmund Vestey said that the order for *Dunedin Star* had been placed not by him personally, but by the Blue Star Line, and his brother Lord Vestey was working hard in promoting the trade and commerce of the country. Cammell Laird confirmed the order had been placed for another cargo vessel for the company and that two keel plates were laid before the guests left the launching platform.

*1934 advertisement.*

# 20,000 PEOPLE CAN'T BE WRONG

THAT is the number who have booked cruises on the famous Pleasure Liner "ARANDORA STAR" to date. It includes hundreds whose names are household words in the Land. All these discriminating passengers have definitely *preferred* the "Arandora Star." Large numbers have travelled half-a-dozen or more times, while several have records of 15 to 18 cruises on the "Arandora Star" to their credit. The Blue Star Line venture to think that the explanation of the above is summed up in one word—SATISFACTION. May we add your name to the list of Arandora enthusiasts?

## FORTHCOMING CRUISES INCLUDE

AUGUST 4. To Bergen, Oslo, Copenhagen and the Norwegian Fjords. | AUGUST 18. To Norway, Sweden, Denmark, Dantzig, Germany and Holland. | SEPT. 8. To Algiers, Tripoli, Naples (for Pompeii), Barcelona, Gibraltar, Lisbon.

13 Days. From 20 Gns. | 19 Days. From 30 Gns. | 19 Days. From 34 Gns.

SEPT. 29. To Tangier, Philippeville, Alexandria for Cairo, Jaffa for Jerusalem, Cyprus, Port Said, Haifa for Nazareth, Beyrout, Rhodes, Athens, Tunis, Gibraltar. | DEC. 22. To Teneriffe, Gambia, Sierre Leone, Madeira.

30 Days. From 53 Gns. | 20 Days. From 34 Gns.

## ALSO UNIQUE WINTER SUNSHINE CRUISE

To Teneriffe, St. Helena, Cape Town, Durban, Mauritius, Bali, Semarang, Batavia, Singapore, Penang, Colombo, Aden, Port Tewfik for Cairo, Port Said, Bizerta for Tunis. JAN. 26 to APRIL 11, 1935, 75 DAYS. FROM 155 Gns. INCLUSIVE

*For full details and illustrated Cruising Brochure apply:*

# BLUE STAR LINE

Passenger Office: 3 Lower Regent Street, London, S.W.1; Head Office: 40 St. Mary Axe, E.C.3; Liverpool, Birmingham, Manchester, Glasgow, Bradford, Paris and all Principal Agents.

On a voyage from Glasgow to Liverpool on 18 August 1935, *Napier Star* was in a collision with the Cunard liner *Laurentic* in thick fog 40 miles north-west of the Mersey Bar lightship. *Laurentic* took *Napier Star* in tow until tugs arrived from Liverpool, which then took over the task. Both vessels were repaired at Liverpool and *Napier Star* was sent to the Tyne for the job to be completed. *Napier Star*'s cargo was discharged and loaded onto *Fresno Star*, which sailed to New Zealand several days later. *Stuart Star* was on a voyage from Liverpool to Melbourne via Lourenço Marques in 1937. On 17 December she went ashore in thick fog near Hood Point Lighthouse and she broke her back and was abandoned.

The firm of Frederick Leyland & Company Limited was acquired in 1935 and it became a holding company, owning a number of the vessels in the Blue Star Line fleet. *Dunedin Star* was delivered in February 1936, followed by *Sydney Star* from Harland & Wolff at Belfast the following month. *Melbourne Star* was launched on 7 July 1936, and *Brisbane Star* in September that year. Both vessels were built by Cammell Laird & Company Limited at Birkenhead. The Imperial Star class of vessels proved very successful as they were fast ships of 17 knots and reduced the voyage time for the carriage of frozen meat from Australia and New Zealand.

An order was placed with Burmeister & Wain in 1937 for three vessels, which were later referred to as the 'C' class. *California Star* emerged in 1938, followed by *Canadian Star* and *Columbia Star*. *Adelaide Star* was ordered in 1938 from Burmeister & Wain and was launched on 30 December the following year. However, she was seized during fitting out and was never actually delivered to the Blue Star Line. *Millais* was acquired from the Lamport & Holt Line in 1938, becoming *Scottish Star*, and *Gothic Star* was broken up at Savona.

At the beginning of the Second World War, the Blue Star Line fleet comprised thirty-nine ships of approximately 380,000 tons and twenty-nine of these were lost during the hostilities. One of the first casualties was the *Ionic Star*, which was on a voyage from Rio de Janeiro and Santos to Liverpool. On 17 October 1939, she ran aground west of Formby Point, near the Mersey Bar lightship. She broke her back and was declared a total loss, but a small proportion of her cargo of fruit and cotton was recovered.

On 2 December that year, *Doric Star* was on a voyage from Sydney and Auckland to the United Kingdom with a cargo of refrigerated mutton, lamb, cheese and butter and a quantity of wool in bales in the 'tween decks. She was in the South Atlantic, some 1,200 miles from the Cape of Good Hope and 660 miles east by south of St Helena. The Admiralty had warned all British ships on 1 October that a German raider might be operating off the east coast of South America. This followed the sinking of the Booth Line vessel *Clement*, 75 miles south-east of Pernambuco, Brazil, on 30 September. The captain and chief engineer were taken on board the raider, which was, in fact, the pocket battleship *Admiral Graf Spee*. During October, *Admiral Graf Spee* sank four British ships on the trade route to the Cape. At 1 p.m. on 2 December a heavy shell exploded 100 yards from the *Doric Star* and this was followed by a second shell.

Captain Stubbs of *Doric Star* wrote:

I ordered the wireless operator to transmit the raider distress call, also signalled the engine room for all possible speed. After the second shot I realised it was impossible to escape so stopped the engines and ordered the wireless operator to amplify the message and state battleship attacking. By this time I could read the daylight Morse lamp from the battleship signalling 'Stop your wireless,' but I took no notice of this signal. As the battleship approached I gave orders to the engine room to stand by for scuttling, and as it appeared that our wireless call had not been heard I ordered the Chief Engineer to start and scuttle. A few minutes later the wireless operator reported that our message had been repeated by another British vessel and also a Greek vessel, so I countermanded the orders for

*Doric Star* and the *Admiral Graf Spee*, 2 December 1939. (Wallace Trickett)

scuttling, then threw overboard all confidential papers and books, breech of gun, ammunition and rifles, also all papers about cargo. After the distress call had been transmitted I ordered the wireless operator to cease transmitting, as the battle ship was exhibiting a notice: 'Stop your wireless or I will open fire.' The *Doric Star*, a 12-knot ship, with one anti-submarine gun aft, had no alternative but to obey.

A motor-boat was sent from the battleship and *Doric Star* was boarded by three officers and thirty men. Captain Stubbs was confined to his cabin and questioned and the wireless room was searched for codes and ciphers. Two of her holds were opened after Captain Stubbs told the boarding party that he was only carrying wool. As this was the last cargo to be loaded, the Germans were satisfied and the crew were given ten minutes to collect lifebelts, blankets and personal effects and were then transferred to the battleship by launch. Seven shells were fired at *Doric Star* and she was finally sunk by a torpedo. The following day the Shaw, Savill vessel *Tairoa* was attacked and sunk by *Admiral Graf Spee* and the crew joined the survivors of *Doric Star* on the battleship. Most of the 196 prisoners were transferred to the *Altmark* on 6 December. The *Graf Spee* sailed south-west towards the River Plate and was in contact with the British cruisers *Ajax*, *Achilles* and *Exeter* on 13 December. *Exeter* was badly damaged, and *Graf Spee* was followed by *Ajax* and *Achilles*. The German battleship anchored off Montevideo shortly after midnight and a German officer spoke to the prisoners: 'Gentlemen, for you the war is over. We are now in Montevideo harbour. Today you will be free.' The crew who had been transferred to the German raider *Altmark* were kept prisoner on board until she was captured by HMS *Cossack* in Josing Fjord, Norway, on the night of 16 February 1940. They finally arrived at Leith the following day.

*Stanfleet* was purchased from the Stanhope Shipping Company by the Zubi Steam Ship Company Limited in 1939 and was passed to Blue Star

ownership as *Pacific Star*. On 14 February 1940, 350 miles from Land's End on a voyage from Buenos Aires with a cargo of frozen meat and 1,000 tons of butter, *Sultan Star* was torpedoed and sank. She was commanded by Captain W. H. Bevan and had a crew of seventy-two officers and men. At 4.30 a.m. she was torpedoed on the starboard side aft and one member of her crew died in the explosion. She quickly began to settle and Captain Bevan gave the order to abandon ship. He went to the wireless office and told Mr P. Winsor, the First Wireless Officer, to leave the ship immediately. However, Mr Winsor informed him that he would when he had managed to contact other vessels. Captain Bevan remained with his ship until the last minute, and when he left his lifeboat nearly capsized and was swamped. Mr Winsor was seen hanging on to some wreckage and was eventually dragged into one of the boats. However, he had managed to alert other vessels to their plight, and two of the vessels escorting HMS *Exeter* home from the River Plate, the *Vesper* and *Whitshed*, arrived on the scene to rescue the survivors. The escorts managed to locate the U-boat, which they attacked with depth charges and destroyed. They picked up the submarine's crew, who were landed at Plymouth the following day. Captain Bevan was officially commended and Mr Winsor awarded the MBE and the Lloyds War Medal for Bravery at Sea.

In his report, Captain Bevan said, 'I think this wireless officer, Mr P. Winsor, is one of the bravest men I have ever met since going to sea.' *The London Gazette* of 24 May 1940 reported the incident as follows:

The Radio Officer continued to broadcast the SOS and the master stood by him. The ship's stern was under water, and the water was over the after end of the boat deck. The ship was going and it seemed certain death to stay another moment. He [Captain Bevan] dived over the side and struck out for the boat, which was standing by for him. As he was hauled into the boat, he looked for back for Winsor. The ship was now standing on her stern, her bows were in the air and water was going down the funnel, when he saw Winsor leave the wireless office and dash for the side. He was sliding down a rope when the ship went down. The next time he was seen he was clinging to some wreckage. The *Sultan Star* carried a deck cargo of some 200 tons in heavy barrels. These broke loose as she sank. There was the danger of bursting boilers, so the master waited for the maelstrom to die down, 'til it was safe to bring his boat to rescue Winsor. He could hear his groans as he was caught and pounded and crushed between the barrels. At last they lifted him on board, more dead than alive. It was not long before the destroyers arrived. They picked up the men from the *Sultan Star*'s boats and sank the enemy. The doctor in one of them saved Winsor's life. Winsor's gallantry and devotion to duty had brought help to his shipmates and destruction to the enemy.

*Adelaide Star* was renamed *Seeburg* when completed by the Germans on 19 November 1940. She was managed by the Hamburg America Line and used as a depot and target practice ship for the 27th U-boat flotilla. *Seeburg* was mined and sunk by the Russians off Heistevnest in Danzig Bay on 4 December 1944. She was partly raised by the Poles in 1952 and it was found that she had extensive damage to her stern. However, the engines were in good condition and she was beached at Gdynia, repaired and renamed *Dzierzynski*. In 1963 she grounded in the River Scheldt, broke her back and was scrapped at Antwerp.

*Avelona Star* was sunk by U-43 off Cape Finisterre on 30 June 1940. She had sailed from Buenos Aires for London via Santos and Freetown under the command of Captain George Ernest Hopper with a cargo that included 8,800 tons of frozen meat. She reached Freetown on 15 June, sailing the next day with the commodore of a convoy of thirty-four ships which had gone on ahead. At 10.00 a.m. on 30 June one of the ships was torpedoed and the commodore ordered an 'emergency turn'. The convoy continued to zigzag, later returning to its original course. However, twelve hours later, at 9.30 p.m.,

*Avelona Star* was torpedoed on the starboard side forward. It was described as: 'A dull thud and a huge column of water. The ship seemed to lift, and then settled with a twenty degree list to starboard. She righted herself, and then the foremost boiler blew up with clouds of smoke, ashes and steam which hid everything.' She was abandoned and later sank. The *Beignon* picked up the survivors but she was later torpedoed and abandoned. The crew of the *Beignon* and survivors of *Avelona Star* were in the water for some time but were eventually rescued by the destroyers *Vesper* and *Windsor* at 5.00 a.m. the following day. The 110 survivors from both ships were eventually landed at Plymouth and four of *Avelona*'s crew were lost.

*Wellington Star* was sunk on 16 June by U-101, also off Cape Finisterre on the return leg of her maiden voyage. *Wellington Star* had been damaged while she was fitting out at Belfast when war broke out in September 1939. She left Melbourne on 12 May, under the command of Captain Trevor Williams, with a general cargo of wool and refrigerated foodstuffs. It was a fine day, with a fresh breeze from the northward, a slight sea and full visibility. At 11.02 a.m. she was torpedoed on the starboard side between Nos 1 and 2 hatches and began to sink by the head. The captain gave orders to abandon ship and the four boats, containing the crew of sixty-nine officers and men, were lowered into the water. The ship was then hit with another torpedo and the submarine came to the surface, shelled her and set her on fire. The crew were questioned and then the submarine left them. At 4.45 p.m. *Wellington Star* rolled over and sank. The *Pierre LD* rescued most of the crew and they were taken to Casablanca. However, the boat containing Captain Williams took eight days to reach Oporto but no lives were lost in the incident.

*Arandora Star*, loaded with 1,673 people on board, including Italian and German internees and prisoners of war, was sunk west of Bloody Foreland on 3 June 1940 with a loss of 805 lives. She left Liverpool on 1 July, sailing unescorted at 15 knots and zigzagging. At 6.15 a.m. the next day she was torpedoed 75 miles west of the Bloody Foreland, County Donegal. Chief

Officer Mr F. B. Brown and Third Officer Mr W. H. Tulip were both on duty on the bridge. Four lookouts were posted but there was no sign of a submarine. The torpedo struck and exploded on the starboard side at the after engine room, which immediately flooded. All the engine room crew in this area were drowned or killed by the blast. The main and emergency generators were not working and the ship was in complete darkness. One boat on the starboard side and davits were damaged. It was reported that following the explosion most of the Germans and Italians rushed on deck, making it difficult for the crew to lower the boats.

Ten out of the twelve boats were lowered but these were overcrowded by prisoners going down the side on ladders and falls. However, many of the Italians still refused to leave the sinking ship. Captain Moulton had to leave the ship at 7.15, still attempting to get the Italians to take to the rafts. The Chief Officer later said, 'I was picked up by a boat after being in the water about twenty minutes. I saw nothing of the officers who left at the same time as I did. The vessel turned over and sank stern first almost immediately, and I think they must have been trapped as she came over.' At 9.30 a.m. a Sunderland flying boat of Coastal Command of the Royal Air Force was on the scene, dropping first-aid outfits, food and cigarettes in watertight bags. The aircraft circled around until 1.00 p.m., when the destroyer HMCS *St Laurent* arrived at full speed. She was later assisted by HMS *Walker*. The 868 survivors were landed at Greenock the following day. Captain Moulton and twelve other officers, together with forty-two of the crew of *Arandora Star*, lost their lives. Thirty-seven military guards were drowned, with 470 Italians and 243 Germans. The total death toll was 805 people of the 1,673 on board.

*Above: Arandora Star.*

*Below: Arandora Star* at Copenhagen.

*Auckland Star*, which was a sister of *Wellington Star*, was torpedoed and sunk by U-99 off Ireland on 28 July 1940 on a voyage from Townsville, Sydney, Cape Town and St Vincent, Cape Verde, to the United Kingdom, under command of Captain Rattray MacFarlane. She was about 80 miles west of Dingle Bay, Ireland, and was travelling at 16½ knots in a northerly breeze and a slight sea. At 4.00 a.m. she was torpedoed on the port side abreast of Nos 5 and 6 holds. Thirty minutes later, the captain gave orders for *Auckland Star* to be abandoned. A second torpedo was fired at 4.55 and another at 5.15, which both hit the ship. Several minutes later she rolled over to port, and sank by the stern. The crew had taken to the four boats, one of which reached Slyne Head on 30 July and the other three sailed to within 12 miles of Dingle, County Kerry. They were towed ashore the following day by a fishing boat.

On 18 December 1940 *Napier Star* was also sunk by a German U-boat. She had sailed from Liverpool to New Zealand three days earlier. On board were eighty-two officers and crew and seventeen passengers. When 300 miles to the southward of Iceland in a full gale, she was torpedoed on the port side at 3.55 p.m. She immediately listed to port and began to settle by the stern. Captain William Walsh gave the order to abandon ship and four boats were lowered. The Second Officer, Mr John Wilson Thompson, later reported that he left the ship with a boatload of twenty people, including six passengers, three of whom were women. As the boat pulled away, *Napier Star* was hit by another torpedo and sank twenty minutes later. The wind rose to a full gale and everyone on board was seasick. Four people died of exposure during the night and the gale continued for the rest of the day. Another man died of exposure that afternoon and all on board were suffering from cold and exhaustion. At 8.30 a.m. on 20 December a light from a ship was seen through the wind and spray. Flares were set off and the ship started to head towards them. The vessel was the Swedish steamer *Vaalaren* and as they came closer ladders were lowered and the survivors were hauled on board by ropes. They were landed at Liverpool three days later. The fifteen people who were rescued were the only survivors of the sinking, in which eighty-four people lost their lives. Consequently, in the first year of hostilities the Blue Star Line lost seven ships by enemy action and one by marine hazard, totalling around 95,000 gross tons.

*Almeda Star* was sunk by U-96 on 17 January 1941, 200 miles west of the Outer Hebrides, in heavy weather. Her 194 passengers and 166 of her crew were all lost. She had sailed from Liverpool on 15 January and on 17 January sent out a signal of distress. She had been torpedoed 35 miles north of Rockall and no further messages were received from her. Naval vessels were sent to search for any survivors but nothing was found belonging to her. No trace was ever found of the ship or the 360 people on board.

On 29 January *Afric Star* was sunk by the German raider *Kormoran*, who picked up her crew and transferred them to German ships, which later landed them at Bordeaux. *Afric Star* sailed from Rio de Janeiro on 15 January 1941 for the United Kingdom via St Vincent, Cape Verde Islands, with a cargo of meat. She was commanded by Captain Clement Ralph Cooper with a crew of seventy-two, two naval gunners and two women passengers. Early on 29 January she sighted a ship flying the Russian ensign which remained in sight for several hours. The ship finally caught up with her around 2.00 p.m. and as she approached she hoisted the German flag, showed her guns and opened fire. *Afric Star* caught fire and the crew abandoned the ship.

The German raider *Kormoran* took the crew on board and fired at *Afric Star* until she sank. Several days later the crew were transferred to the German supply tanker *Nordmark*, which was flying the American flag under the name of *Dixie*. They were later moved to the *Portland*, which was on a voyage from Chile to Bordeaux, part of German-occupied France. When a fire broke out on *Portland* a German guard shot a passenger and a crew member of *Afric Star*. They both died. Portland had around 300 people on board from sunken vessels and arrived at Bordeaux on 14

March. One of *Afric Star*'s deck boys was sent to Naples, where he was placed on a ship to Turkey and later transferred to a British hospital ship, which took him to Alexandria. He was placed on several vessels and finally arrived back in England via the Cape of Good Hope in June 1943.

*The London Gazette* of 11 December 1945 printed details of the award of the British Empire Medal to Able Seaman Arthur Ernest Fry of the *Afric Star*, and to Able Seamen Lynch and Merrett of other vessels:

> The *Portland* was captured by the Germans and, with a prize crew on board, was used to transport 327 prisoners to Bordeaux. A small group of prisoners led by Fry determined to regain control of the ship and bring her into a British port. An attempt was made to set the cargo on fire, in the hope that the smoke would be seen by British naval craft. The enemy succeeded in putting out the fire, though not until considerable damage had been done to the ship and cargo. The Germans sentenced Fry to death and his assistants to long terms of imprisonment on charges of mutiny and arson. The three men were subsequently repatriated and are now in this country. Fry was the chief ringleader and displayed courage and determination. Lynch played a prominent part in planning and preparing for the attempted mutiny and fire. Merrett willingly participated in the execution of the plans and assisted Fry in the final preparations for starting the fire. Fry, Lynch and Merrett, knowing they faced almost certain death, were very brave men.

On a voyage from Buenos Aires, *Rodney Star* was sunk by a torpedo in May 1941. She sailed from Buenos Aires on 29 April, for Santos and St Vincent, Cape Verde Islands, and was commanded by Captain Samuel John Clement Phillips. In the early morning of 16 May, about 420 miles south-west of Freetown, she was torpedoed at 5.50 a.m. on the starboard side abreast of No. 3 hold and started to list heavily to starboard. The captain gave orders to abandon ship at 6.02 a.m. and the boats quickly left the listing vessel.

A second torpedo was fired at the vessel at 6.20 a.m., which hit the port side. Two of the lifeboats had been damaged in the initial explosion and these were inspected by the crew in the serviceable boats, who took food, water and other stores from them. At 6.50 a third torpedo exploded on the starboard side of the vessel, forward of the funnel. *Rodney Star* then broke her back, with the bow and stern lifting into the air. Several minutes later, the submarine appeared and fired seventy-eight rounds at the ship. Captain Phillip's boat was picked up by a destroyer after six days and they were landed at Takoradi; Chief Officer Mr J. Maclean's boat made 298 miles and they were rescued by a French passenger vessel on 24 May. The two other lifeboats were also picked up after two days and the crew landed at Dakar. However, those landed at Dakar were handed over to the Vichy French but were exchanged for the crew of a French ship.

*Melbourne Star* and *Sydney Star* reached Malta safely in convoy in July that year. However, *Imperial Star* was bombed while on a Malta convoy on 27 September and later sank, but *Dunedin Star* managed to reach Malta safely. *Britanica* was requisitioned by the Admiralty in 1941 as an auxiliary vessel and later as a store ship at Scapa Flow. *Tacoma Star* was bombed during an air raid while she was berthed in dock at Liverpool on 4 May 1941. She sank and was later refloated and repaired. However, on the way to join a convoy on 1 February 1942, commanded by Captain R. G. Whitehead, she was torpedoed and sunk by U-109, 380 miles from Hampton Roads. No trace was found of her by the search vessels and she was declared lost with all ninety-four hands on board. Between 12 January and the end of that month, the German U-boats in the Caribbean and off the east coast of America destroyed thirty-nine ships of nearly 250,000 gross tons.

On 12 February 1942 the *Empire Star*, under command of Captain Selwyn N. Capon, together with the Blue Funnel vessel *Gorgon*, under escort of HMS *Durban* and *Kedah*, sailed from Singapore for Batavia with evacuated naval, military and RAF personnel and civilian refugees.

Japanese forces had driven south through the Malay Peninsula, attacking Singapore on 6 February. The captain recorded that *Empire Star* carried more than 2,160 people and was attacked by Japanese aircraft just after 9.00 a.m. She received three direct hits, which killed fourteen people and severely wounded another seventeen. The ship was on fire in three places but these were eventually extinguished by a team led by the Chief Officer, Mr Joseph Lindon Dawson. The ship was attacked by bombers for the next four hours and a lifeboat was demolished by one of the bombs.

Captain Capon was assisted by Captain George Wright of the Singapore Pilot Service and the Third Officer, Mr James Peter Smith. Captain Capon later observed that 'both of [them] all through coolly kept the attacking aircraft under close observation, keeping me at the same time advised of their manoeuvres and their probable and eventual angle of attack'. He also stated that:

> Throughout this long and sustained attack the ship's company, one and all behaved magnificently, each going about his allocated duty with a coolness and spirit of courage, unquestionably deserving of the highest praise. It was fortunate that the damage caused by the three direct hits did not seriously damage the ship's fire service, and prompt action and yeoman service by the fire parties under the direction of the Chief Officer, Mr J. L. Dawson, prevented any serious fire developing in the initial critical stage of the attack.

Captain Capon later wrote,

> Each one of us on board at the time, simply did our duty; what, under circumstances of any such emergency, was commonly expected and required of us. In such circumstances, as I feel sure you will understand and appreciate, it is team work which so materially counts and that, in a great measure, accrues from example and leadership born of a high sense of duty.

He drew attention to the Chief Officer, Mr J. L. Dawson; the Third Officer, Mr J. P. Smith; the Senior Second Engineer, Mr H. C. Weller; and the Chief Steward, Mr C. E. Ribbons, 'who went to the greatest lengths in doing everything possible under most trying and exacting conditions for both Service personnel and the civilian refugees then carried, and more especially in instilling amongst the latter that element of comforting assurance which means so much in eliminating in such circumstances any suggestion of or tendency towards panic'.

Captain Capon had been awarded an OBE in the First World War and became a Commander of the Most Excellent Order of the British Empire. The Chief Officer, Mr J. L. Dawson, and the Chief Engineer, Mr R. F. Francis, were both awarded the OBE; the Second Officer, Mr D. Golightly, the Senior Second Engineer, Mr H. C. Weller, and J. P. Smith, the Third Officer, were all awarded the MBE. The British Empire Medal was given to W. Power, the boatswain, and S. Milne, the carpenter.

*Scottish Star* was lost on 20 February 1942 when she was also torpedoed by a German U-boat. She had sailed from Liverpool to Montevideo in convoy on 2 February. The convoy dispersed on 12 February and *Scottish Star* continued her voyage to South America. On 19 February, about 700 miles east-north-east of Trinidad, she was hit by a torpedo abreast of No. 3 hold on the starboard side at 9.05 p.m. The hatches were blown off and the holds and engine room quickly flooded. Captain Edgar Norton Rhodes gave the order to abandon ship at 9.30 and the four boats were safely lowered. The German U-boat briefly came to the surface, fired five rounds then disappeared again. Three of the boats were picked up by HMS *Diomede* and the fourth boat reached Barbados on 27 February, a voyage of nearly 600 miles. Four men in the engine room lost their lives.

The company had taken responsibility for *Empire Glade* from the Ministry of War Transport in October 1941, and *Empire Galahad*, *Empire Might*, *Empire Highway*, *Empire Lakeland* and *Empire Strength* the following year. On 28 November 1942, *Empire Glade* was attacked by a submarine when she was in a position 840 miles north-east of Trinidad. The submarine opened fire on her at 4.53 a.m. The gunfire was returned from *Empire Glade*, but during the incident a cabin boy lost his life and five members of her crew were wounded. Captain Duff was later awarded the George Medal and Lloyds War Medal for Bravery at Sea. The Chief Engineer, Mr John Bell Parker, was awarded the OBE, and the Chief Officer, Second Officer, and Second Engineer received the MBE. Mr H. Shakeshaft and Frank Simmons were awarded the British Empire Medal. The company took over responsibility for *Empire Castle* in January 1943.

Returning from South America with a cargo of frozen meat, *Avila Star* was torpedoed and sunk by U-201 on 6 July 1942. She had sailed from Buenos Aires with a refrigerated cargo on 12 June, under command of Captain John Fisher, and carried a crew of 166 and thirty passengers. In the evening of 5 July she was passing through a recognised submarine area and all on board were wearing their life jackets. The ship's surgeon, Doctor Maynard Crawford, described the torpedo attack at 9.05 p.m. as 'a tremendous rending crash and shock, which was like the tearing up of thousands of frosted aluminium boxes'. She quickly tilted over to starboard when the torpedo hit the starboard side in the boiler room and the electric lights went out and plunged everyone into darkness. As the boats were being lowered a second torpedo struck the ship, flinging many of the occupants into the water. After the ship sank many people, including the captain, were in the water holding onto life-rafts and pieces of debris. Captain Fisher soon lost his strength and drifted away. Some were rescued by the crew and passengers who were in the life-boats, but others died in the water. The Portuguese destroyer *Lima*, which was sailing from Lisbon to Ponta Delgada in the Azores, arrived on the scene the next morning and rescued the survivors in three of the boats. As two other boats were still missing, the Portuguese captain, Rodriguez, searched for more than twenty-four hours without success.

On 23 July one of the boats spotted two seaplanes, which circled and dropped life-jackets with bottles, and tins of biscuits. Another plane dropped a cylinder containing part of a chart of the West African coast and a message saying that help would soon arrive. At 10.00 a.m. on 25 July the mast of a vessel was sighted and the crew and passengers in the boat were rescued by the Portuguese sloop *Pedro Nunes*. Twenty-eight people had survived twenty days in the lifeboat, one died aboard the *Pedro Nunes* and two others in hospital after reaching Lisbon on 26 July. They had drifted to about 100 miles off the West African coast when they were found by the Portuguese ship. Lifeboat No. 6 was never seen again and of the total of 199 persons on board the *Avila Star*, seventy-three people lost their lives.

*The London Gazette* of 24 November 1942 announced that the Chief Officer, Mr E. R. Pearce; the First officer, Mr M. B. M. Tallack; the Second Officer, J. L. Anson; Miss M. E. Ferguson; and the Boatswain, Mr J. A. Gray, were awarded the British Empire Medal. The Chief Officer was also recognised by Lloyd's and was awarded the Corporation's War Medal for Bravery at Sea. Mr R. T. Clarke, the Third Officer, was also awarded the OBE.

Only five out of a convoy of fourteen vessels reached Malta at the end of Operation Pedestal in August 1942. *Melbourne Star* and *Brisbane Star* were two of the vessels that reached Valetta with their precious cargo.

*Viking Star* was lost on 25 August 1942 when she was torpedoed and sunk 180 miles south-west of Freetown. She was sailing from Buenos Aires to the United Kingdom with a cargo of frozen meat and 200 tons of fertilizer, under the command of Captain James Edward Mills. About 180 miles to the south of Freetown she was torpedoed on the port side at 4.50 p.m. She immediately started to list to port and the captain gave the orders to abandon ship, and the two starboard boats were lowered. However, one of the boats was waterlogged and the occupants swam to a drifting raft. The occupants of the second boat attempted to bail out the other boat that was damaged. However, when they realised that the boat could not be used they transferred the stores and water and cast her adrift. Both boats had drifted about half a mile from *Viking Star*, which was torpedoed again. The explosion broke her back and she quickly sank by the bow.

The U-boat surfaced and came to question the crew in the lifeboat; her captain boasted that he had sunk nine ships in the last four days and that his total was fifty-two ships sunk. There were over thirty men in the lifeboat; six were on one of the rafts and seven on another. Two other rafts were drifting some distance away. The following morning, as the weather began to deteriorate, two rafts were lashed together and acted as a sea anchor for the lifeboat. It was decided to remain in that position as a Sunderland flying-boat had been seen just five hours before the vessel was torpedoed. Later in the day, smoke was seen on the horizon. The Third Officer, Mr J. Rigiani, issued rations to the thirteen men on the rafts on the basis that these would last for at least twenty-five days. He calculated that one biscuit, one spoonful of pemmican, one Horlicks malted milk tablet, one piece of chocolate and a small dipper of water per man each morning and night would be sufficient. The rafts also contained an axe, one weather cloth, a compass, an emergency light, some smoke signals, two spoons, two dippers, a small coil of lashing, six blankets and paddles. The men took turns in sleeping on the rafts as were very cold as they were sitting in the water for long periods. As the weather began to deteriorate on 27 August, it became difficult to keep the lifeboat a safe distance from the rafts and after two of the crew were transferred the boat separated from the raft. The wind continued to blow and on 29 August the lifeboat was caught in heavy surf. Everyone was swept overboard and they were washed onto a sandy beach. The crew managed to haul the boat, with the food and provisions, up the beach. The Second Officer, Mr F. Jones, and Able Seaman F. Mayes were later mentioned by the Chief Officer, Mr F. MacQuiston, as 'setting a fine example'. The lifeboat and the other rafts all managed to get ashore on the coast of Liberia.

Mr J. Rigiani, the Third Officer, described the voyage in the rafts following the sinking.

I decided that we were making a course approximately east-south-east at about twelve to fifteen miles a day. If the wind held there would be a chance to hit land before the Guinea current swept us around the bulge of Africa and into the Gulf of Guinea. The course was materially assisted by energetic paddling to keep the wind astern. The knowledge that the land lay some 150 miles to the eastward was of great importance to our spirits, despite the facts that many were suffering from open wounds and cuts, with little or no clothing to protect them from the alternative heat of the sun and the extreme chill of frequent rain squalls, and the accumulating and depressing ordeal of spending every six hours sitting in salt water. Each morning and evening the food ration was issued and the men tackled it with gusto. Occasionally a fish was caught and the diet was varied with raw fish. Unfortunately we could not take advantage of the rain storms to eke out the water ration owing to the fact that our blankets and weather cloth were continually soaked in sea water.

At 6.00 p.m. on 28 August, they sighted a raft about 3 miles away. On 30 August it was decided to issue the men with an extra ration of malted milk tablets. Rigiani continued, '6.00 a.m., food and drink. The sea was choppy but the sun broke through the cloud bank and it became warm. At about 8.00 a.m. we sighted smoke to the southward, and later made out the masts, funnel and finally hull of a steamer.' However, after attempting to attract its attention, the vessel passed without seeing them. Rigiani noted that, 'The men were rather depressed; but not for long. The warmth of the sun was invigorating. They stretched out as best they could and for the first time since leaving the ship they felt warm.'

The rafts were beginning to attract the attention of sharks, which came very close to it. On 31 August the wind had increased; the provisions had become wet but fortunately the wind moderated and turned into a gentle breeze. Another raft was sighted just before dusk and it was still in sight the following morning. They paddled towards it and took off Mr Boardman. The three rafts were lashed together and spirits were raised when they discovered the provisions and water on Boardman's raft. In the afternoon land was sighted and they paddled towards it. However, during the night heavy rainstorms developed and in the morning the land was not in sight anymore.

At 9.00 p.m. they sighted a bright flashing light to the south-east and headed towards it during the night. At daylight on 3 September, they observed 'a hump of rock, apparently an island, with a lighthouse on it, away to the south-east, distant about nine or ten miles'. Rigiani later wrote that:

> As I was afraid of slipping past this to the southward, I ordered a course to be hauled further round to the northward and continue paddling. At noon we cut the third raft adrift to facilitate progress. The men were by now weak from exhaustion, but they kept gamely on, and in the late afternoon we were rewarded by seeing the island recede further round to the starboard quarter, and finally about 5.00 p.m. a line of low land broke to the eastward from north to south, distant about five miles. A double issue of food and drink put new energy into us, and we paddled on through the night. About midnight the heavy swell changed into long rollers and I realised we were close to the land. After another hour we suddenly heard the roar of surf and found ourselves in heavy breakers. We made an attempt to close in on the breakers; but the seas were too high and I realised that it was essential to keep off the shore until morning. Suddenly a very high breaker tossed the raft completely over and all hands were swept in. Everyone soon managed to get back onto the raft but all the food, water and provisions had been swept overboard. For the rest of the night we clung to the rafts and by the mercy of God were not swept by any more breakers.

The following day the land was about half a mile away and they took the raft towards the breakers. Rigiani ordered them to take to the waters and swim ashore. When they were all on the beach, it was realised that Boardman was missing but everyone else reached the safety of the island. Shortly after, a group of people arrived and told them that they had landed in Liberia. The following morning they set off to find a town or village and walked along the sand for two hours to Lata. Along the way they found Mr Sullivan, the Chief Radio Officer, who had been alone on a raft and had also drifted ashore. A launch arrived at midnight and took them to a Dutch trader's house, 'where they were treated with every hospitality, and their wounds dressed'. Eight people were lost from *Viking Star*, which included Abel Seaman R. Boardman, who perished near the beach on the landing in Liberia. Mr F. MacQuiston, the Chief Engineer, was awarded the MBE, with the citation, 'By his leadership and skill Chief Officer MacQuiston brought thirty six people to safety, and his efforts led to the early rescue of the other survivors.'

*Tuscan Star* was also sunk by a U-boat on 6 September 1942. She was on a voyage from Buenos Aires via Santos and Freetown to the United Kingdom, and was commanded by Captain Edgar Norton Rhodes. She was loaded with frozen meat and carried twenty-five passengers and eighty-eight crew. *Tuscan Star* was struck by two torpedoes at 9.00 p.m. on the starboard side in the engine room, and also in No. 5 hold. She quickly started to sink by the stern with a list to starboard and the captain gave the order to abandon the ship. It was a very efficient operation as all the boats were away within ten minutes and she sank within minutes of the crew getting off the vessel.

The U-boat surfaced and a German officer quizzed the crew in English and left. It returned later with Mr Gill, the Second Radio Officer, who they had rescued. They ordered one of the boats to come alongside and gave the survivors tins of food. The U-boat captain said that he was sorry, 'but I have to do my duty'. It was later discovered that the Third Officer's boat was taking in water and there was not enough room to bale her out. Several women and children were then transferred to the captain's boat. The following afternoon some of the boats separated but at 3.00 p.m. the captain's boat saw the smoke of a steamer and headed towards her course. It was the Orient liner *Otranto*, which picked them up about an hour and a half later. They all reached Freetown the next day and Liverpool on 25 September. The survivors in the other boats also reached safety. However, nine members of the crew lost their lives when the ship exploded.

*Andalucia Star* was lost near Freetown on 6 October 1942. She was the last of the 'A' class ships to be sunk during the hostilities and all but seven of those on board were rescued by HMS *Petunia*. She was commanded by Captain James Bennett Hall and was on a voyage from Buenos Aires and Freetown to the United Kingdom. She carried eighty-three passengers and a crew of 170. At 10.00 p.m., about 180 miles south-west of Freetown, she was torpedoed twice in Nos 5 and 6 holds. It was quickly established that the ship was sinking as the main engine room flooded, and orders were given to abandon ship. All of her boats were successfully launched, but No. 2 boat tipped over and the occupants ended in the water. A stewardess, Mrs L. A. Green, and a steward lost their lives.

A third torpedo was fired at her twenty minutes later, which struck on the port side. Unfortunately, two of the boats were alongside but they managed to escape the blast without any serious injury. The captain and four men who were still on board were making their way to the stern when they suddenly discovered a male passenger. They launched a raft but could not find the passenger, who had since wandered away from them. One member of the crew lost his life when he had a heart attack. *Andalucia Star* sank about 10.25 p.m. It was decided that the boats should remain together and the following morning they set off for Freetown. The next morning HMS *Petunia* sighted them and they were taken on board and landed at Freetown.

On 23 October 1942 *Empire Star* was attacked by a torpedo on a voyage to Cape Town and remained fairly stable. She was on a voyage from Liverpool and was unescorted. Captain Capon was still in command of the vessel and at 3.43 p.m., about 570 miles north of the Azores, she was struck by the torpedo, which exploded on the starboard side amidships. The engine room quickly flooded and the lights went out. A heavy list to starboard developed and the passengers and crew took to the lifeboats. As they left the ship, she appeared to right herself and Mr L. Vernon, the Chief Officer, considered returning to the vessel. However, the U-boat then fired two more torpedoes and she sank stern first. Soon after she sank the survivors in the boats heard a loud explosion underwater, which may have been caused by an item of *Empire Star*'s cargo, but they thought that it was odd that the submarine did not surface. It was normally the practice of the U-boats to surface and question the crew after sinking their vessel. However, it was later reported that the submarine did survive and was sunk in the Caribbean the following year.

It was established that all apart from the four men killed in the engine room had survived the sinking, and it was decided that the boats would remain together during the night. However, the strong wind and heavy spray made this task very difficult. The following morning the boats had separated and Captain Capon's boat, with thirty-eight people on board, was never seen again. The weather continued to deteriorate but they were sighted by HMS *Black Swan*, which took on board the occupants of the First Officer's boat at 6.15 p.m. on 25 September, and later picked up the passengers and crew in the Third Officer's boat.

Considerable damage was caused to *Pacific Star* when she was hit by a torpedo from U-509 on 27 October 1942 but she was able to continue towards Las Palmas. She had sailed from Freetown on 18 October in a convoy of about forty vessels and an escort of five corvettes. On 27 October the convoy Commodore warned all the ships that U-boats were in the vicinity and the course was altered 30 degrees to starboard, and later back to its original track. *Pacific Star* was torpedoed forward on the starboard side at the centre of No. 1 hatch. Initially it was possible to steer the ship but when it became difficult to stop the inflow of water into her holds the captain decided to abandon ship, and the ninety-seven people on board took to the lifeboats. Captain Evans decided to remain close to the ship as he felt he may be able to save her but it became clear that this was impossible and they sailed for the nearest land. All the crew survived and Captain G. L. Evans was later awarded the OBE.

On 30 November 1942 *Dunedin Star* collided with an object off the Skeleton Coast and was beached. The story of the shipwreck is told in *Skeleton Coast* by John H. Marsh, which describes the loss of the vessel and the efforts made to save the crew and recover the ship and her cargo.

The first Blue Star vessel to be lost in 1943 was *California Star*, which was torpedoed on 4 March and sank. She was on a voyage from Australia and New Zealand to Liverpool via the Panama Canal with a cargo of refrigerated cargo and other goods. At 7.30 p.m. she was torpedoed twice, about 380 miles north-west of Flores, in the Azores. The torpedoes exploded on the starboard side of No. 3 hatch and the two boats on that side of the ship were damaged. As the remaining boats were being lowered, the ship was struck by a third torpedo just below boat No. 2. The boat disintegrated and all the occupants lost their lives. As it was clear that the ship was sinking, the captain dived into the water to swim to a raft and the vessel was struck with another torpedo and sank. Soon after the vessel disappeared, the submarine surfaced and continued its voyage. Later that day Captain Foulkes discovered that the First Officer, Mr Cameron, had been taken prisoner by the submarine. It was decided that the captain would take the boat and attempt to reach Flores. The voyage took eleven days where Captain Foulkes instigated the search for the remaining crew in the rafts. However, the search produced no results and fifty-one people out of the seventy-four on board were lost.

Several days after *California Star* left the United States, her sister *Canadian Star* also sailed in a convoy. Ten ships, including *Canadian Star* were lost. She was commanded by Captain R. D. Miller and left New York on 8 March in a convoy of forty-two ships. She was carrying twenty-two passengers and a crew of sixty-nine. *Canadian Star* was struck by two torpedoes on the port side which disabled the engine room as one torpedo actually hit one of the cylinders in the main engine. It was decided to abandon ship by boats Nos 1 and 3. However, boat No. 3 hung by the bows as it was being lowered and the occupants were dropped into the water. No. 1 boat was launched before all starboard rafts were in the water. No. 3 boat was righted in the water. The sea conditions were atrocious and the boats and rafts were capsizing in the heavy seas. HMS *Anemone* and *Pennywort* rescued many of the survivors and then returned to the convoy. There were ninety-one people on *Canadian Star* when she was torpedoed and thirty-two lost their lives. Mr P. H. Hunt, the Chief Officer, and Mr R. H. Keyworth, the Third Officer, were both awarded the MBE.

*Empire Lakeland* sailed from New York to Liverpool on 23 February but left the convoy because she could not keep up with the other ships. On 11 March, off Rockall, she was torpedoed and sunk and all of her crew were lost. *Celtic Star* left Freetown on 28 March for Montevideo and Buenos Aires and was torpedoed the following day. She was commanded by Captain J. H. A. Mackie MBE, who was Chief Officer on *Sydney Star* on her voyage to Malta in August 1941. She was torpedoed just after 10.00 p.m. on 29 March and was abandoned. At 10.12 she was hit by another torpedo and two of her boats were wrecked. People had been thrown off the vessel into the water and were swimming around trying to find life-rafts. The lifeboat containing the Chief Officer was approached by the Italian submarine, which took an Able Bodied Seaman as a prisoner of war. Two lives were lost and the survivors were rescued by HMS *Westwater*. Captain Mackie was awarded the OBE and Third Officer, Mr J. Nuttall, the MBE.

*Melbourne Star* was sunk by a torpedo on 2 April 1943. She had sailed from Liverpool to Sydney via the Panama Canal on 22 March, with thirty-one passengers and eighty-six crew and a cargo of torpedoes and ammunition. When 480 miles south-east of Bermuda, she was hit by two torpedoes at 3.00 a.m. It appears that the ship sank within two minutes, leaving eleven people on rafts. The U-boat approached the two rafts, questioned the crew members and then left. One of the rafts drifted away and after three very rough days the wind abated and the seas became calm. The survivors managed to supplement the rations by catching fish, which they ate raw. Thirty-eight days after their ship had sunk, on 9 May, they were rescued by an American flying boat and were landed in Bermuda. Of the eleven people who took to life-rafts, only four survived.

On 21 April 1944 *Royal Star*, on a voyage from Buenos Aires to Malta, Taranto and Alexandria, was damaged by bombers north-east of Algiers. She had sailed in convoy from Algiers the previous day with frozen meat, dehydrated meat and eight naval torpedoes. At 9.00 p.m., when off Cape Bengut, the convoy was attacked by low flying bombers and she was struck with a torpedo. The ship was taking in water and around 11.00 p.m. an American destroyer came close but was unable to tow *Royal Star* to safety. Just after midnight, Captain McDonald started to broadcast SOS messages until the batteries ran down around 2.50 a.m. As the ship continued to take on water, the captain gave the order to abandon ship. He remained on board when she was taken in tow by the Admiralty tug *Athlete*, which arrived from Algiers, but she later sank. It was the company's final war loss. Captain T. F. McDonald was later awarded the OBE.

On 5 June 1944, the Lamport & Holt Line was acquired on behalf of the Blue Star Line by the Union Cold Storage Company's subsidiary Frederick Leyland & Company Limited. An offer of £1 25d was offered for each 33d share and it was accepted by more than 85 per cent of the shareholders. The company's head office moved from St Mary's Axe to 19 West Smithfield, London EC1 on 1944.

Six American-built ships were placed under Blue Star Line management in 1944. They were the *Empire Anvil*, *Empire Javelin*, *Samannan*, *Saminver*, *Samnid* and *Samtay*. At the end of the war *Empire Anvil* and *Saminver* were returned to the United States; *Empire Javelin* was lost; *Samtay* was purchased by Ropners; and *Samannan* and *Samnid* were acquired by the Blue Star Line in 1947, becoming *Oregon Star* and *Pacific Star*. *Empire Javelin* left Southampton for Le Havre on 28 December 1944 with 1,448 American servicemen on board. She was torpedoed in the English Channel but only seven lives were lost as the survivors were transferred to the escorting French frigate *L'Escaramouche* and LSTs.

The Blue Star Line was given management responsibility for the Empire-type vessel *Empire Talisman* in 1944, and she was later placed on bare-boat charter to the company. She was purchased by the line in 1949 and renamed *Tacoma Star*. *Empire Wisdom* was transferred to Blue Star from Clan Line management in 1944 and she later became *Royal Star* and *Caledonia Star*. The Booth Steamship Company was taken over in 1946 along with its interests in the Booth American Shipping Corporation, together with the Associated Mersey & Hudson Wharfage Corporation, the South-End Stevedoring Company and the Amazonas Engineering Company, as well as the Booth agencies on the Amazon. *Empire Clarendon* was acquired and renamed *Tuscan Star*, later becoming *Timaru Star* and *California Star*.

In 1945 a contract was signed with Cammell Laird & Company Limited at Birkenhead for the construction of four passenger and cargo vessels for the South American route. *Argentine Star* was delivered in June 1947 and *Brasil Star* in October that year. *Empire Star* was purchased from the Admiralty in 1946. She was launched as *Empire Mercia* and was designed with accommodation for thirty-six first class and ninety-six tourist class passengers. She had six cargo holds and a total insulated space of 443,159 cubic feet. On her departure from Glasgow in 1947, she reintroduced the link between the Scottish port and South African and Australian ports by the Blue Star Line.

*Fresno Star* was sold for scrap in July 1947 and was sent to the yard of Thos W. Ward at Inverkeithing to be broken up. *Celtic Star* was transferred to Lamport & Holt Line and was renamed *Murillo*. The Marine Court in Copenhagen decided that the non-delivery of *Adelaide Star* had been 'an act of war' and that the Blue Star Line could make recourse to Germany to recover some of the costs of the vessel. The court later awarded the company 10 million kroner, which represented insurance and interest since its seizure in 1940. However, in October 1947 the Copenhagen Maritime Court decided against the Blue Star Line and it was ordered to pay 100,000 kroner costs.

*Albion Star* was broken up at Briton Ferry in 1948 when six vessels were introduced into the fleet. *Paraguay Star*, *Uruguay Star*, *Rhodesia Star*, *South Africa Star*, *Imperial Star* and *Melbourne Star* came into service for the company's services. *Imperial Star* and *Melbourne Star* were built as the largest ships in the post-war fleet and were designed with a service speed of 17 knots. Twelve passengers were also carried in single and double rooms.

Since the termination of the war ship-owners operated partly under requisition and when this was terminated under the Shipping Advisory and Allocation Committee (SAAC), it gave the industry a larger measure of self-government but was not interpreted as freedom as there was a control of freight rates and tonnage was 'steered' into areas most needed to lift essential government-sponsored cargo. The situation changed in 1949 when new tonnage was beginning to come into service on a regular basis, which had been ordered when owners began to replace war losses and build up their fleets. Consequently, this allowed a larger measure of commercial working and it was found that there was no longer any need to steer tonnage to a particular area, or any need for freight control. However, a small amount of tonnage was still operated under a series of licences.

The situation at the time was further complicated by currency and finance problems and restrictions on commerce, with an embargo on certain imports by the South African government. Political disturbances, such as those in China and Indonesia, meant further uncertainty for British ship-owners who needed to maintain modern and efficient fleets

*Brasil Star* Dining Room.

*Above left: Brasil Star* Smoking Room.

*Above right: Brasil Star* Lounge.

*Below: Brasil Star* double cabin.

to enable them to compete with foreign competitors. The ship-owners began to put pressure on the Chancellor of the Exchequer 'to see fit to give some relief to our industry, upon which our whole welfare depends, not only in peace but at war as well'. They referred to the high cost of building, which necessitated large amounts being put away to cover interest, depreciation, and high taxation on funds which were then ploughed back into the business.

On 27 July 1949 the Union Cold Storage Company Limited changed its name to Union International Company Limited. The following year, at the Annual General Meeting, its assets were transferred to the Union Cold Storage Company Limited. This company had been registered in 1929 as United Cork Industries Limited. All vessels registered in the name of Frederick Leyland & Company Limited were transferred to the Blue Star Line or Union International Company Limited. *Tudor Star* and *Norman Star* were broken up, and *Adelaide Star, Dunedin Star, English Star, Scottish Star* and *Tasmania Star* were introduced in 1950.

Another 'Empire' type vessel joined the fleet in 1951 when *Vasconia* was acquired from the Cunard Line and renamed *Fresno Star*. The Austasia Line was formed in Singapore the following year, operating services between Singapore, Malayan and Australian ports. The *Clement* from Booth Line was transferred to the new venture and renamed *Malay*. She had been ordered by the Booth Line as *Clement* and launched as *Malay Star*, when taken over by the Blue Star Line. *Wellington Star* was introduced in 1952 and was claimed to be the largest refrigerated ship in the world with a capacity of 594,560 cubic feet. Lamport & Holt's *Millais* was another 'Empire' type vessel and she was transferred to the Blue Star Line and renamed *Oregon Star* in 1952. However, she only had a brief time in the fleet as she was sold two years later. *Dryden* also came from Lamport & Holt and was renamed *Fremantle Star*. Sir Edmund Vestey, Bart died in 1952.

*Drover* was built in 1923 and completed as *Copeland* for the Clyde Steam Ship Company. She was sold to G. Heyn & Sons' Head Line and renamed *North Down* in 1946. She was acquired by the Blue Star Line in October 1954 and renamed *Drover* but was soon disposed of when she was purchased by the Belfast Steamship Company and renamed *Ulster Herdsman*. There was clearly nothing mechanically wrong with the ship as she survived under that name until 1964, when she was broken up at Passage West.

In 1953 an order was placed for a motor tanker which was launched as *Pacific Star* on 22 January 1954 by William Hamilton & Company Limited, Port Glasgow. She was Blue Star Line's only tanker and was owned by the Booth Steam Ship Company and bare-boat chartered to the Blue Star Line. *Pacific Star* was transferred to Blue Star ownership in 1961.

In June 1954 the Donaldson Line decided to move out of its services from Glasgow to the Pacific coast of North America and these were acquired by the Blue Star Line with the vessels *Carmia, Corrientes* and *Gracia*. *Carmia* was delivered as *Empire Flag* for the Ministry of War Transport in 1943 and was managed by the New Zealand Shipping Company. In 1946 she was sold to the Donaldson Line, becoming *Carmia*. When she was purchased by the Blue Star Line in March 1954, she was renamed *Victoria Star*. *Corrientes* was to have been renamed *Oakland Star* but was sold to Williamson & Company of Hong Kong and renamed *Inchmay*. *Gracia* became *Oregon Star*. *Delius* was transferred to the Blue Star Line, becoming *Portland Star*, and *Delane* was also transferred from Lamport & Holt Line, becoming *Seattle Star*. *Defoe* was renamed *Geelong Star* for the Australian services.

The Norwegian refrigerated vessel *Mosdale* was acquired by Blue Star Line in May 1954 and it was intended that she would be renamed *Trinidad Star* and placed on the West Indies banana trade service. However, she became *Albion Star* and transferred to Lamport & Holt Line, who renamed her *Balzac*. *Trojan Star*, the oldest vessel in the fleet, was broken up at Blyth in 1955. She had suffered a serious fire when 1,700 miles from Colombo on 7 October 1954. The fire was brought under control but it was not until eleven days later that it was finally extinguished at Colombo. Repairs were made when *Trojan Star* reached Brisbane and on her return to Britain it was decided that she should be scrapped.

Orders were placed for four refrigerated cargo vessels with Bremer Vulkan at Vegesack. They were to be propelled by MAN oil engines, developing 10,000 bhp, with a service speed of 17 knots. This order caused great controversy in maritime and shipbuilding circles as British shipyards felt that they were in a position to provide the vessels for a British shipping company. However, an order was placed with Cammell Laird & Company Limited for the construction of a refrigerated cargo ship of 14,500 tons at Birkenhead. *Canberra Star*, *Hobart Star*, *Newcastle Star*, *Gladstone Star* and *Townsville Star* entered service during 1956–57. They were all, except *Newcastle Star*, registered in the name of the Salient Shipping Company Limited of Bermuda. *Auckland Star*, delivered in 1958 at Birkenhead, was also placed under this company. The ships were bare-boat chartered to the Blue Star Line. These were followed by *Queensland Star* and *Rockhampton Star* for the Australian routes and *Canadian Star* for service to Canada.

The Crusader Shipping Company Limited was a partnership with the New Zealand Shipping Company, Port Line and Shaw Savill & Albion Line. It was formed in 1957 to operate services between New Zealand and Japan. The first vessel in the fleet was named *Crusader* and was built by the Valmet Shipyard at Helsinki. She was a refrigerated motorship designed for the carriage of fruit, frozen meat and fish. She was followed

*Above: Newcastle Star.*

*Below: Canberra Star* and the Shaw, Savill & Albion vessel *Icenic*. (Chris Finney)

# BLUE STAR LINE

### SOUTH AFRICA

EXPRESS LINER SERVICE TO

| | |
|---|---|
| **CAPETOWN**<br>Due 28th Jan. | **PORT ELIZABETH**<br>Due 30th Jan. |
| **EAST LONDON**<br>Due 1st Feb. | **DURBAN**<br>Due 3rd Feb. |
| **LOURENCO MARQUES**<br>Due 6th Feb. | **BEIRA**<br>Due 8th Feb. |

———

## M.V. "CANBERRA STAR"

will receive cargo at :-

| | |
|---|---|
| **NEWPORT** | 6 SHED, ALEXANDRA DOCK<br>From 21st Dec. until 30th Dec. |
| **GLASGOW** | 58 STOBCROSS QUAY<br>From 23rd Dec. until 6th Jan. |
| **LIVERPOOL** | CLOSING 9th Jan.<br>(Loading berth and receiving date to be advised later) |

REFRIGERATED SPACE AVAILABLE

INSURANCE EFFECTED AT COMPETITIVE RATES

For further particulars rates of freight, etc. apply:-

# BLUE STAR LINE
LTD,
**ALBION HOUSE, LEADENHALL STREET, LONDON, E.C.3**
TELEPHONE ROYAL 4567
GLASGOW : 93 HOPE STREET (CENTRAL 5133)
CHAM : 6 VICTORIA SQUARE    MANCHESTER : 556 ROYAL EXCHANGE
LIVERPOOL : LAMPORT & HOLT LINE LTD., ROYAL LIVER BUILDING (CENTRAL 5650)
For Other Agents See Overleaf

by *Saracen* and *Knight Templar*. The New Zealand Shipping Company's *Turakina*, Shaw Savill's *Amalric*, Port Line's *Port Montreal* and *Canterbury Star* all operated on this service, which was later extended to the Pacific coast of North America and the Pacific islands.

*Ulster Star* was delivered by Harland & Wolff at Belfast in 1959 and *Vancouver Star* was sold and broken up. *Fremantle Star* was delivered in 1960 for the Australian trade and *Carroll* and *Crome* were transferred from Lamport & Holt, becoming *Norman Star* and *Roman Star*. They were sent to the Middle Docks at South Shields, who converted them to carry edible oils. All of the refrigerated space was taken out and tanks for the carriage of the oils were fitted. The Austasia Line started a new service from Australia to New Guinea, North Borneo and Sarawak in April 1960 but the route did not prove successful. *Chatham* and *Constable* were transferred from Lamport & Holt and renamed *Mendoza Star* and *Santos Star* in 1962. They were placed on the London to River Plate ports service, and later from the River Plate to Barcelona, Marseilles and Genoa.

*Pacific Star* was sold in 1961 after only seven years in service for the company. However, the line announced in 1962 that they would be operating a new service from Australia to United States and Canadian east coast ports. It was a voyage that would take twenty-four days and would terminate at Montreal in summer and Halifax, Nova Scotia, in the winter months. *Townsville Star* sailed from Brisbane on 25 August 1962 on the first sailing to United States ports and Montreal. The service was later maintained by *Montreal Star, Halifax Star, America Star* and *New York Star*. Blue Star Line was joined by the German Columbus Schiffahrts GmbH in 1964, offering fortnightly sailings in both directions. *Santos Star* was lengthened by Harland & Wolff at Belfast and *Mendoza Star* at Hoboken in 1963. Fifty 5-foot sections were fitted and the cargo capacity was increased by 1,000 tons.

*Canberra Star* sailing list.

*Above: America Star.* (Chris Finney)

*Right:* Fairfield Shipbuilding & Engineering Company Limited advertisement, June 1960.

It was decided to transfer the Booth Line's *Anselm* to the Blue Star Line in 1963 and she was renamed *Iberia Star* for the London to Buenos Aires route. She was sent for conversion at Vegesack and emerged with her accommodation reduced from 180 to ninety passengers. She had operated on Booth Line's service from Liverpool to the Amazon since she was introduced into that service in 1961. *Iberia Star* was chartered to the Austasia Line in 1965, becoming *Australasia* with Blue Star Line as owners. She was joined by the Booth Line vessel *Hubert* in October 1964. *Hubert* was renamed *Malaysia* and both ships were registered in Singapore in 1971. *Iberia Star* was broken up in 1973.

*Orient* was acquired in 1964 and renamed *Waveney Star* for feeder services from Continental ports to London. The small vessel *Julia Anna* was purchased in 1965, renamed *Orwell Star* and used for feeder services from the Tyne, Middlesbrough and the Humber to London. *Waveney Star* became *Waveney* in 1965 and *Orwell Star* was renamed *Orwell* the following year.

*Napier Star* took the honour of making the 100th call by a Blue Star vessel at the port of Timaru on 31 March 1963. It was claimed that the cargo of 268,000 cases of butter and 55,000 cases of cheese that arrived on *Auckland Star* in November 1963 was the biggest cargo of dairy produce ever to leave New Zealand. The refrigerated vessels *Norefjell*, *Parthenon* and *Piraus* were purchased in 1964–65 and renamed *Genova Star*, *Padova Star* and *Barcelona Star* for the South America–Mediterranean service. The three vessels were later transferred to the subsidiary Calmedia SpA di Nav, Cagliari, becoming *Calabella*, *Calarossa* and *Calasetta* respectively.

*Australia Star* was broken up at Faslane in 1964 and *Brisbane Star* at Osaka in 1965, when *Napier Star* was declared a constructive total loss. She gone aground off Bahia Potrero, Uruguay, on 20 July 1965 and then went aground near Montevideo. Following an inspection in dry-dock it was decided that it was uneconomic to repair her and that she should be scrapped. A new *Australia Star* emerged from Austin & Pickersgill in 1965 which had the distinction of having the largest heavy lift gear ever built into a ship. Following her completion she was towed to Hamburg, where her 300-ton Stulcken derrick was fitted, and she entered service for the Blue Star Line in May 1966. Orders were placed for three new vessels in September and October 1965, one with Bartram at Sunderland and the other two from Bremer Vulkan of Vegesack.

In 1965 the Mersey Docks & Harbour Board, in conjunction with the Blue Star Line, announced that they were to build a fully mechanised discharging berth for meat and other refrigerated foodstuffs at Alexandra Dock, Liverpool. The shed at the north side of Alexandra Branch Dock No. 2 was to be demolished and a new aluminium structure, 775 feet long and 85 feet wide, would be built. Specialised equipment designed to the requirements of the Blue Star line would be installed. This consisted of two portable elevators, each with a capacity of 3,000 packages, or 100 tons an hour, fed by telescopic belt conveyors and chutes. Overhead conveyors ran the length of the shed and were connected to the cold store across the Dock Road. Packages destined for direct delivery to road or rail transport would be transferred to other belts at ground floor. Alternatively, cargo discharged to conveyors on the quay would be sorted on the belts and manually turned on to short conveyors to take goods direct to lorries or railway wagons. Around 80,000 tons of frozen meat and 85,000 tons of dairy products were discharged at the Port of Liverpool each year and it was anticipated that the new facilities would substantially increase the total.

At the launch of the *Australia Star* (2) at Sunderland on 11 May 1965, Mr Kenneth Douglas, managing director of Austin & Pickersgill, referred to the problem of keeping to promised delivery dates. He said:

It is very disappointing that as soon as order books begin to fill up, we experience delays in receiving supplies of equipment from sub-contractors, and labour troubles serve to accentuate the difficulties ship-builders face,

# REFRIGERATION

## for

**Passenger Liners**

**Cargo Vessels**

**Tankers**

**Trawlers**

**Yachts**

# J & E HALL
### LIMITED

DARTFORD · KENT

**Telephone: Dartford 23458**

A member of the Hall-Thermotank group

---

# *BLUE STAR LINE

## EXPRESS LINER SERVICES

The Blue Star Line, one of the world's leading maritime enterprises, offers most modern facilities for the safe carriage of all types of refrigerated and general cargoes.

**AUSTRALIA**
**NEW ZEALAND**
**SOUTH AFRICA**
**SOUTH AMERICA**
Via LISBON, and the CANARY ISLANDS
**NORTH PACIFIC COAST**

It is always safe to

## SHIP BY BLUE STAR LINE

ALBION HOUSE, LEADENHALL STREET, LONDON E.C.3.
Tel : ROYal 4567

Passenger Office :
**3, LOWER REGENT STREET, LONDON S.W.1.**
Tel : WHitehall 2266

# m.v. AUSTRALIA STAR

**MAIN PARTICULARS**

**HULL**

| | |
|---|---|
| Length B.P. | 485' 0" |
| Breadth moulded | 70' 0" |
| Depth to Upper Deck | 41' 9" |
| Depth to Second Deck | 29' 9" |
| Depth to Third Deck | 21' 0" |
| Draught | 30' 0" |
| Deadweight | 12170 tons |
| Cargo Capacities - Grain | 626,000 cu.ft. |
| Bale | 567,500 cu.ft. |
| Refrigerated | 109,200 cu.ft. |
| Bunkers (Total) | 2,700 tons |
| Water Ballast (Total) | 2,600 tons |
| Gross Tonnage | 10,916 tons |
| Net Tonnage | 6,404 tons |
| Service Speed | 20 knots |

**MACHINERY**

One 8 cylinder, two stroke, single acting, turbo-charged Diesel engine, 'Vickers-Sulzer' 8RD 90, 17600 B.H.P. at 119 R.P.M. arranged for Bridge control.

**AUXILIARY MACHINERY**

| | |
|---|---|
| 4 diesel alternators | 400 k.w. each |
| 1 diesel emergency/harbour alternator | 90 k.w. |

**CARGO GEAR**

| | |
|---|---|
| 1 'Stulcken' derrick | 300 tons |
| 4 derricks | 10 tons each |
| 3 - 3 ton traversing electric deck cranes | |
| 1 - 3 ton fixed electric deck crane | |
| 1 - 5 ton traversing electric deck crane | |
| 2 - 5 ton fixed electric deck cranes | |

Upper deck hatch covers, 'single-pull' steel W.T. type with hydraulic chain drive lower deck hatch covers. Flush, folding, steel type with hydraulic operation.

## AUSTIN & PICKERSGILL LTD
*SHIPBUILDERS*
SOUTHWICK SUNDERLAND

---

1964 advertisements.

Austin & Pickersgill Limited advertisement, November 1966.

*Australia Star* (2). (Chris Finney)

through their inherent delays with a consequent necessity for overtime in being able to quote firm delivery dates and prices. It is patent to anyone who takes a reasonable view of things that this gives no great encouragement to ship-owners to place orders in United Kingdom yards.

The first meeting of Associated Container Transportation Limited (ACT) was held in London on 12 January 1966. It was a joint venture by Ellerman Lines, Blue Star Line, Ben Line, Harrison Line and Port Line to discuss the funding of the new large container vessels that would be needed to transport cargos around the world. The first new build for the consortium was *ACT 1*, which was delivered in 1969 as part of the Australia Europe Container Services (AECS). The Associated Container Transportation left

the AECS in 1972, together with the Australia National Line. However, they became part of the group again in 1977, which was later renamed the Australia New Zealand Europe Container Service (ANZECS). ACT survived until 1991, when the ships were sold or transferred. *ACT 3*, *ACT 4*, *ACT 5*, *ACT 6* and *ACT 10* went to the Blue Star Line and a partner company.

*Timaru Star* was delivered by Bartram & Sons, at Sunderland, in July 1967 for the New Zealand routes. *Southland Star* entered service in May 1967, followed by *New Zealand Star* in September. The two Bremer Vulkan vessels were fitted with Stulcken heavy lift derricks. Each vessel incorporated engine room control from the bridge and offered a refrigerated capacity of 562,627 cubic feet. *Fresno Star* was broken up at Kaohsiung in 1966 and the feeder ships were placed under the management of G. T. Gillie Blair Limited and they lost the word 'Star' from their names. *Crouch* and *Deben* were added to the coaster fleet to join *Orwell* and *Waveney*.

The Donaldson Line's interests in the South African trade were acquired by the Blue Star Line in 1967 and Donaldsons were placed into voluntary liquidation. *South Africa Star* was broken up in Japan and *Scottish Star* was trapped with fourteen other ships in the Great Bitter Lake on the Suez Canal during the Arab-Israeli War in June 1967. There were in fact two *New Zealand Star* vessels in the fleet in 1967. One was sold to be broken up in July after giving the company thirty-three years' service and the other was introduced into the New Zealand route later that year.

*Canadian Star* was sent to the Birkenhead yard of Cammell Laird & Company Limited in 1967 and emerged able to carry sixty 29-foot containers. *Columbia Star* was broken up at Kaohsiung in 1968, *Orwell* was sold and *Dunedin Star* was transferred to the Lamport & Holt Line. A new partnership was formed with the Port Line in 1968 for their ships engaged in the Australasian services. It was known as Blue Star Port Lines (Management) Limited and coordinated all management services for the vessels engaged in that trade.

The container ship *ACT 1* was laid down on 11 January 1968 at the yard of Bremer Vulkan and was launched on 18 October that year. She sailed on her maiden voyage to Australia on 22 March 1969. *California Star* was broken up at Kaohsiung in 1969 and *Paraguay Star* suffered a serious fire at her berth at the Royal Victoria Dock in London. Following an inspection, it was decided that she was uneconomic to repair and she was sold and towed to Hamburg, where she was broken up.

ACL found that there was no link between Australia and the Far East. Consequently, Blue Star, Ellerman and Port Line applied to the Australian Northbound Conference to contribute vessels to this trade and the application was rejected. However, the three companies decided to set up the Atlas line to provide a service from Adelaide, Melbourne, Sydney and Brisbane to Japanese ports and Hong Kong. The first sailing was taken by *Rockhampton Star* in September 1967, followed by *Gladstone Star*, *Port St Lawrence* and *Hobart Star*. After a short time the Atlas Line was invited to purchase a minority interest in any container service that may be developed between Australia and the Far East. However, this offer was never exercised.

The consortium involved in running the Australia-Europe Container Service consisted of Overseas Containers Limited (OCL), Hapag Lloyd, Nedlloyd, Messageries Maritimes, ACT and the Australian National Line. In September 1972 the ACT/ANL group withdrew from the consortium to operate a service from Tilbury and Liverpool to Australia and New Zealand. They also operated from Australia and New Zealand to the United States and Canada. *California Star* and *Columbia Star* were delivered in 1971 and were able to carry 871 20-foot containers or equivalents comprising of 746 general and 125 insulated. The service from Europe to the Pacific coast of North America was operated in conjunction with the Danish East Asiatic Company and was known as ScanStar. *Imperial Star*, *Empire Star* and *Caledonia Star* were disposed of and scrapped and the feeder ships *Crouch* and *Deben* were sold.

The ScanStar consortium was joined by the Johnson Line of Sweden early in 1972, forming Johnson ScanStar. The fleet comprised of five Johnson vessels, two Blue Star ships and two East Asiatic container ships, providing a weekly service from Gothenburg–European ports–United States Pacific ports–Vancouver and return in sixty-three days. *America Star*, *Halifax Star* and *New York Star* were sent to Sandfjord, Norway, to be 'jumboised' by increasing their capacity. Their refrigeration plants were up-rated to provide for the carriage of bananas, in addition to their meat and fruit cargos. They emerged in 1973 being 540 feet 5 inches long, with their deadweight tonnage increased from 8,400 to 11,700. *America Star*'s first voyage was to South Africa to load deciduous fruit for Cardiff and

# BLUE STAR LINE

## SOUTH AMERICAN SERVICE

### SCHEDULE 1970 (JAN.-DEC.)

| SOUTHBOUND | | | | | | | NORTHBOUND | | | | | | |
|---|---|---|---|---|---|---|---|---|---|---|---|---|---|
| dep. London | Lisbon | Las Palmas | Rio de Janeiro | Santos | Montevideo | arr. Buenos Aires | dep. Buenos Aires | Montevideo | Santos | Rio de Janeiro | Lisbon | arr. Rotterdam | arr.* London |
| 9 Jan. | 12 Jan. | 15 Jan. | 24 Jan. | 25 Jan. | 28 Jan. | 29 Jan. | 5 Feb. | 6 Feb. | 9 Feb. | 10 Feb. | 21 Feb. | 24 Feb. | 27 Feb. |
| 30 Jan. | 2 Feb. | 5 Feb. | 14 Feb. | 15 Feb. | 18 Feb. | 19 Feb. | 26 Feb. | 27 Feb. | 2 Mar. | 3 Mar. | 14 Mar. | 17 Mar. | 20 Mar. |
| 13 Feb. | 16 Feb. | 19 Feb. | 28 Feb. | 1 Mar. | 4 Mar. | 5 Mar. | 12 Mar. | 13 Mar. | 16 Mar. | 17 Mar. | 28 Mar. | 31 Mar. | 3 Apr. |
| 13 Mar. | 16 Mar. | 19 Mar. | 28 Mar. | 29 Mar. | 1 Apr. | 2 Apr. | 9 Apr. | 10 Apr. | 13 Apr. | 14 Apr. | 25 Apr. | 28 Apr. | 1 May |
| 3 Apr. | 6 Apr. | 9 Apr. | 18 Apr. | 19 Apr. | 22 Apr. | 23 Apr. | 30 Apr. | 1 May | 5 May | 6 May | 17 May | 20 May | 23 May |
| 17 Apr. | 20 Apr. | 23 Apr. | 2 May | 3 May | 6 May | 7 May | 14 May | 15 May | 19 May | 20 May | 31 May | 3 June | 6 June |
| 15 May | 18 May | 21 May | 30 May | 31 May | 3 June | 4 June | 11 June | 12 June | 16 June | 17 June | 28 June | 1 July | 4 July |
| 5 June | 8 June | 11 June | 20 June | 21 June | 24 June | 25 June | 2 July | 3 July | 7 July | 8 July | 19 July | 22 July | 25 July |
| 3 July | 6 July | 9 July | 18 July | 19 July | 22 July | 23 July | 30 July | 31 July | 4 Aug. | 5 Aug. | 16 Aug. | 19 Aug. | 22 Aug. |
| 24 July | 27 July | 30 July | 8 Aug. | 9 Aug. | 12 Aug. | 13 Aug. | 20 Aug. | 21 Aug. | 25 Aug. | 26 Aug. | 6 Sept. | 9 Sept. | 12 Sept. |
| 14 Aug. | 17 Aug. | 20 Aug. | 29 Aug. | 30 Aug. | 2 Sept. | 3 Sept. | 10 Sept. | 11 Sept. | 15 Sept. | 16 Sept. | 27 Sept. | 30 Sept. | 3 Oct. |
| 4 Sept. | 7 Sept. | 10 Sept. | 19 Sept. | 20 Sept. | 23 Sept. | 24 Sept. | 1 Oct. | 2 Oct. | 6 Oct. | 7 Oct. | 18 Oct. | 21 Oct. | 24 Oct. |
| 25 Sept. | 28 Sept. | 1 Oct. | 10 Oct. | 11 Oct. | 14 Oct. | 15 Oct. | 22 Oct. | 23 Oct. | 26 Oct. | 27 Oct. | 7 Nov. | 10 Nov. | 13 Nov. |
| 16 Oct. | 19 Oct. | 22 Oct. | 31 Oct. | 1 Nov. | 4 Nov. | 5 Nov. | 12 Nov. | 13 Nov. | 16 Nov. | 17 Nov. | 28 Nov. | 1 Dec. | 4 Dec. |
| 6 Nov. | 9 Nov. | 12 Nov. | 21 Nov. | 22 Nov. | 25 Nov. | 26 Nov. | 3 Dec. | 4 Dec. | 7 Dec. | 8 Dec. | 19 Dec. | 22 Dec. | 24 Dec. |
| 27 Nov. | 30 Nov. | 3 Dec. | 12 Dec. | 13 Dec. | 16 Dec. | 17 Dec. | 24 Dec. | 25 Dec. | 28 Dec. | 29 Dec. | 1971 9 Jan. | 12 Jan. | 15 Jan. |
| 18 Dec. | 21 Dec. | 24 Dec. | 1971 2 Jan. | 3 Jan. | 6 Jan. | 7 Jan. | 14 Jan. | 15 Jan. | 18 Jan. | 19 Jan. | 30 Jan. | 2 Feb. | 5 Feb. |

LOW SEASON SAILINGS ARE SHOWN IN RED

*All sailings are subject to alteration or cancellation without notice*

\* Exceptionally passengers may be disembarked at Southampton before Rotterdam

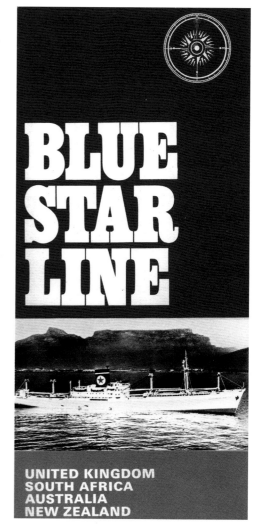

Blue Star Line schedule, 1970.

BLUE STAR LINE

UNITED KINGDOM
SOUTH AFRICA
AUSTRALIA
NEW ZEALAND

Gothenburg. *New York Star* took frozen fish from Las Palmas to Japan, which was also loaded at Villa Cisneros, Luanda, Walvis Bay and Cape Town. The fish was loaded direct from Japanese and Russian trawlers and fish factory ships. *Halifax Star*'s first voyage in her new guise was from South Africa to Southampton with a cargo of deciduous fruit.

The Royal Mail passenger vessel *Aragon* made her final departure from Buenos Aires to London in January 1969. This ended the line's passenger service between Britain and the River Plate, on which direct sailings were first introduced in June 1869. However, this service is older, since from 1851 passengers could travel there by the Royal Mail Line, although they had to change to a local vessel at Rio de Janeiro. Consequently, the Blue Star Line became the sole British company to maintain a regular passenger service between the United Kingdom and South America.

However, the passenger service from London to South American ports was terminated in 1972 after forty-five years and *Argentina Star*, *Brasil Star* and *Uruguay Star* were sent to the breakers at Kaohsiung. They were replaced by *Montevideo Star*, *Brasilia Star* and *Buenos Aires Star* and later *Ulster Star*. In August 1972 *Melbourne Star* was sold and after taking a final cargo, she was broken up at Kaohsiung. *English Star* followed her in 1973 and *Australia Star* was sold to Costa Armatori SpA of Naples and renamed *Cortina* that year. A joint company formed by the Blue Star Line and Robert M. Sloman of Hamburg launched the motorship *Starman* at the Lowestoft shipyard of Brooke Marine Limited on 17 September 1973. She was a heavy lift ship designed for the transportation of heavy equipment.

Early in 1974 Blue Star Ship Management was formed, which took responsibility for the management of Blue Star Line, Lamport & Holt and Booth Line vessels. It began its operations at Albion House, Liverpool, in January 1975. *Afric Star* was delivered in February 1975. She was the first of six 'A' class refrigerated vessels and was owned by the Glencairn

Brooke Marine Limited advertisement.

Shipping Company, on bare-boat charter to the Blue Star Line. She was followed by *Avila Star* and *Andalucia Star*, which berthed in the Pool of London prior to entering service. *Adelaide Star* suffered severe engine damage on a voyage from Timaru to Liverpool on 8 March 1975. She returned to Britain and discharged her cargo but was found to be beyond economical repair and was sold and broken up in Korea. Her sister *Tasmania Star* was broken up at Kaohsiung later that year.

*Almeria Star* entered service in November 1976. She was delivered to the Transport Exchange Company Limited, with Blue Star Ship Management as managers. Her sister *Almeda Star* was delivered to Avelona Star Limited, as was the *Avelona Star*. Both were also placed on bare-boat charter to the Blue Star Line and managed by Blue Star Ship Management. *Labrador Clipper* and *Newcastle Clipper* were acquired from Maritime Fruit Carriers when the company ran into financial difficulties in 1976. They were actually purchased from Maritime Midland Bank Limited and renamed *Tuscan Star* and *Trojan Star* respectively.

The container ship *Australia Star* was delivered to Brodies (London) Limited with Blue Star Ship Management as managers in 1978. Her sister, *New Zealand Star*, was launched on 20 July 1978 and entered service in January the following year. They were designed to carry 721 TEUs. *New Zealand Star* of 1967 was renamed *Wellington Star*, *Brasilia Star* was broken up at Kaohsiung and *Avila Star* was sold to Kornelius Olsen for further trading. *Townsville Star* of 1957 was sold after delivering 160,000 carcases of meat from Australia to Odessa, arriving at Kaohsiung on 14 July 1980, and broken up by Nan Long Steel & Iron Company. *Rockhampton Star* was sold for further trading in 1981 and survived another two years before she was demolished at Chittagong.

*Andalucia Star* and *Avelona Star* were chartered by the British government during the Falkland Island conflict in 1982 and both were fitted with a helicopter pad aft. *America Star* was sold to Vermerar Cia Nav of Panama and renamed *Golden Princess* for further trading and *Halifax Star* was broken up in China the following year.

A fire broke out in the engine room of *English Star*, which was one of four new ships being fitted out by Harland & Wolff at Belfast. It caused approximately £1 million of damage and delayed her entry into service. HRH the Duchess of Kent, accompanied by Edmund Vestey, named *English Star* on 25 January 1985. It was pointed out at the ceremony that it was twenty-five years since *Ulster Star* was completed and fifty years since Harland & Wolff built *Imperial Star*, their first ship for the Blue Star Line. *Scottish Star* was delivered in March 1985, followed by *English Star*, *Auckland Star* and *Canterbury Star*. After ten years' service with the company, *Andalucia Star*, *Almeria Star*, *Almeda Star* and *Avelona Star* were sold for further trading.

The joint service by Blue Star Line, Houlder Brothers, Lamport & Holt Line and Royal Mail Line was renamed the Brisa Service in 1986 and a new consortium was formed with Hamburg Sud-Amerika, Alianca, Cie Maritime Belge, Havenlijn, SEAS (D'Orbigny), Rotterdam Zuid-Amerika and Nedlloyd, with a fleet of nine ships on South American routes. At the end of 1986 *Afric Star* was sold and *Columbia Star* was transferred to the Austasia Line and renamed *Mandama*. *Perseus* was chartered in 1986 to operate from the Falkland Islands to Japan with squid caught off the islands. Lion Shipping Limited, Hong Kong, was formed that year to manage seven refrigerated vessels. *California Star* was transferred to the Austasia Line in 1987 and renamed *Mulbera*.

By 1990 the debt inside the Vestey empire increased to £420 million and many of the tax loopholes that the organisation had taken advantage of were closed by the British government in 1991. It was estimated at the time that the organisation had legally avoided paying more than £88 million in tax. The Vestey family fortune was estimated at £2 billion, they had 23,000 employees and owned 250,000 head of cattle on several continents. It was reported in 1978 that the Dewhurst chain of butchers paid £10 tax on a profit of more than £2.3 million. More than fifty-five banks were owed money and Union International assets were estimated at £50–100 million. A consortium of the banks, coordinated by Lloyds, called on a halt to the spending and demanded cutbacks and economies. The business was changing as the supermarkets were developing their own wholesaling operations with specialist butchery sections. They were able to take advantage of the economics of scale when purchasing items such as meat, fruit and other items. Union International had also invested heavily in the property boom with money borrowed from the banks.

Edmund Hoyle Vestey had joined the business and became chairman of the Blue Star Line in 1971. He held that post for twenty-five years and was President of the General Chamber of British Shipping in 1981/82. He owned a sporting estate in Sutherland, which was purchased by the family in the 1930s and extended to more than 100,000 acres. However, a large proportion was sold off under the devolved Scottish administration's land reforms. He also owned farmland in the Borders and the Thurlow estate in Suffolk. Edmund was High Sheriff of Essex in 1977 and was appointed a deputy Lord Lieutenant of Essex in 1978, and of Suffolk in 1991.

Despite the Vestey family putting £35 million into the business, it was decided to put Union International into administrative receivership in 1995. A spokesperson for the family said in March 1995 that the family were very saddened by the demise of Union International, as it was one of the original parts of their business. However, the Vesteys retained their interests in property and farming and the shipping interests of the Blue Star Line were sold to P&O Nedlloyd for £60 million in 1998. The refrigerated ships were retained by the Vestey organisation under the ownership of Albion Reefers. These were operated by Star Reefers, formed by the merging of the reefer fleets of Hamburg Sud and Albion Reefers. Blue Star later took over the minority interest of Hamburg Sud. Star Reefers dates back to the mid-1990s and was the result of various single ship acquisitions and corporate mergers. Its origins go back to vessels owned by Irgens Larsen AS, and through Kvearner Shipping AS and Swan Shipping AS. Equity was injected into the company by Siem Industries Incorporated in 2000 and it was renamed Star Reefers Incorporated the following year. Star Reefers, with a fleet of twenty-four ships, was sold in July 2001 to Norwegian interests, who later joined with the Japanese NYK Line, forming NYK Star Reefers Limited. The new company operated a fleet of seventy-four ships. The sale ended the ninety years' association of the Vestey family with the shipping industry and an era in British shipping history.

*America Star*, *Melbourne Star*, *Sydney Star* and *Queensland Star* retained the Blue Star Line colours on the Australia and New Zealand to the west coast of America service. *America Star* ended her career in Blue Star Line colours in February 2003. Reederei Blue Star was formed in 2002 as the management company of P&O Nedlloyd Limited. P&O Nedlloyd stated that it created Reederei Blue Star to diversify its resources for chartered ships. It placed an order in April 2002 for five 2,500 TEU vessels on time charter for five years, followed by an order for an additional four vessels the following year. P&O Nedlloyd Limited was acquired by AP Muller-Maersk in 2006, combining it with Maersk Sealand, forming the Maersk Line. Reederei Blue Star continued to operate as part of the Maersk Line.

The following vessels were operated by P&O Nedlloyd Maersk:

| | | | |
|---|---|---|---|
| *P&O Nedlloyd Adriana* | 2003 | 24,833 grt | 34,282 dwt |
| 200.55 x 30.20 x 11.50 metres | | IMO 9275024 | |
| *Nedlloyd America* | 1992 | 48,508 grt | 50,620 dwt |
| 266.00 x 32.27 x 12.50 metres | | IMO 8915677 | |
| (*Ekali* – 2013, Broken up – 2014) | | | |
| *P&O Nedlloyd Juliana* | 2003 | 26,833 grt | 12,743 dwt |
| 210.07 x 30.20 x 11.50 metres | | IMO 9275036 | |
| *P&O Nedlloyd Lyttleton* – see *Brisbane Star* (2)/*Singapore Star* | | | |
| *P&O Nedlloyd Marita* | 2003 | 26,833 grt | 34,295 dwt |
| 210 x 30.20 x 11.50 metres | | IMO 9275048 | |
| *P&O Nedlloyd Maxima* | 2003 | 26,833 grt | 34,314 dwt |
| 210.07 x 30.20 x 16.70 metres | | IMO 9283708 | |
| (*Rio Thelon* – 2012) | | | |
| *P&O Nedlloyd Mondriaan* | 2004 | 93,511 grt | 97,517 dwt |
| 335 x 42.80 x 14.00 metres | | IMO 9289922 | |
| (*Maersk Sana* – 2006) | | | |
| *P&O Nedlloyd Nina* – see *Choyang Sydney* | | | |
| *P&O Nedlloyd Pallister Bay* – see *ACT 7* | | | |
| *P&O Nedlloyd Pegasus Bay* – see *ACT 8* | | | |
| *P&O Nedlloyd Taranaki* – see *Australia Star* (4) | | | |

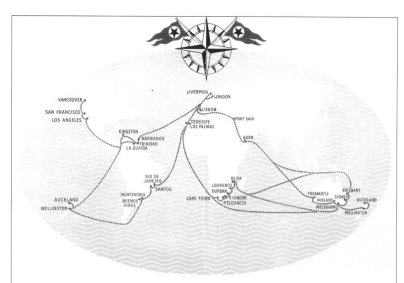

# *Blue Star Liners span the World*

**A NEW AND IMPROVED SERVICE BETWEEN THE UNITED KINGDOM, SOUTH AFRICA, AUSTRALIA AND NEW ZEALAND**

Years of experience in the passenger trades of the seven seas have gone into the design, arrangement and equipment of these vessels. As a result the accommodation and general facilities compare very favourably with those of the large liners, with the added advantage of a strictly limited number of passengers.

On these compact vessels there are the utmost conveniences, for you have an easy and constant access to every facility without negotiating flights of stairs and exposure to the elements if the weather should be inclement.

## *All outside Staterooms*

Blue Star Line brochure.

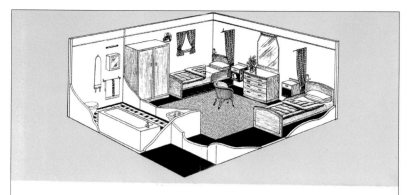

# *Comfort - Relaxation - Good Service*

While these modern Blue Star Liners are essentially cargo vessels the passenger accommodation has been thoughtfully and carefully planned, and although they vary somewhat both in the number of passengers carried, and in layout of the passenger's accommodation this folder can but depict the general attractiveness of the Cabins and Public Room.

These staunch vessels represent the most advanced ideas in ship design and general construction: the excellent deck space provided, affords the greatest possible relaxation, while the good service on board from the Captain downwards leaves nothing undone which would contribute to the comfort, pleasure and enjoyment of your trip.

With all these amenities so specially designed for a limited number of passengers, a voyage on one of these vessels will truly be an experience calculated to remain in your memory for all time.

## *Outdoor Salt Water Plunge*

BLUE STAR LINE

| | | | |
|---|---|---|---|
| *Maersk Nottingham* | 2004 | 26,833 grt | 34,300 dwt |
| 200.55 x 30.20 x 11.50 metres | | IMO 9275050 | |
| *Maersk Sarnia* | 2005 | 93,511 grt | 97,543 dwt |
| 335.36 x 42.80 x 20.78 metres | | IMO 9289946 | |

On 18 June 2009, the German Komrowski Shipping took over the management of Reederei Blue Star from the AP Muller/Maersk Group, with the ships remaining on charter to Maersk. The managing director of Komrowski stated that:

> All the vessels are owned by German KG funds and have long standing charter party contracts with Maersk Line as the prime charterer. The charter contracts with Maersk would remain unchanged and had not been renegotiated. Blue Star will be part of the Komrowski Group but will continue to operate under its own name. We have a lot of respect for Blue Star and want to keep the name.

The Komrowski group was established in 1912 and was originally founded as a trading company. It took up shipping and ship management functions in 1923 and has developed these ever since. It is also involved in international trading and financial services with a number of overseas offices.

The deal brought Komrowski's fleet to fifty-two vessels under management and its total box-ship capacity to 190,000 TEUs. To date, Komrowski had only managed feeder-ships of up to 1,700 TEUs and the fleet included four heavy lift vessels and eight bulk carriers between 57,000 dwt and 75,200 dwt. The company also had an additional ten vessels on order, four 1,085-TEU feeder-ships and six bulkers of 57,000 dwt and 75,200 dwt respectively.

In 2009 Blue Star managed thirty-four vessels, comprising nine 2,500-TEU feeder-ships, nine box-ships of around 4,200 TEUs, five vessels of 3,600 TEUs and eleven container ships with an 8,400-TEU capacity.

| Charter Name | Owner's Name | TEU Capacity | BLT |
|---|---|---|---|
| *Nedlloyd Adriana* | *Adriana Star* | 2,556 | 2003 |
| *Nedlloyd Juliana* | *Juliana Star* | 2,556 | 2003 |
| *Nedlloyd Marita* | *Marita Star* | 2,556 | 2003 |
| *Maersk Nottingham* | *Regina Star* | 2,556 | 2004 |
| *Nedlloyd Valentina* | *Valentina Star* | 2,556 | 2004 |
| *Nedlloyd Teslin* | *Rio Teslin* | 2,556 | 2004 |
| *Nedlloyd Maxima* | *Rio Thelon* | 2,556 | 2004 |
| *Maersk Nolanville* | *Rio Taku* | 2,556 | 2004 |
| *Nedlloyd Evita* | *Rio Thompson* | 2,556 | 2004 |
| *Nedlloyd Europa* | *Europa Star* | 3,604 | 1991 |
| *Nedlloyd Asia* | *Asia Star* | 3,604 | 1991 |
| *Nedlloyd America* | *America Star* | 3,604 | 1992 |
| *Nedlloyd Africa* | *Africa Blue Star* | 3,604 | 1992 |
| *Nedlloyd Oceania* | *Oceania Star* | 3,604 | 1992 |
| *Maersk Miami* | *Hong Kong Star* | 4,181 | 1994 |
| *Nedlloyd Honshu* | *Honshu Star* | 4,181 | 1995 |
| *MSC Almeria* | *Jervis Star* | 4,224 | 1992 |
| *MSC Dalton* | *Repulse Star* | 4,224 | 1992 |
| *MSC Darlington* | *Newport Star* | 4,224 | 1993 |
| *Maersk Dauphin* | *Providence Star* | 4,224 | 1994 |
| *MSC Dartford* | *Singapore Star* | 4,224 | 1994 |
| *Maersk Delano* | *Shenzen Star* | 4,224 | 1994 |
| *Maersk Delmont* | *Colombo Star* | 4,224 | 1995 |
| *Maersk Stralsund* | *Marilyn Star* | 8,400 | 2005 |
| *Maersk Saigon* | *Maria Star* | 8,400 | 2006 |
| *Maersk Seoul* | *Marlene Star* | 8,400 | 2006 |
| *Maersk Sana* | *Mondriaan Star* | 8,450 | 2004 |

| Maersk Santana | Manet Star | 8,450 | 2005 |
|---|---|---|---|
| Maersk Sarnia | Michelangelo Star | 8,450 | 2005 |
| Maersk Sydney | Miro Star | 8,450 | 2005 |
| Maersk Seville | Mahler Star | 8,466 | 2006 |
| Maersk Sheerness | Mendelssohn Star | 8,466 | 2006 |
| Maersk Sofa | Menotti Star | 8,466 | 2007 |
| Maersk Singapore | Monteverdi Star | 8,466 | 2007 |

ER Capital Holding and Komrowski Holdings completed the merger of their ship management activities into a combined German ship-owning group known as Blue Star Holdings in December 2011. The subsidiary ER Schiffahrt was responsible for managing the new activities. The joint managed fleet under the umbrella of Blue Star Holdings consisted of 137 vessels; twenty-five bulk carriers, four multipurpose units and 108 containerships (including two ships managed for the Norwegian ship-owning group SinOceanic ASA). Blue Star Holdings said that its strategy was aimed at growth, attracting other ship-owning companies as partners and increasing its fleet to over 200 vessels. The company said that it is open to talks with other ship-owning companies who would be interested in joining the new group as partners. They felt that:

> Synergies in terms of economies of scale, for example when marketing vessels or in crewing and procurement as well as in operational areas such as implementing new environmental regulations, can be best gained once a group reaches a certain size. Furthermore, banks will in future focus their ship financing activities on profitable companies which can support financing on the strength of their balance sheets. This is why structures are required now to be successful in the future.

Star Reefers is 73.5 per cent owned by the Siem Industrial Group and has plans to attract further business outside the perishable products sector.

The company had posted a poor performance in 2011 of a US $124 million net loss compared to a profit of $2.4 million the previous year, with a loss of $39,000 in the first quarter of 2012. There were problems of an ageing fleet of fuel-inefficient ships and a lack of investment in modern vessels, coupled with the lowered demand in Europe and poor harvests in South America, which had lessened the chance of a peak shipping season. Siem Industries is a diversified holding company with interests in the oil and gas services industry, the ocean transport of refrigerated cargoes and automobiles, potash mining in Germany, finance and Swedish industry. The company was formed in 1980 but can trace its history back to the nineteenth century. It is incorporated in the Cayman Islands and has offices in Norway, London and Monaco. The Ores Trust is the largest shareholder, with 66.8 per cent of the share capital. For the year ended 31 December 2012, they reported a consolidated net income of US $246.5 million, and the year ended 31 December 2013 a consolidated net income of US $159.3 million. In March 2014 the company announced that four of their Star-class ships had gained a 4½-year charter with Chiquita's Great White Fleet, commencing in June 2014.

In 2014 the Vestey Family's farming interests are concentrated in Brazil, where the group manage cattle breeding and rearing programmes as well as sugar cane production for the ethanol and sugar companies. They have planted eucalyptus trees and have wine investments in the Australian Adelaide Hills and Victoria. They also remain involved in the premium quality meat mail order market through Donald Russell Limited, which is based in Aberdeenshire.

# FLEET LIST

1. *Lizanka/Broderick* (1890)
4,331 grt, 2,842 n, 364.8 x 47 x 26.9 feet, yard no. 248.
Steel, single screw, triple expansion, 3 cyls, 415 NHP, steam pressure 160 lbs, two double ended boilers by Blair & Company, Stockton. 10 knots. Two decks.
B. R. Ropner & Son, Stockton-on-Tees.

19.6.1890    Launched as *Pakeha* for Shaw Savill & Albion Limited.
8.1890    Delivered.
18.9.1909    Purchased by the Vestey Brothers, renamed *Lizanka* and registered in London by William P. Outram.
31.10.1910    Chartered to the Russian Ministry of Fisheries, Vladivostok, and was used as the mother ship for the Siberian salmon fishing fleet. Owned by Emma E. Rulcovius and later J. M. Erikson.
4.1911    Returned to the Vestey Brothers and renamed *Broderick*, owned by the Broderick Steam Ship Company, London.
1.1912    Managed by the Blue Star Line.
29.4.1918    On a voyage from London to Puerto Cabello she was torpedoed and sank by UB-57 off Hastings.

2. *Brodmore* (1890)
4,045 grt, 2,642 n., 365 x 47 x 26.9 feet, yard no. 392.
Steel, single screw, triple expansion, 3 cyls, 415 NHP, steam pressure 160 lbs, two double ended boilers by Central Marine Engineering Company, West Hartlepool. 10 knots. Two decks.
B. William Gray & Company, West Hartlepool.

4.6.1890    Launched as *Rangatara* for Shaw Savill & Albion Company and her thinner funnel distinguished her from her sister *Lizanka*. Laid down for Christopher Furness, West Hartlepool.
16.4.1909    Purchased by David Daniel Jones, London.
3.12.1909    Renamed *Count Muravieff* when chartered by the Russian Ministry of Fisheries. Owned by Emma E. Rulcovius and later J. M. Erikson.
1910    Became *Graf Muravjev*.
18.4.1911    Sold to Mark Hinchliff, London.
2.5.1911    Renamed *Brodmore*, owned by M. Hinchliff and J. Ragg and the Brodmore Steam Ship Company, Josiah Calderbank Ragg, Liverpool, as managers.
1912    Managed by the Blue Star Line.

27.2.1917 Torpedoed and sank by UB-43, north-west of Marsa Susa, North Africa, on a voyage from Majunga to the United Kingdom. Her master was taken as a prisoner of war.

### 3. *Brodland* (1891)

2,989 grt, 1,949 n., 310 x 41.2 x 17.8 feet.

Steel, single screw, triple expansion, 3 cyls, 272 NHP, steam pressure 160 lbs, 2 single ended boilers by Westgarth, English & Company, Middlesbrough. 9 knots. One deck and spar deck.

B. Craig Taylor & Company, Stockton-on-Tees.

9.4.1891 Launched as *Highland Mary* for the Nelson Line

1900 Company became Nelson Line (Liverpool) Limited.

1.1912 Renamed *Brodland*, owned by the Brodland Steam Ship Company, Blue Star Line as managers.

1.2.1912 She made the first official sailing of the Blue Star Line with a cargo of coal from Barry Dock to Buenos Aires.

20.1.1913 On a voyage from Port Talbot to Punta Arenas with a cargo of coal, she grounded on Aberavon beach and was wrecked. Crew were rescued using a breeches buoy.

### 4. *Brodstone* (1896)

4,927grt, 3,181 n., 400.4 x 48.2 x 29 feet, yard no. 225.

Steel, single screw, triple expansion, 3 cyls, 485 NHP, steam pressure 200 lbs by D. Rowan & Sons Limited, Glasgow. 10 knots. Two decks.

B. Charles Connell & Company, Scotstoun.

5.3.1896 Launched as *Indraghiri* for Thomas B Royden's Indra Line, Liverpool.

4.1896 Delivered.

1901 Transferred to the Indra Line Limited, T. Royden as managers.

11.1910 Purchased by the Vestey brothers and renamed *Brodstone*, William Raphael Outram Limited, Liverpool, as managers.

1912 Managed by the Blue Star Line, owned by the Brodstone Steam Ship Company. She sailed from Barry Dock to Shanghai with a cargo of coal, returning with frozen pork, and was then placed on the River Plate service.

1915 Operated as a food transport for the British Expeditionary Force in France.

15.8.1917 On a voyage from Cardiff to Zarate, she was torpedoed and sunk by UB-40, west of Ushant. Five of her crew lost their lives.

### 5. *Brodvale/Tudorstar/Tudor Star* (1) (1899)

5,987 grt, 3,906 n., 440 x 54.3 x 29 feet, yard no. 540.

Steel, single screw, triple expansion, 3 cyls, 515 NHP, steam pressure 160 lbs, 3 double ended boilers by G. Clark, Sunderland. 11 knots. Two decks.

B. Sir James Laing & Sons, Sunderland.

11.3.1899 Launched as *Tomoana* for Tyser & Company, owned by the Tomoana Steam Ship Company.

16.6.1899 Maiden voyage from London to Australia.

1903 Owned by Tyser Line Limited.

1912 Renamed *Brodvale*, owned by the Brodvale Steam Ship Company, managed by the Blue Star Line.

1920 Renamed *Tudorstar*, owned by the Union Cold Storage Company Limited with Blue Star Line (1920) as managers.

19.12.1922 Ship was flooded and part of the bridge was damaged during a severe Atlantic gale.

28.12.1922 She reached Greenock.

1929 Renamed *Tudor Star*.

8.1934 Sold to SA Ricuperi Metallici.

6.10.1934 Arrived at Savona, Italy, and broken up.

6. *Brodmount/Stuartstar* (1899)

5,706 grt, 3,071 n., 420 x 54 x 28 feet, yard no. 360.

Steel, single screw, triple expansion, 3 cyls, 491 NHP, steam pressure 160 lbs, 3 single ended boilers by builder. 11 knots. Two decks, well deck aft covered.

B. R. & W. Hawthorn Leslie & Company Limited, Hebburn on Tyne.

15.11 1898    Launched as *Wakanui* for the New Zealand Shipping Company, registered in Plymouth.

2.1899    Maiden voyage from London to New Zealand.

4.1913    Renamed *Brodmount*, owned by the Brodmount Steam Ship Company, Blue Star Line as managers.

1919    Re-boilered.

1920    Renamed *Stuartstar*, owned by the Union Cold Storage Company Limited, managed by Blue Star (1920) Limited.

4.10.1923    Grounded at the Hook of Holland during a gale on a voyage from Zarate to Rotterdam with a cargo of frozen meat, and broke her back. The wreck became a danger to navigation and was demolished by explosives.

7. *Brodliffe/Tuscanstar* (1898)

5,464 grt, 3,505 n., 420 x 54 x 28 feet, yard no. 359.

Steel, single screw, triple expansion, 3 cyls, 491 NHP, steam pressure 160 lbs, 3 single ended boilers by builder. 11 knots. Two decks, well deck aft covered.

B. R. & W. Hawthorn Leslie & Company Limited, Hebburn on Tyne.

1.9.1898    Launched as *Morayshire* for the Elderslie Steam Ship Company, Glasgow.

12.1898    Delivered.

1900    Completed three voyages from Australia to South Africa as a Boer War supply ship.

10.8.1910    Sold to the Scottish Shire Line.

1911    In collision with the Thames collier *Axwell*, which sank. The Inquiry found that *Morayshire* was on the wrong side of the stream.

30.3.1915    Renamed *Brodliffe*, owned by the Brodliffe Steam Ship Company, Blue Star Line as managers.

3.4.1917    Avoided a torpedo fired by a German U-boat.

15.4.1920    Renamed *Tuscanstar*, owned by the Union Cold Storage Company Limited, managed by Blue Star (1920) Limited. It is reported that she was later renamed *Tuscan Star*.

1.1929    Purchased by G. & S. Rizzuto of Italy and renamed *Fortunestar*.

1936    Sold to Ignacio Messina Cia, renamed *Semien*.

1942    She was damaged by fire and taken over by the Swiss Nautilus S.A. and renamed *Lugano*.

1948    Returned to Ignacio Messina and operated on their South American meat route.

30.7.1952    Arrived at Savona and broken up.

8. *Brodness* (1894)

5,537 grt, 3,584 n., 420 x 54 x 28 feet, yard no. 324.

Steel, single screw, triple expansion, 3 cyls, 491 NHP, steam pressure 160 lbs, 3 single ended boilers by builder. 11 knots. Two decks, well deck aft covered.

B. R. & W. Hawthorn Leslie & Company Limited, Hebburn on Tyne.

1.9.1894    Launched as *Banffshire* for Elderslie Steam Ship Company.

11.1894    Delivered.

1910    Owned by Turnbull Martin & Company's Scottish Shire Line.

7.6.1915    Purchased by Brodness Steam Shipping Company, managed by Blue Star Line.

31.3.1917    Torpedoed off Anzio on a voyage from Genoa to Port Said. The sinking was claimed by the submarines U-3 and U-6.

9. *Brodhurst/Miltonstar* (1914)

3,071 grt, 2,109 n., 304.3 x 44.7 x 27.2 feet, yard no. 311.

Steel, single screw, triple expansion, 3 cyls, 1,460 NHP by builder. 9½ knots. One deck and shelter deck. Refrigerated.

B. Clyde Ship Building & Engineering Works, Port Glasgow.

31.10.1914    Launched as *Yula* for W. H. Stott Limited. Acquired on the stocks and handed over as *Brodhurst*, owned by the Brodland Steam Shipping Company with Blue Star Line as managers.

15.1.1915    Owned by Brodhurst Steam Shipping Company.

14.4.1920    Owned by the Union Cold Storage Company Limited. Blue Star Line (1920) Limited as managers.

25.10.1920    Renamed *Milton Star*.

11.1927    Renamed *Dnepr* when sold to Chenamskaya Azovskaya Kontora Sovtorgflot, Odessa, to operate on the Odessa–Novosibirsk–Marseilles route.

2.1933    Transferred to operate from Vladivostok.

1941–45    Operated on services from Vladivostok to Vancouver and Washington State.

8.1945    Operated as a supply ship to the Kurile Islands.

1958    Employed by the Magadanskova Fish Trust as a base at Nagovo Bay.

7.1970    Converted to a warehousing and accommodation base ship.

1978    Broken up.


10. *Brodholme/Gothicstar/Gothic Star* (1) (1899)

5,673 grt, 3,628 n., 420.5 x 54.7 x 28.8 feet, yard no. 333.

Steel, single screw, triple expansion, 3 cyls, 493 NHP, 3 single ended boilers, steam pressure 160 lbs by builder. 11 knots. Two decks.

B. Clydebank Engineering & Shipbuilding Company, Port Glasgow.

16.12.1898    Launched.

2.1899    Delivered to Elderslie Steam Ship Company, Turnbull Martin, as *Nairnshire*.

1910    Transferred to Scottish Shire Line.

2.6.1915    Purchased by the Brodholme Steam Ship Company, renamed *Brodholme*. Blue Star Line as managers.

10.6.1918    Damaged by torpedo from the German submarine UC-53 but managed to reach port.

1920    Owned by the Union Cold Storage Company Limited, managed by Blue Star (1920) Limited and renamed *Gothicstar*.

1929    Renamed *Gothic Star*.

4.7.1938    Arrived at Savona to be broken up.


11. *Brodfield* (1899)

5,455 grt, 3,498 n., 420.4 x 54 x 28.6 feet, yard no. 370.

Steel, single screw, triple expansion, 3 cyls, 505 NHP, 3 single ended boilers, steam pressure 160 lbs by builder. 11 knots. Two decks.

B. R. & W. Hawthorn Leslie & Company, Hebburn on Tyne.

7.1899    Launched.

9.1899    Delivered as *Surrey* to the Federal Steam Navigation Company.

1901    Operated as a Boer War transport between New Zealand and Cape Town on her inward voyages.

25.2.1915    Collided with a mine off Dunkirk and was beached near Deal and towed into Dover.

20.6.1915    Arrived at Tilbury and beached, prior to discharging her cargo. Examined by underwriters and declared a total loss.

6.8.1915    Purchased by Brodstream Steam Ship Company, Blue Star Line as managers.

15.12.1915    On completion of repairs she was renamed *Brodfield*, owned by the Brodfield Steam Shipping Company and managed by the Blue Star Line.

13.11.1916    On a voyage from Le Havre to Barry in ballast she was wrecked near Church Point, Scilly Isles. The crew were all saved.

12. *Brodlea/Saxonstar/Saxon Star* (1) (1899)

5,455 grt, 3,498 n., 420.4 x 54 x 28.6 feet, yard no. 369.

Steel, single screw, triple expansion, 3 cyls, 505 NHP, 3 single ended boilers, steam pressure 160 lbs by builder. 11 knots. Two decks.

B. R. & W. Hawthorn Leslie & Company, Hebburn on Tyne.

| | |
|---|---|
| 11.3.1899 | Launched as *Kent* for the Federal Steam Navigation Company. |
| 6.1899 | Delivered. |
| 1900 | Employed transporting New Zealand troops for the Boer War on her second inward voyage. |
| 14.10.1915 | Owned by the Brodlea Steam Shipping Company, managed by the Blue Star Line (1920) Limited, renamed *Brodlea*. |
| 4.1920 | Renamed *Saxonstar*, owned by the Union Cold Storage Company Limited, managed by Blue Star (1920) Limited. |
| 4.1929 | Renamed *Saxon Star*, owned by the Blue Star Line. |
| 1933 | Laid up on the River Tyne. |
| 8.1934 | Sold to SA Ricuperi for £8,000. |
| 17.9.1934 | Arrived at Savona and broken up. |

13. *Brodmead/Romanstar/Roman Star* (1) (1895)

5,628 grt, 3,660 n., 420 x 54 x 28.7 feet, yard no. 330.

Steel, single screw, triple expansion, 3 cyls, 505 NHP, 3 single ended boilers, steam pressure 160 lbs by builder. 11 knots. Two decks.

Passengers: 26 first class, 250 'tween deck.

B. R. & W. Hawthorn Leslie & Company, Hebburn on Tyne.

| | |
|---|---|
| 25.4.1895 | Launched as *Rakaia* for the New Zealand Shipping Company. |
| 6.1895 | Delivered. |
| 1909 | Transported the first consignment of frozen meat from Nelson to the United Kingdom. |
| 13.2.1915 | Owned by the Broadmead Steam Shipping Company, renamed *Broadmead*. |
| 7.9.1917 | Torpedoed in the Mediterranean by UB-49 and the master, Captain D. Macqueen, was killed on the bridge. She managed to escape the German submarine and later docked at Gibraltar. |
| 4.1920 | Owned by the Union Cold Storage Company Limited, renamed *Romanstar* and managed by the Blue Star Line. |
| 20.8.1925 | Loaded the first consignment of South African fruit for the United Kingdom. |
| 5.1929 | Renamed *Roman Star*, owned by the Blue Star Line (1920) Limited. |
| 1933 | Laid up on the River Tyne. |
| 8.1934 | Sold to S. A. Ricuperi for £8,000. |
| 29.9.1934 | Arrived at Savona to be broken up, joining *Saxon Star* (1) and *Tudor Star* (1). |

14. *Montilla/Gaelicstar/Gaelic Star* (1) (1917)

5,595 grt, 3,528 n., 389.8 x 53.2 x 24.7 feet, yard no. 693.

Steel, single screw, triple expansion, 3 cyls, 548 NHP, 3 single ended boilers, steam pressure 200 lbs by D. Rowan & Company, Glasgow. 12 knots. Two decks and shelter deck.

Passengers: 12.

B. Russell & Company, Port Glasgow.

| | |
|---|---|
| 22.2.1917 | Launched as *Montilla* for the Montilla Steam Ship Company, managed by the Blue Star Line. |
| 8.1917 | Delivered. |
| 5.1920 | Renamed *Gaelicstar*, owned by the Union Cold Storage Company Limited, Blue Star Line (1920) Limited as managers. |
| 4.1929 | Owned by the Blue Star Line (1920) Limited, renamed *Gaelic Star*. |

8.1949     Sold to Cia Genovese di Nav a Vapori SA, Genoa, renamed *Capo Noli*.

1950     Purchased by Gestione Escercizio Navi, Genoa, and retained the same name.

1956     Transferred to Gestioni Esercizio Navi Sicilia GENS, Italy.

1.7.1959     Arrived at Trieste and broken up.

### 15. *Rubiera/Ionicstar/Ionic Star* (1) (1917)

5,602 grt, 3,528 n., 389.8 x 53.2 x 24.7 feet, yard no. 694.
Steel, single screw, triple expansion, 3 cyls, 548 NHP, 3 single ended boilers, steam pressure 200 lbs by D. Rowan & Company, Glasgow. 12 knots. Two decks and shelter deck.
Passengers: 12.
B. Russell & Company, Port Glasgow.

28.6.1917     Launched as *Rubiera* for Rubiera Steam Ship Company Limited, Blue Star line as managers.

12.1917     Delivered.

5.1920     Renamed *Ionicstar*, owned by the Union Cold Storage Company Limited, Blue Star Line (1920) Limited as managers.

1929     Became *Ionic Star* (1).

17.10.1939     On a voyage from Brazil she went aground on the approach to the Mersey, and broke in two, 1 mile west of Formby Point.

### 16. *Camana/Celticstar/Celtic Star* (1) (1917)

5,575 grt, 3,528 n., 390.7 x 53.2 x 24.7 feet, yard no. 289.
Steel, single screw, triple expansion, 3 cyls, 548 NHP, 3 single ended boilers, steam pressure 200 lbs by D. Rowan & Company, Glasgow. 12 knots. Two decks and shelter deck.
Passengers: 12.
B. Dunlop, Bremner & Company, Port Glasgow.

3.12.1917     Launched.

6.1918     Completed as *Camana*, owned by the Camana Steam Ship Company, Blue Star line as managers.

4.1920     Owned by the Union Cold Storage Company Limited, renamed *Celticstar* with Blue Star Line (1920) as managers.

1929     Renamed *Celtic Star*.

18.11.1934     Became the largest vessel to pass under Tower Bridge to berth at New Fresh Wharf in the Pool of London.

1935     Funnel replaced with a shorter version from *Avelona Star* (1).

18.10.1939     She was damaged when she collided with another vessel while in a convoy off the Cape Verde Islands.

28.3.1943     Sailed from Freetown on a voyage from Manchester, Greenock to Montevideo and Buenos Aires with cargo and mail.

29.3.1943     Torpedoed by the Italian submarine *Giuseppe Finzi*. She was hit in the No. 2 hold, starboard side, and immediately began to sink. Boats 1 and 2 were successfully launched and she sank so quickly that the men still on board were forced to jump into the sea. Two lives were lost and the sixty-three survivors were picked up by HMS *Wastwater*. One member of crew was taken prisoner by the Italians and cigarettes and matches were given to the men in the boats.

### 17. *Royalstar/Royal Star* (1) (1919)

7,918 grt, 4,910 n., 465 x 58.5 x 37.1 feet, yard no. 438.
Steel, twin screw, triple expansion, 2 x 3 cyls, 1,138 NHP, 3 double ended boilers, steam pressure 200 lbs by builder. 12 knots. Two decks and shelter deck.
B. Workman Clark & Company, Belfast.

22.11.1918     Launched as *War Charon* for the Shipping Controller as a Standard 'G' type.

*Celtic Star* (1).

2.1919        Completed as *Royalstar* (1) for the Royalstar Steam Shipping Company, Blue Star Line as managers.

5.1920        Owned by the Union Cold Storage Company Limited, Blue Star Line (1920) Limited as managers.

11.1926        Damaged by an unchartered rock in the Malacca Strait and managed to reach Singapore, where she docked stern first.

1929        Renamed *Royal Star* (1).

1934        She was bunkered with the incorrect fuel, which solidified in her double bottom. Following her arrival at Smith's Dock, South Shields, steam pipes were fitted and when these were heated the fuel was able to be pumped out.

11.3.1941        Damaged off Stonehaven, Scotland, by bombs and gunfire.

20.4.1944        On a voyage from Buenos Aires to Malta, Taranto and Alexandria, she was damaged by German aircraft north-east of Algiers.

One crew member lost their life.

21.4.1944        Taken in tow by the Admiralty tug *Athlete*, but she continued to take in water and sank at 11.07 that morning. This was Blue Star Line's final war loss in the Second World War. Seventy-eight of the crew survived.

18. *Albionstar/Albion Star* (1) (1919)

7,920 grt, 4,908 n., 465 x 58.5 x 37.1 feet, yard no. 439.

Steel, twin screw, triple expansion, 2 x 3 cyls, 1,138 NHP, 3 double ended boilers, steam pressure 200 lbs by builder. 12 knots. Two decks and shelter deck.

B. Workman Clark & Company, Belfast.

6.3.1919        Launched as *War Hecuba* for the Shipping Controller as a Standard 'G' class, Commonwealth & Dominion Line Limited as managers.

11.6.1919        Following trials as *Albionstar*, she was owned by the Albionstar Steam Shipping Company, managed by the Blue Star Line.

6.1919        Maiden voyage from the United Kingdom to China and Japan.

5.1920        Owned by the Union Cold Storage Company Limited, Blue Star Line (1920) Limited as managers.

1929        Renamed *Albion Star* (1).

1930–32        Laid up.

1940        Deck house fitted between the bridge and funnel.

23.4.1948        Arrived at Briton Ferry and broken up by Thos W. Ward.

19. *Fresno Star* (1) (1919)

7,948 grt, 4,908 n., 465 x 58.5 x 37.1 feet, yard no. 572.

Steel, twin screw, triple expansion, 2 x 3 cyls, 1,138 NHP, 3 double ended boilers, steam pressure 200 lbs by builder. 12 knots. Two decks and shelter deck.

B. Barclay Curle & Company.

12.7.1919     Launched as *War Apollo* for the Shipping Controller as a Standard 'G' type. Became *Woodarra*, owned by the British India Steam Navigation Company.

26.11.1919     Trials.

8.1929     Purchased by the Blue Star Line (1920) Limited, and renamed *Fresno Star* (1) for service on the Pacific coast of America.

1933     Owned by the Union Cold Storage Company Limited, Blue Star Line Limited as managers.

1935     Ownership transferred to Frederick Leyland & Company.

14.7.1947     Arrived at Inverkeithing and broken up by Thos W. Ward.

20. *Tacoma Star* (1) (1919)

7,924 grt, 4,908 n., 465 x 58.5 x 37.1 feet, yard no. 440.

Steel, twin screw, triple expansion, 2 x 3 cyls, 1,138 NHP, 3 double ended boilers, steam pressure 200 lbs by builder. 12 knots. Two decks and shelter deck.

B. Workman Clark & Company, Belfast.

30.4.1919     Launched. She was laid down as *War Theseus* for the Shipping Controller as a Standard 'G' type. Handed over to the British India Steam Navigation Company as *Wangaretta*.

4.1929     Purchased by the Blue Star Line (1920) Limited with *Woodarra*, renamed *Tacoma Star* (1).

1933     Owned by the Union Cold Storage Company Limited, Blue Star Line Limited as managers.

1935     Ownership transferred to Frederick Leyland & Company.

3.5.1941     Damaged by an air raid and sank in Liverpool Docks.

7/8.5.1941     Struck by incendiary bombs and further damaged.

1.6.1941     Raised and dry-docked.

1.2.1942     On a voyage from Buenos Aires to the United Kingdom she was hit by a torpedo fired from U-109, 380 miles off Hampton Roads en route to join a convoy to the United Kingdom. A distress signal was heard but there was no other trace of the ship. Eighty-five people lost their lives.

21. *Pacific Star* (1) (1920)

7,951 grt, 4,954 n., 449.1 x 58.5 x 37.1 feet, yard no. 574

Steel, twin screw, triple expansion, 2 x 3 cyls, 1,138 NHP, 2 double and 3 single ended boilers, steam pressure 200 lbs by builder. 12 knots. Two decks and shelter deck.

B. Barclay Curle & Company.

1919     Laid down as *War Jupiter* for the Shipping Controller.

29.10.1919     Launched as *War Jupiter* for the Shipping Controller as a Standard 'G' type. Delivered to the New Zealand Shipping Company as *Otaki*.

4.2.1920     Sailed on her maiden voyage from Glasgow to New Zealand via the Panama Canal.

31.5.1934     Purchased by the Clan Line, renamed *Clan Robertson*. Cayzer Irvine & Company Limited as managers.

1935     Sold to J. A. Billmeir's Stanhope Shipping Company, renamed *Stanfleet*.

1939     Purchased by the Zubi Steam Ship Company Limited, renamed *Pacific Star*. Later acquired by the Blue Star Line.

27.10.1942     On a voyage from Rosario to Liverpool via Freetown in Convoy SL125, she was hit by a torpedo from U-509 and changed her course to head for Gibraltar. As the weather deteriorated, she changed course again for the Canary Islands.

28.10.1942     She continued to take on water and it was decided to abandon ship, with the ninety-seven crew and gunners taking to the lifeboats before she sank.

22. *Empirestar/Empire Star* (1)/*Tudor Star* (2) (1919)

7,199 grt, 4,524 n., 423.4 x 56 x 28.7 feet, yard no. 714.

Steel, single screw, triple expansion, 3 cyls, 696 NHP, 4 double ended boilers, steam pressure 200 lbs by J. G. Kincaid & Company, Greenock. 12 knots. Two decks and shelter deck.

B. Lithgows, Port Glasgow.

2.1919     Delivered as *Empirestar*, owned by the Empirestar Steam Ship Company, Blue Star Line as managers.

10.1920    Owned by the Union Cold Storage Company Limited, Blue Star Line (1920) Limited as managers.

25.10.1927    Involved in the rescue of passengers and crew from the Italian vessel *Principessa Mafalda*, 200 miles off Brazil. The vessel had lost its propeller shaft and was sinking. Despite the efforts of *Empirestar* and others, 303 people lost their lives in the incident.

1929     Renamed *Empire Star* (1) when the cowal top of the funnel was removed. Owned by the Blue Star Line.

1935     Renamed *Tudor Star* (2) so the name could be given to a new vessel.

1949     Owned by the Union International Company Limited, Blue Star Line Limited as managers.

1950     Sold to NV Scheepsloperij en Machinehandel, Holland.

27.2.1950    Arrived at Hendrik Ido Ambacht, Holland, and broken up.

23. *Magicstar* (1893)

5,534 grt, 3,403 n., 420 x 54 x 28.7 feet, yard no. 316.

Steel, single screw, triple expansion, 3 cyls, 534 NHP, 2 single ended boilers, steam pressure 160 lbs by builder. 11 knots. Two decks and shelter deck.

Passengers: 25 first class.

B. R. & W. Hawthorn Leslie & Company, Hebburn on Tyne.

10.10.1893    Launched as *Buteshire* for the Elderslie Steam Ship Company.

12.1893    Delivered.

1910     Owned by the Scottish Shire Line.

1915     Purchased by Houlder Brothers, Bollington Grange Steam Ship Company Limited, renamed *Bollington Grange*.

1916     Transferred to Furness Houlder Argentine Lines, renamed *Canonesa*.

1.5.1918    Torpedoed by UB-57 off Worthing and beached. Salvaged and sent to Southampton for repairs to be completed.

1919     Owned by the Broadway Steam Ship Company, renamed *Magicstar*, managed by the Blue Star Line.

1920     Union Cold Storage Company Limited as owners, Blue Star Line (1920) Limited as managers.

1929     Laid up.

1930     Broken up at Inverkeithing by Thos W. Ward Limited.

24. *Almeda* (1)/*Normanstar*/*Norman Star* (1) (1919)

6,996 grt, 4,432 n., 415.6 x 56.2 x 25.5 feet, yard no. 290.

Steel, single screw, triple expansion, 3 cyls, 662 NHP, 3 single ended boilers, steam pressure 200 lbs by builder. 12 knots. Two decks and awning deck.

B. Dunlop Bremner & Company, Port Glasgow.

19.4.1919    Launched as *Almeda* for the Almeda Steam Ship Company, Blue Star Line Limited as managers.

10.1919    Delivered to the Normanstar Steam Ship Company as *Normanstar*.

1920     Owned by the Union Cold Storage Company Limited, Blue Star Line (1920) Limited as managers.

1929     Renamed *Norman Star* (1).

16.1.1941    Damaged by bombs at Avonmouth.

1949     Ownership transferred to the Union International Company, Blue Star Line Limited as managers.

7.3.1950     Arrived at Blyth and broken up by Hughes Bolckow Shipbreaking Company Limited.

**25. *Lusiada/Vikingstar/Viking Star* (1) (1920)**
6,445 grt, 3,928 n., 400.3 x 52.3 x 28.5 feet, yard no. 225.
Steel, single screw, triple expansion, 3 cyls, 517 NHP, 3 single ended boilers, steam pressure 180 lbs by Dunsmuir & Jackson Limited, Glasgow. 10 knots. Two decks and shelter deck.
B. Napier & Miller Ltd, Glasgow.
28.11.1919    Launched as *Lusiada* for the Lusiada Steam Ship Company, Brazil, Blue Star Line as managers. Brazilian flag.
3.1920     Delivered as *Vikingstar* for the Blue Star Line (1920) Limited, London.
1929     Renamed *Viking Star* (1).
25.8.1942     On a voyage from Buenos Aires to the United Kingdom via Freetown she was hit by two torpedoes from U-130. She quickly broke in two and sank within minutes. A lifeboat with thirty-six of her crew on board reached land on 29 August, and two other life-rafts with twelve people reached the coast of Liberia on 4 September. Thirty-three members of her crew lost their lives.

**26. *Doricstar/Doric Star* (1) (1921)**
10,441 grt, 8,503 n., 499.8 x 64 x 37 feet, yard no. 731.
Steel, single screw, 2 double reduction geared turbines, 1,398 NHP, 6 single ended boilers, steam pressure 200 lbs by Metropolitan Vickers Electric Company, Manchester. 14 knots. Three decks and shelter deck.
B. Lithgows, Port Glasgow.
24.2.1921     Launched as *Doricstar* for Eastman's Limited, managed by the Blue Star Line for the China frozen pork service.

10.1921     Completed.
1929     Renamed *Doric Star*.
1933–34     Lengthened to 529.8 feet at Jarrow with the fitting of a new bow. Speed increased to 15 knots.
1938     Owned by the Union Cold Storage Company Limited, Blue Star Line Limited as managers.
2.12.1939     On a voyage from Auckland and Cape Town to the United Kingdom she was sunk by gunfire and a torpedo from the German battleship *Admiral Graf Spee* in the South Atlantic. The crew were taken aboard *Altmark* and were later rescued by HMS *Cossack* off Norway. Captain Stubbs was taken prisoner on board *Admiral Graf Spee* and was released just before she was destroyed in the River Plate.

*Doric Star.*

**27. *Britanica* (1913)**

1,350 grt, 774 n., 220 x 42.1 x 9.9 feet, yard no. 790.

Steel, twin screw, comp inv, 2x2 cyls each fired by one single ended boiler, steam pressure 140 lbs by Dunsmuir & Jackson Limited, Glasgow. 10 knots. One deck.

B. Cammell Laird & Company Limited, Birkenhead.

22.1.1913    Launched as *Doon* for the Royal Mail Steam Packet Company and based in Buenos Aires as a feeder vessel. Argentine flag.

4.1913    Delivered.

1919    Employed on the Europe–United Kingdom feeder services. Sold to the Las Palmas Produce Company, Argentina, and renamed *Britanica*.

1923    Sold to the Anglo South American Meat Company, Buenos Aires.

1924    Purchased by the Union Cold Storage Company Limited, Blue Star Line as managers. Her registration allowed her to trade to Brest or Hamburg.

1926    Managed by Soc. Anon. Frigorifico Anglo, Argentina.

1927    British flagged, managed by the Blue Star Line (1920) Limited.

1936    Owned by the Blue Star Line Limited.

25.11.1941    Operated as a store ship at Scapa Flow.

1.1946    Designated as a cold meat store at Singapore.

1.9.1947    Sailed from Singapore to London and laid up in the Thames.

2.1948    Laid up at the Royal Victoria Dock, London, with engine problems. Sold to L. & J. Engelen, Boom, Belgium, and converted to carry scrap metal between Antwerp and Willebroek, Belgium.

**28. *Kaolack* (1917)**

1,843 grt, 1,021 n., 268.8 x 35.8 x 19.1 feet, yard no. 222.

Steel, twin screw, two decks.

B. Ateliers et Chantiers de la Loire, St Nazaire.

15.6.1916    Launched for De Chanaud & Cie, Paris.

1.1917    Delivered to Soc. Coloniale d'Alimentation Frigorifique.

1921    Owned by Cie Francaise du Froid.

1924    Purchased by the Union Cold Storage Company Limited for the Almeria–Shanghai–Kobe salt trade.

1925    Quarantined at Taku Bar with cholera, one crew member died.

1933    Laid up on the River Tyne.

1935    Sold to the Crete Shipping Company, London, with Stelp & Leighton as managers.

1938    Owned by Claude Angel & Company, Cardiff, and used as a Spanish Civil War blockade runner.

25.11.1938    Damaged by bombs at Valencia.

1939    Owned by the Zubi Shipping Company.

1946    Sold to Empresa Nacional Elcano de la Marine Merrcante, renamed *Artico*.

1949    Operated as a fish factory storage ship by Industrias Pesquerias Africanas SA and based at Morocco.

1955    Owned by Empresa Nacional Elcano de la Marine Merrcante.

1959    Broken up at Cadiz by Sidero Metalurgica Navarra.

**29. *Trojanstar/Trojan Star* (1) (1916)**

9,257 grt, 5,612 n., 473.8 x 60 x 36.6 feet, yard no. 99.

Steel, twin screw, triple expansion, 3 cyls plus double reduction geared turbine with hydraulic coupling, 1,106 NHP, 5 single ended boilers, steam pressure 200 lbs by builder. 13 knots. Two decks and shelter deck.

B. Ateliers et Chantiers de France, Dunkirk.

9.11.1916    Launched as *Aberdeenshire* for the Scottish Shire Line and taken over by the French government, completed as *La Perouse* for Soc. Gen. d'Armaments Maritimes, Le Havre. Passengers: 300.

1920         Completed two voyages for the French Line, laid up.

1923         Chartered to the Northern Steamship Company.

1924         Owned by the Union Cold Storage Company Limited, Blue Star Line (1920) Limited as managers, renamed *Trojanstar*. Refrigerated space installed. Passengers: 12

1926         Owned by Blue Star Line (1920) Limited.

10.1928      Engine room fire after a steam pipe burst.

1929         Renamed *Trojan Star* (1).

1933         Converted to oil burning by Smith's Dock, South Shields. Added an extra 2 knots to her speed.

5.1934       On a voyage from Auckland to London the oil in the double bottom tanks became very thick and could not be pumped and she was forced to return to port.

1935         Two Bauer Wach exhaust steam turbines were added to each screw, and superheaters to the boilers, by Smith's Dockyard at North Shields. Her speed was increased by 2 knots and larger bunkers were installed.

23.3.1938    Collided with the German sail training vessel *Albert Leo Schlageter* in the Dover Straits. The German vessel later became the Portuguese *Sagres*.

27.8.1954    Sailed from Newport on her final voyage, which included a fire off Colombo, a leaking stern gland and an engine breakdown. She returned to London in April the following year.

25.5.1955    Arrived at Blyth and broken up by Hughes Bolckow Shipbreaking Company Limited.

30. *Stuartstar* (2)/*Stuart Star* (1) (1926)
11,884 grt, 7,430 n., 475.8 x 67.3 x 45.2 feet, yard no. 957.
Steel, twin screw, 2 x 2 single reduction geared turbines, 1,582 NHP, 4 boilers, steam pressure 200 lbs by Parson's Marine Steam Turbine Company, Newcastle. 14 knots. Four decks.

*Trojan Star* (1).

B. Palmer's Company, Newcastle.

15.3.1926    Launched as *Stuartstar* for Blue Star Line (1920) Limited.

7.1928       A pulverised coal burning boiler was installed, which proved economical and successful.

5.1929       Renamed *Stuart Star* (1)

1935         Major re-building was completed by decking over the wells.

20.11.1937   Sailed from Liverpool to Australia via Lourenço Marques.

17.12.1937   At 10.00 in thick fog she went aground at Hood Point Light, near East London, and when the stern broke off she became a total loss. She was on a voyage from Glasgow and Liverpool to Lourenço Marques and Melbourne.

**31. *Rodneystar/Rodney Star* (1) (1927)**

11,803 grt, 7,416 n., 476 x 67.3 x 45.2 feet, yard no. 785.
Steel, twin screw, 2 x 2 single reduction geared turbines, 1,582 NHP, 4 boilers, steam pressure 200 lbs by builder. 14 knots. Four decks.
B. Palmer's Company, Newcastle.

| | |
|---|---|
| 14.4.1926 | Launched as *Rodneystar*. |
| 1.1927 | *Delivered*. |
| 1929 | Renamed *Rodney Star*. |
| 1935 | Major rebuilding similar to *Stuartstar*. |
| 16.5.1941 | On a voyage from Buenos Aires to the Clyde, she was torpedoed three times by U-105, 400 miles off Freetown. The ship broke in two and the crew of eighty-three took to the lifeboats and were fired upon by the submarine. However, they were all later picked up by a destroyer and taken to Takoradi. |

**32. *Africstar/Africa Star* (1) (1926)**

11,867 grt, 7,425 n., 476 x 67.3 x 45.2 feet, yard no. 958.
Steel, twin screw, 2 x 2 single reduction geared turbines, 1,582 NHP, 4 boilers, steam pressure 200 lbs by builder. 14 knots. Four decks.
B. Palmer's Company, Newcastle.

| | |
|---|---|
| 11.5.1926 | Launched. |
| 11.1926 | Delivered and refrigeration plant fitted. |
| 1929 | Renamed *Africa Star* (1). |
| 29.1.1941 | On a voyage from Rio de Janeiro to London via St Vincent, Cape Verde Islands, she was sunk by the German raider *Kormoran*, which was disguised as a Russian vessel. One member of her crew lost his life but seventy-three men were taken to Bordeaux for internment by the German cargo vessel *Portland*. |

**33. *Raleighstar/Napierstar/Napier Star* (1) (1927)**

10,583 grt, 6,527 n., 476 x 67.3 x 45.2 feet, yard no. 786.
Steel, twin screw, 2 x 2 single reduction geared turbines, 1,582 NHP, 4 boilers, steam pressure 200 lbs by builder. 14 knots. Four decks.
B. Lithgow's, Port Glasgow.

| | |
|---|---|
| 5.8.1926 | Launched as *Raleighstar*, for Blue Star Line (1920) Limited. |
| 3.1927 | Delivered as *Napierstar*. |
| 1929 | Renamed *Napier Star*. |
| 1934 | Lengthened and fitted with a Maierform bow. |
| 18.8.1935 | Sailing from Glasgow to Liverpool, she collided head on with the White Star vessel *Laurentic* 40 miles from the Mersey Bar lightship. *Laurentic* took *Napier Star* in tow until the salvage tugs arrived to take over. On arrival at Liverpool her cargo was transferred to *Fresno Star* (1) and *Napier Star* was sent to the Tyne to be repaired. She was lengthened by 24 feet and a Maier bow was fitted. The wells fore and aft were plated over and a forecastle added. |

*Napier Star* (1).

18.12.1940    On a voyage from Liverpool to New Zealand with a crew of sixty-eight, one gunner and sixteen passengers, she was torpedoed by U-100, 300 miles south-west of Ireland. Two passengers and twelve of the crew were rescued from a lifeboat by the Swedish cargo vessel *Vaalaren*. Her crew of fifty-nine and twelve passengers lost their lives.

34. *Almeda* (2)/*Almeda Star* (1) (1926)
12,838 grt, 7,826 n., 535 x 68.3 x 43 feet, yard no. 919.
Steel, twin screw, 2 x 2 Parson's 22,000 rpm turbines (1 HP + 1 LP with astern incorporated in LP). Single reduction geared to 120 rpm. 8,000 IHP, 3 double and 2 single Howden boilers, 200 psi by builder. 17 knots. After funnel was a dummy. Three decks and part of 4th deck.
Passengers: 180 first class.
B. Cammell Laird & Company Limited, Birkenhead.
29.6.1926    Launched as *Almeda* as the first of three sisters for Blue Star Line (1920) Limited.
12.1926    Delivered.
16.2.1927    Operated the first Blue Star Line London to South America passenger service.
7.5.1929    Renamed *Almeda Star* (1)
1935    Lengthened by 65.7 feet and a Meier bow fitted. 14,935 grt.
Passengers: 150 first class.
28.5.1937    On a voyage to Tilbury she grounded in fog outside Boulogne, re-floated the following day.
1937    Mainmast removed.
22.12.1940    During an air raid in Liverpool she sustained considerable damage while anchored in the River Mersey. She returned to the docks for repairs. That night 299 German aircraft attacked Merseyside between 19.45 and 04.20, causing considerable damage to the docks and to the West Float of Birkenhead, which was particularly badly hit. *Llangibby Castle* was hit by incendiaries in Alexandra Dock and the fires were quickly extinguished. However, the fire in an adjoining shed spread to the ship, causing damage. The Brocklebank cargo vessel *Mahronda* was damaged by a bomb exploding in her No. 1 hold, setting her cargo on fire. The Mersey Docks & Harbour Board grab hopper dredger was sunk in Langton Dock, but was re-floated the following February. *Pando* was damaged in Canada Dock. She had only been completed by Harland & Wolff at Belfast several months earlier. Ellerman Wilson Line's *Silvio* was sunk in Alexandra Dock, with the loss of one of her crew. The damage to *Silvio* was so extensive that she was broken up later where she lay.
17.1.1941    She was sunk by a torpedo from the German submarine U-96, 250 miles west of the Outer Hebrides, in a gale. The 194 passengers, 137 of her crew and twenty-nine gunners lost their lives. She was on a voyage from Liverpool to the River Plate. U-96 had sunk the Pacific Steam Navigation Company passenger vessel *Oropesa* the previous day. Her crew of 137, twenty-nine gunners and 194 passengers lost their lives.

35. *Andalucia*/*Andalucia Star* (1) (1927)
12,846 grt, 7,830 n., 535 x 68.3 x 43 feet, yard no. 920.
Steel, twin screw, 2 x 2 Parson's 22,000 rpm turbines (1 HP + 1 LP with astern incorporated in LP). Single reduction geared to 120 rpm. 8,000 IHP, 3 double and 2 single Howden boilers, 200 psi by builder. 17 knots. After funnel was a dummy. Three decks and part of 4th deck.
Passengers: 180 first class.
B. Cammell Laird & Company Limited, Birkenhead.
21.9.1926    Launched as *Andalucia* for Blue Star Line (1920) Limited.
3.1927    Delivered to the Blue Star Line.
27.5.1929    Renamed *Andalucia Star* (1).
1935    Lengthened by 65.7 feet and a Meier bow fitted. 14,935 grt.
Passengers: 150 first class.
1937    Mainmast removed.

*Andalucia Star* (1).

6.10.1942    On a voyage from Buenos Aires to Liverpool, she was hit by two torpedoes from U-107 in nos 5 and 6 holds. 242 passengers and crew were rescued by HMS *Petunia* but one passenger and three of the crew lost their lives. The survivors arrived at Freetown the following day and were brought to the United Kingdom by the *President Doumer*. She was the final 'A' class ship to have been sunk in the hostilities.

## 36. *Arandora/Arandora Star* (1) (1927)

12,838 grt, 7,818 n., 535 x 68.3 x 43 feet, yard no. 921.
Steel, twin screw, 2 x 2 Parson's 22,000 rpm turbines (1 HP + 1 LP with astern incorporated in LP). Single reduction geared to 120 rpm. 8,400 IHP at 120 rpm, 3 double and 2 single Howden boilers, 200 psi by builder. 17 knots. After funnel was a dummy. A lift was installed. Three decks and part of fourth deck.

Passengers: 162 first class.
B. Cammell Laird & Company Limited, Birkenhead.

14.1.1927    Launched as *Arandora*, for Blue Star Line (1920) Limited.

5.1927    Delivered.

1929    She was sent to the Fairfield Ship Building & Engineering Company and converted to a cruise liner. Renamed *Arandora Star*.

15.6.1929    First cruise from Immingham to Norway but later based at Southampton. Passengers: 400. Fitted with a swimming pool, ballroom and shopping centre.

1931    Painted with a white hull and red band.

1935    White hull with blue band.

1936    Mainmast removed during refit.

1937    Transferred to Frederick Leyland & Company Limited, Blue Star Line Limited as managers.

1938    During the annual overhaul at Southampton, a Vent-Axia ventilation system was installed in all public rooms and main cabins.

3.9.1939    At the outbreak of war she was bound for New York and was sent back to Southampton and laid up at Falmouth.

12.12.1939    Operated as a test ship for net defences against torpedo attacks at Avonmouth.

1939    Converted to a troopship.

4.6.1940    Evacuated 1,600 troops from Narvik to Glasgow. Then sailed to Brest and Quiberon Bay, bringing back troops to the United Kingdom. She was under constant air attack when the men were being taken on board by boats. She later returned to France, embarking, 1,700 people from St Jean de Luz, arriving at Liverpool on 29 June.

30.6.1940    Embarked German and Italian internees for St John's, Newfoundland. Sailed from Liverpool with 479 German, 734 Italian male internees and 86 German prisoners of war, guarded by 200 troops and a crew of 174.

2.7.1940    Torpedoed by U-47 at 06.15, 75 miles west of Bloody Foreland, and sank within sixty-five minutes. The Canadian destroyer HMCS *St Laurent* arrived at the scene at noon and rescued 868 people from the sea. In all, 805 people lost their lives and it was claimed that if the Italians had not refused to leave the ship until she sank, more might have been saved. There were fifty-five of *Arandora Star*'s crew and thirty-seven soldiers who lost their lives in the sinking.

### 37. *Avelona/Avelona Star* (1) (1927)

13,376 grt, 7,818 n., 535 x 68.3 x 43 feet, yard no. 515.

Steel, twin screw, 2 x 2 Parson's 22,000 rpm turbines (1 HP + 1 LP with astern incorporated in LP). Single reduction geared to 120 rpm. 8,400 IHP, 3 double and 2 single Howden boilers, 200 psi by builder. 17 knots. After funnel was a dummy. A lift was installed. Three decks and part of 4th deck.

Passengers: 162 first class.

B. John Brown & Company Limited, Clydebank.

6.12.1926    Launched for Blue Star Line (1920) Limited.

20.5.1927    Maiden voyage from London to Madeira, Rio de Janeiro, Santos, Montevideo and Buenos Aires.

1928    Admiralty top removed from funnels.

5.1929    Renamed *Avelona Star* (1).

1931    As the Depression caused the passenger figures to fall dramatically, it was decided to convert her into a cargo vessel at Greenock. The passenger accommodation was removed and the bridge located nearer the bow.

1934    The carrying capacity was modified to 651,699 cubic feet (18,454 m) refrigerated, which gave her the largest capacity of any vessel afloat.

4.8.1939    At Dakar when war was declared and sailed directly to Buenos Aires to load meat.

*Top: Arandora Star.*

*Above: Arandora Star in the Mersey.*

5.1940        Sailed from Buenos Aires for Freetown to join a convoy.

16.6.1940     Convoy of thirty-three ships left Freetown.

30.6.1940     Torpedoed by U-43 at 09.30 when south-west of Land's End, and sank the following day. The French vessel *Beignon* rescued eighty survivors and was later torpedoed by U-30. The destroyers HMS *Vesper* and HMS *Windsor* were escorting the convoy and picked up 120 men, but four of *Avelona Star*'s crew lost their lives.

### 38. *Avila/Avila Star* (1) (1927)

12,872 grt, 7,878 n., 535 x 68.3 x 43 feet, yard no. 514.

Steel, twin screw, 2 x 2 Parson's 22,000 rpm turbines (1 HP + 1 LP with astern incorporated in LP). Single reduction geared to 120 rpm. 8,000 IHP, 3 double and 2 single Howden boilers, 200 psi. by builder. 17 knots. After

*Avelona Star* (1).

funnel was a dummy. Three decks and part of 4th deck.

Passengers: 162 first class.

B. John Brown & Company Limited, Clydebank.

22.9.1926     Launched as *Avila* for Blue Star Line (1920) Limited.

3.1927        Delivered.

1928          Admiralty top removed from funnels.

5.1929        Renamed *Avila Star*.

25.11.1934    Arrived on the Tyne for lengthening by 39 feet and the fitting of a Maierform bow by Palmer's Shipbuilding & Iron Company Limited, Jarrow.

3.1935        Returned to service.

5.7.1942      On a voyage from Buenos Aires to Freetown and Liverpool with a crew of 171 and twenty-five passengers, she had called at Freetown and was torpedoed just after midnight by U-201, 90 miles west of the Azores. The second torpedo struck the ship near a lifeboat which was being lowered and threw the occupants into the sea. The captain left the ship last and he was never seen again. As the weather deteriorated the lifeboats became separated and the Portuguese destroyer *Lima* rescued 110 people from three of the boats, and they were put ashore at Punta Delgada in the Azores.

22.7.1942     Another lifeboat was spotted by an aircraft and the Portuguese sloop *Pedro Nunes* was sent to them. The fifth lifeboat was never traced and sixty-two people lost their lives.

### 39. *Oregonstar/Oregon Star* (1) (1914)

5,714 grt, 3,620 n., 426.3 x 54.1 x 29.3 feet, yard no. 464.

Steel, single screw, quad expansion, 4 cyls, 747 NHP, 4 single ended boilers, steam pressure 220 lbs by NE Marine Engineering Company Limited, Newcastle. 12 knots. Two decks and shelter deck.

Passengers: 12.

B. Hawthorn Leslie & Company Limited, Hebburn on Tyne.

1913            Ordered by William Milburn & Company.

12.2.1914       Launched.

29.5.1914       Delivered to the Commonwealth & Dominion Line as *Port Albany*.

2.1929          Purchased by the Union Cold Storage Company Limited, renamed *Oregonstar*, Blue Star Line (1920) Limited as managers.

5.1929          Renamed *Oregon Star* (1).

13.11.1932      Suffered a serious fire on the buoys at Palmer's Shipbuilding & Iron Company Limited yard on the Tyne during an annual overhaul.

24.11.1932      Dry-docked and declared a total loss.

1933            Anchored in the River Tyne.

1934            Sold by the insurance underwriters to Hughes Bolckow to be broken up at Blyth, where she arrived on 1 May.

## 40. *Sultan Star* (1) (1930)

12,306 grt, 7,684 n., 486.1 x 70.2 x 36.4 feet, yard no. 955.

Steel, twin screw, 3 double reduction geared turbines to each screw, 1,870 NHP, steam pressure 230 lbs by builder. 14 knots. Three decks.

Passengers: 12. Crew: 72.

B. Cammell Laird & Company Limited, Birkenhead.

4.10.1929       Launched for Blue Star Line (1920) Limited.

2.1930          Inaugurated the service to New Zealand.

1933            Owned by the Union Cold Storage Company Limited, Blue Star Line Limited as managers.

12.1933         Made Blue Star's first call at Timaru.

1935            Owned by Frederick Leyland & Company.

14.2.1940       On a voyage from Buenos Aires to Liverpool, she was torpedoed by U-48 off Land's End at 16.30. She was in company of HMS *Exeter*, which was returning damaged from the Battle of the River Plate, and the battleship HMS *Barham* and destroyers HMS *Vesper* and HMS *Whitshed*. It was thought the German submarine had been following the group and when *Sultan Star* left them to head for the Thames, she was attacked and sank. HMS *Vesper* and *Whitshed* fired depth charges and picked up the survivors from *Sultan Star*. It was recorded that the submarine was sunk but records show she actually survived until 1945. One of her crew of seventy-six lost his life.

## 41. *Tuscan Star* (1) (1930)

11,449 grt, 7,075 n., 471 x 68.3 x 35.1 feet, yard no. 990.

Steel, twin screw, oil, 2 strike single acting 2 x 8 cyls, 1,994 NHP, 15 knots. By Sulzer Brothers, Winterthur, fitted by Palmer's.

B. Palmer's, Newcastle.

31.10.1929      Launched as the first motorship for the Blue Star Line (1920) Limited.

4.1930          Delivered for the New Zealand service.

1933            Owned by the Union Cold Storage Company Limited, Blue Star Line Limited as managers.

1935            Owned by Frederick Leyland & Company, same managers.

17.12.1939      Attacked by German bombers in the English Channel.

6.9.1942        With a crew of seventy-seven, twelve gunners and twenty-five passengers, she was torpedoed twice by U-109 in the South Atlantic between Freetown and Santos. She sank within fifteen minutes with a loss of forty-one of her crew, eight gunners and three passengers. She was on a voyage from Buenos Aires, Santos and Freetown to Liverpool. Sixty-two people survived.

## 42. *Brodstone* (2) (1935)

72 grt, 6 n., 75.6 x 18.1 x 7.1 feet, yard no. 652.

Steel, single screw, oil, 8 cyls 4 stroke, single acting, 122 NHP, 8 knots by Mirrlees, Bickerton & Day, Manchester. One deck. Tug.

B. Alexander Hall & Company, Aberdeen.

23.10.1934 Launched for service on the River Thames.

1935 Delivered as owned by Frederick Leyland, managed by the Blue Star Line. She was operated by the Union Cold Storage Company Limited and was the only vessel to wear their funnel colours.

1939 Renamed *Elizabeth Brodstone*.

1946 Sold to Gaselee & Son, renamed *Vespa* for their Thames services.

## 43. *Imperial Star* (1) (1935)

12,427 grt, 7,672 n., 543 x 70.4 x 32.9 feet, yard no. 933.
Steel, twin screw, oil, 4 stroke B&W type single acting 2 x 10 cyls, 1,631 NHP. 17 knots by builder. Three decks and part fourth.
Passengers: 12.
B. Harland & Wolff Limited, Belfast.

9.10.1934 Launched by remote by Lord Bledisloe, Governor General of New Zealand, and Lady Vestey named the vessel.

1.1935 Delivered to the Blue Star Line Limited.

10.1940 She was attacked by a surfaced German submarine and when she returned the fire, the vessel dived and *Imperial Star* was able to continue her voyage.

1.1941 Owned by Frederick Leyland & Company Limited, Blue Star Line Limited as managers.

12.3.1941 Berthed in Brocklebank Dock, Liverpool, she was bombed by German fighter planes.

9.1941 In convoy to Malta as part of Operation Halbard with cargo and troops. From Gibraltar the convoy was escorted by HMS *Prince of Wales*, *Nelson* and *Rodney*, the aircraft carrier *Ark Royal*, five cruisers and eighteen destroyers.

27.9.1941 At 20.32 she was hit by an aerial torpedo from an Italian aircraft which took off the rudder and both propellers. Over 300 troops

and some crew were taken off by the destroyer HMS *Heythorp* and a line was made from the destroyer *Oribi* in an attempt to tow the vessel to safety. However, this proved unsuccessful and *Imperial Star* was taking water and settling by the stern.

28.9.1941 It was decided to abandon the tow at 01.20 and 141 people were taken off her before three depth charges were attached and hit by gunfire from *Oribi*. The Italian submarine was sunk during this procedure.

## 44. *New Zealand Star* (1) (1935)

12,436 grt, 7,677 n., 542.9 x 70.4 x 32.9 feet, yard no. 934.

*Imperial Star* (1).

Steel, twin screw, oil, 4 stroke B&W type single acting 2 x 10 cyls, 1,631 NHP. 17 knots by builder. Three decks and part fourth.

Passengers: 12.

B. Harland & Wolff Limited, Belfast.

| | |
|---|---|
| 22.11.1934 | Launched for the Blue Star Line Limited. |
| 3.1935 | Delivered for the New Zealand service. |
| 1940 | Owned by Frederick Leyland & Company Limited, Blue Star Line Limited as managers. |
| 1950 | Transferred to Lamport & Holt Line, retained the same name. |
| 1953 | Moved to the Booth Line, same name. |
| 29.7.1967 | Sailed from Osaka for Kure. |
| 8.1967 | Broken up by Shimabun KK, Etajima Island, Kure, in Crusader Shipping Company's colours. |

*New Zealand Star* (1) berthed in Gladstone Dock, Liverpool.

### 45. *Australia Star* (1) (1935)

12,614 grt, 8,001 n., 542 x 70.4 x 32.3 feet, yard no. 939.

Steel, twin screw, oil, 2 stroke B&W type double acting 2 x 6 cyls, 2,463 NHP. 17 knots by builder. Three decks and part 4th.

Passengers: 12.

B. Harland & Wolff Limited, Belfast.

| | |
|---|---|
| 8.1.1935 | Launched. She differed from the first two vessels of the Imperial Star class as she had a poop and split bridge superstructure. Owned by Frederick Leyland & Company Limited, managed by the Blue Star Line Limited. |
| 4.1935 | Delivered for the New Zealand service. |
| 3.5.1941 | She was damaged by incendiaries in dock at Liverpool during the 'May Blitz'. That night saw the worst of the attacks, which took place between 22.30 and 05.00 when 300 German aircraft dropped around 360 tonnes of bombs and more than 49,700 incendiaries. The docks and area around them were the main targets for the bombers and 406 people lost their lives in Liverpool, fifty-seven in Bootle and sixteen in Litherland. The Brocklebank cargo vessel *Malakand* was berthed in Huskisson Branch No. 2 Dock, with more than 1,000 tons of ammunition and bombs. She was set on fire by an incendiary and an attempt was made to scuttle her but she later blew up. *Tacoma Star* (1) was hit by a bomb and settled on the bottom of the dock. She was later re-floated, repaired in drydock and returned to service. |
| 9.9.1944 | While in convoy in the Caribbean Sea, 150 miles from Cristóbal, she was in collision with the *Hindoo* and sank her. She rescued the survivors and docked at Cristóbal for repairs. *Hindoo* was a United States-owned vessel under the Panamanian flag and sank with a loss of three lives. *Hindoo* was not fitted with radar, although it was installed on *Australia Star*. The vessels were unlit and the night was dark and cloudy. *Hindoo* was moving at 10 knots and *Australia Star* at 15 knots. The collision |

occurred at 21.32, when *Australia Star* struck the port side of *Hindoo*. A later Court of Inquiry found that although *Hindoo* had contributed to the collision, *Australia Star* was at fault by not using its radar equipment. The judgement widened the law of negligence by stating that if a vessel is equipped with radar, it is duty bound to use it when visibility becomes or threatens to become impaired or limited in any manner.

1950        Owned by the Blue Star Line Limited.

15.6.1964    Arrived at Faslane and broken up by Shipbreaking Industries Limited.

*Australia Star* (1).

### 46. *Dunedin Star* (1) (1936)

12,891 grt, 8,020 n., 551 x 70.4 x 32.2 feet, yard no. 1009.

Steel, twin screw, oil, 2 x 20 cyls, 12,000 BHP. 17 knots by Sulzer Brothers, Winterthur.

One deck plus shelter deck.

Passengers: 12.

B. Cammell Laird & Company Limited, Birkenhead.

29.10.1935    Launched.

2.1936        Delivered to the Union Cold Storage Company Limited, Blue Star Line Limited as managers.

9.1941        Part of the Malta convoy Operation Halbard (see also *Imperial Star* (1)).

29.11.1942    On a voyage from Liverpool to Saldanha Bay, Aden and Egypt, she struck a submerged rock off the west coast of Africa.

30.11.1942    As she was taking on water, she was beached on the Skeleton Coast. When the rescue ships *Manchester Division* and *Temeraire* reached the scene, they discovered that sixty-three survivors had reached the shore. The rescue ships took off the remaining fifty-three people on board and an attempt was made by the Cape Town tug *Sir Charles Elliot* to assist the people on the shore, but this was unsuccessful. The tug proceeded back to Cape Town but it was also wrecked 40 miles further on, when it ran out of coal. The minesweeper *Nerine* arrived and attempted to get some food to those on the shore but she had to leave because of a lack of fuel. An aircraft dropped supplies but when it attempted to land it got stuck in the sand. On 2 December a convoy of eight rescue vehicles left Windhoek, 600 miles away. HMSAS *Nerine* arrived with a surf boat and rescue experts on board.

10.12.1942    The surf boat from *Nerine* managed to rescue seventeen people before it was wrecked and a ship's lifeboat managed to take eleven people and then twenty-six survivors. By 12 December the land convoy was 4 miles away and a second convoy was forty miles behind it. Both convoys arrived back at Windhoek on 24 December.

1.1943        The ex-trawler *Crassula* attempted to salvage the mail and other supplies from *Dunedin Star* but when her back broke this was abandoned.

1951      It was reported that brass and other metals were salvaged from the vessel, which was slowly sinking into the sand.

## 47. *Empire Star* (2) (1935)

12,656 grt, 9,187 n., 543 x 70.4 x 32.2 feet, yard no. 957.
Steel, twin screw, oil, 2 x 20 cyls, 12,000 BHP. 17 knots by Sulzer Brothers, Winterthur. One deck plus shelter deck.
Passengers: 12.
B. Cammell Laird & Company Limited, Birkenhead.
26.9.1935      Launched for Frederick Leyland & Company Limited, managed by the Blue Star Line.
12.1935      Delivered.
6.2.1942      The Japanese attack on Singapore commenced.

*Dunedin Star* (1).

12.2.1942      Escorted by HMS *Durban* and HMS *Kedah*, *Empire Star* sailed from Singapore for Batavia. At 08.50 she was attacked by six dive bombers and received three direct hits. A large number of bombers continued the attack and sixteen people were killed and sixty-seven wounded out of the estimated 2,160 aboard. *Empire Star* reached Batavia and was sent to Fremantle to be repaired.
23.10.1942      On a voyage from Liverpool to East London, she was torpedoed by U-615 off the Azores in a storm. As the boats pulled away from the ship, she was hit by two further torpedoes and sank very quickly. Two boats with survivors were picked up by HMS *Black Swan* and a boat containing the captain and thirty-two passengers and crew was never seen again. Four engine room members lost their lives and as she sank a loud explosion was heard underwater. It was thought that the submarine had also perished but she survived and was sunk in the Caribbean the following year. In all, thirty-two people lost their lives and seventy-one survived.

## 48. *Sydney Star* (1) (1936)

12,696 grt, 9,225 n., 542.8 x 70.4 x 32.3 feet, yard no. 958.
Steel, twin screw, oil, 2 stroke B&W type double acting 2 x 6 cyls, 2,463 NHP, 17 knots. By builder. One deck and shelter deck and part third and fourth decks.
Passengers: 12.
B. Harland & Wolff Limited, Belfast.
11.1.1936      Launched for Frederick Leyland & Company Limited, managed by the Blue Star Line Limited. She was designed with a raked stem, cruiser stern and stream-lined funnel with one mast. Her hull was divided by eight watertight bulkheads and had six holds, which were all insulated.
8.1939      Conveyed the Prime Minister of Queensland to the official opening of the Outer Harbour, Port Mackay.

24.7.1941    She was torpedoed at night by E-boats while on the Malta convoy. The 460 troops aboard were transferred in forty minutes to the escorting destroyer *Nestor*. A skeleton crew was left on board when an air attack began at 05.30. Another followed at 07.30, and a third with high level bombs. By this time she was listing badly and was down by the head but against all odds she managed to make port safely. The hole made by the torpedo was 40 feet by 16 feet.

18.8.1941    Dry-docked at Malta and took four months to be repaired by the Malta Dockyard Company.

1950    Owned by the Blue Star Line Limited.

1967    Sold to Embajada Cia Nav. SA and renamed *Kent* for her one-way voyage from Rotterdam to the Far East.

11.8.1967    Arrived at Kaohsiung in tow from Hong Kong and broken up. Yard No. 1014.

*Sydney Star* (1).

### 49. *Melbourne Star* (1) (1936)

12,806 grt, 7,964 n., 548.8 x 70.4 x 32.3 feet.
Steel, twin screw, oil, 2 stroke B&W type single acting 2 x 10 cyls, 2,463 NHP, 17 knots by Sulzer Brothers, Winterthur, installed by builder.
Two decks and part 3rd and 4th deck. Passengers: 12.
B. Cammell Laird & Company Limited, Birkenhead.

7.7.1936    Launched.

11.1936    Delivered to the Union Cold Storage Company Limited, managed by the Blue Star Line Limited.

5.9.1940    She was attacked by German bombers 450 miles west of Ireland and one member of the crew lost his life.

24.7.1941    Attacked by E-boats en-route to Malta but reached Valetta safely.

12.8.1942    During Operation Pedestal to Malta she suffered continuous air attacks but arrived at Valetta safely. In port she was covered with camouflage nets.

1943    Transferred to Frederick Leyland & Company Limited, same managers.

22.3.1943 Sailed from Liverpool to Sydney, via the Panama Canal with a crew of 75, eleven gunners and 31 passengers.

2.4.1943    Torpedoed by U-129 at 03.00, 480 miles from Bermuda in storm conditions on a voyage from Liverpool and Glasgow to Cristobal, Panama and Australia. She was loaded with ammunition and explosives causing the ship to disintegrate very quickly. Eleven of her crew managed to reach rafts in the water. However, only four of her crew of seventy-five, eleven gunners and thirty-one passengers survived and were found by a United States flying boat thirty-eight days later and taken to Bermuda.

### 50. *Brisbane Star* (1) (1937)

12,791 grt, 7,948 n., 551 x 70.4 x 32.3 feet, yard no. 1016.

Steel, twin screw, oil, 2 stroke B&W type double acting 2 x 6 cyls, 2,463 NHP, 17 knots by builder. Three decks and part fourth.

Passengers: 12.

B. Cammell Laird & Company Limited, Birkenhead.

16.9.1936    Launched.

1.1937    Delivered to the Union Cold Storage Company Limited, managed by the Blue Star Line Limited.

1942    Transferred to Frederick Leyland & Company Limited, same managers.

12.8.1942    She was on a voyage from Liverpool and Gibraltar as part of Operation Pedestal to Malta in a convoy of fourteen ships escorted by the battleships HMS *Nelson* and HMS *Rodney*, the aircraft carriers *Victorious*, *Indomitable*, *Furious* and *Eagle* and other cruisers and destroyers. A torpedo hit her bow and she managed to reach Susa in Tunisia. It was decided that she would proceed to Valetta and she left escorted by Spitfires.

14.8.1942    Arrived at Malta safely. Only five ships in the convoy were successful in reaching the island.

1943    When she was repaired, the bow was cut away at 45 degrees to the waterline.

1950    Transferred to the Lamport & Holt Line, same name.

8.1958    Operated the first post-war refrigerated sailing from Southampton, following the rebuilding of the cold store.

1959    Owned by the Blue Star Line Limited.

7.1963    Sold to Margalante Cia Nav. SA, Panama, renamed *Enea*.

1963    Left Rotterdam for Hong Kong and Osaka.

15.10.1963    Arrived at Osaka and broken up.

51. *Auckland Star* (1) (1939)

13,212 grt, 7,960 n., 542 x 70.4 x 32.3 feet, yard no. 1017.

Steel, twin screw, oil, 2 stroke B&W double acting 2 x 6 cyls, 2,463 NHP,

*Brisbane Star.*

17 knots. By builder. Three decks and part fourth.

Passengers: 12.

B. Harland & Wolff Limited, Belfast.

20.6.1939    Launched for the Union Cold Storage Company Limited, Blue Star Line as managers.

11.1939    Delivered.

28.7.1940    Torpedoed by U-99 80 miles off the coast of Ireland, on her first voyage from Townsville. Two more torpedoes were fired at her after she had been abandoned. The crew of seventy-four reached Ireland in three boats.

52. *Wellington Star* (1) (1939)

13,212 grt, 7,960 n., 542 x 70.4 x 32.3 feet, yard no. 1016.

Steel, twin screw, oil, 2 stroke B&W type double acting 2 x 6 cyls, 2,463 NHP, 17 knots by builder. Three decks and part fourth.
Passengers: 12.
B. Harland & Wolff Limited, Belfast.
20.4.1939   Launched for the Union Cold Storage Company Limited, Blue Star Line Limited as managers.
9.1939   Delivered.
16.6.1940   Torpedoed by U-101 at 11.02, 300 miles off Cape Finisterre, also on her first inward voyage from Sydney to Falmouth. The *Pierre LD* took fifty-two survivors to Casablanca and seventeen members of crew in a boat reached Figueria. It was later reported that U-101 had been one of five U-boats that had been waiting to try and locate a troop convoy bringing Australian troops to the United Kingdom. The U-boats never found the convoy, which included the Cunard liners *Queen Mary* and *Mauretania*.

53. *Adelaide Star* (1) (1940)
12,636 grt, 9,209 n., 528 x 70.4 x 32.3 feet, yard no. 646.
Steel, twin screw, oil, 2 stroke B&W double acting 2 x 6 cyls, 2,463 NHP, 17 knots by builder. Three decks and part fourth.
Passengers: 12.
B. Burmeister & Wain Limited, Copenhagen.
30.12.1939   Launched.
9.4.1940   Taken over by the Germans when they invaded Denmark.
6.11.1940   Delivered as *Seeburg* for the German Navy, managed by the Hamburg America Line. Based at Gotenhafen as a depot and target practice ship for the 27th U-boat flotilla.
4.12.1944   Mined and sunk by the Russian submarine SC-407 off Heistevnest, Danzig Bay.
1954   Raised and beached at Gdynia.
1955   Moved to Gdynia Dockyard for repairs to be completed.

1957   Renamed *Dzierzynski* for the Polish Ocean Lines.
19.9.1963   On a voyage from Shanghai to Antwerp and Gdynia, she was in collision with *Fouli* off Ushant. Docked at Brest and Flushing for repairs and at Antwerp she struck a pier at Baudouin Lock. The sea valve collapsed and the engine room flooded. She was beached at Lillo and it was discovered she had a crack at No. 2 hatch.
1.10.1963   She was towed to Liefenshoek, and grounded at No. 92 buoy. Her back broke with the movement of the tides and the two halves were taken to Antwerp, where she was broken up by Jos de Smedt & Company.

54. *George Salt* (1936)
77 grt, 9 n., 75.6 x 19.1 x 8.3 feet, yard no. 225.
Steel, single screw, oil, 8 cyls, 4 stroke SA, 122 NHP, 8 knots by Mirrless, Bickerton & Day, Stockport. One deck. Tug.
B. Henry Robb & Company Limited, Leith.
7.5.1936   Launched.
6.1936   Delivered to Blackfriars Lighterage & Cartage Company, London, managed by Blue Star Line. Owned by Frederick Leyland & Company Limited.
1945   Transferred to Lamport & Holt Line for service at Rio Grande do Sul.
1946   Sold to Cia Nav. das Lagaos, Brazil, renamed *Sao Cristovao*, to operate at Rio de Janeiro.
1955   Based at Rio Grande do Sul again.
1966   Deleted from Lloyds.

55. *Scottish Star* (1) (1917)
7,224 grt, 4,314 n., 434 x 55.3 x 35.2 feet, yard no. 460.
Steel, single screw, quad expansion, 4 cyls, 808 NHP, steam pressure 215 lbs, 2 double ended boilers by Harland & Wolff, Belfast. Three decks.

Passengers: 12.

B. Harland & Wolff Limited, Govan.

7.11.1916    Launched as *Millais* for the Liverpool, Brazil & River Plate Steam Navigation Company Limited.

5.1917    Delivered to the Liverpool, Brazil & River Plate Steam Navigation Company, Lamport & Holt as managers.

1934    Owned by Lamport & Holt Line.

1.1938    Transferred to the Blue Star Line Limited, renamed *Scottish Star*.

11.4.1941    Damaged by bombs 400 miles north-west of Ireland.

2.2.1942    Sailed from Liverpool in convoy on a voyage to Montevideo.

12.2.1942    Left the convoy.

20.2.1942    On a voyage from Liverpool and London to Buenos Aires and Montevideo she was torpedoed by the Italian submarine *Luigi Torelli* at 09.50, 700 miles from Trinidad. Four of her crew of seventy-three lost their lives – most were picked up by HMS *Diomede*.

27.2.1942    The remaining lifeboat reached Barbados safely.


56. *California Star* (1) (1938)

8,293 grt, 5,032 n., 463.9 x 60.2 x 36 feet, yard no. 639.

Steel, single screw, oil, 2 stroke double acting, 6 cyls, 1,236 NHP, 13 knots. By builder. Two decks and part third deck.

Passengers: 12.

B. Burmeister & Wain Limited, Copenhagen.

6.8.1938    Launched for the Union Cold Storage Company Limited, Blue Star Line Limited as managers, for the North Pacific coast service.

12.1938    Transferred to Frederick Leyland & Company Limited, same managers.

5.1939    Owned by the Blue Star Line.

12.6.1940    Operated for the Australian government food service between Australia and the Middle East, supplying their troops in the region. Mainmast removed and replaced by a pole mast.

4.3.1943    Torpedoed by U-515 in convoy, 380 miles north-west of the Azores, on a voyage from Wellington and Cristóbal to Liverpool. A third torpedo exploded under No. 2 lifeboat as it was being launched, killing all aboard. Another lifeboat managed to get to Flores, but thirty-seven of her crew, eight gunners and four passengers lost their lives. Twenty-four people survived.


57. *Canadian Star* (1) (1939)

8,293 grt, 5,032 n., 463.9 x 60.2 x 36 feet, yard no. 640.

Steel, single screw, oil, 2 stroke double acting, 6 cyls, 1,236 NHP, 13 knots. By builder. Two decks and part third deck.

Passengers: 12.

B. Burmeister & Wain Limited, Copenhagen.

20.10.1938    Launched for the Union Cold Storage Company Limited. She was originally ordered as *Canada Star*.

2.1939    Delivered.

2.1939    Transferred to the Union Cold Storage Company Limited, Blue Star Line Limited as managers.

19–20.7.1941    The German submarine U-203 fired two torpedoes at her, south-west of Valentia, on a voyage from Liverpool to Auckland. The torpedoes passed close to her and when the submarine surfaced, both vessels fired at each other. The German commander decided to withdraw, leaving *Canadian Star* to continue her voyage.

30.7.1941    Arrived at Curaçao for repairs.

8.3.1943    Left New York in convoy HX 229, consisting of forty-two ships. She was on a voyage from Sydney and New York to Liverpool.

11.3.1943    West of Newfoundland, the convoy was attacked by a U-boat pack.

18.3.1943      She was hit by two torpedoes from U-221 and sunk south-east of Cape Farewell, Greenland. The corvettes *Anemone* and *Pennywort* picked up fifty-nine survivors, and twenty crew and nine passengers lost their lives.

58. *Columbia Star* (1)/*Patagonia Star* (1) /*Columbia Star* (1939)
8,293 grt, 5,032 n., 463.9 x 60.2 x 36 feet, yard no. 641.
Steel, single screw, oil, 2 stroke double acting, 6 cyls, 1,236 NHP, 13 knots. By builder. Two decks and part third deck.
Passengers: 12.
B. Burmeister & Wain Limited, Copenhagen.
15.2.1939      Launched for the Union Cold Storage Company Limited, Blue Star Line Limited as managers.
5.1939      Delivered.
1950      Transferred to Lamport & Holt Line, same name, managed by the Blue Star Line Limited.
1953      Renamed *Dryden*.
1955      Became *Patagonia Star*, owned by the Lamport & Holt Line, in Blue Star Line colours.
1957      Renamed *Columbia Star*, Lamport & Holt in Blue Star Line colours.
1959      Owned by the Blue Star Line Limited.
1963      Renamed *Dryden*, owned by the Blue Star Line, managed by Lamport & Holt Line.
1966      Transferred to Lamport & Holt Line.
10.11.1968      Arrived at Kaohsiung from Shanghai to be broken up by Yung Tai Steel & Iron Works Company.

59. *Empire Star* (3) (1946)
11,085 grt, 7,027 n., 540.5 x 70.5 x 30.9 feet, yard no. 1303, IMO 5103845.
Steel, twin screw, oil, 2 x 8 cyls B&W type 2 stroke double acting, 16,000 BHP, 17 knots by Harland & Wolff, Govan. Two decks and shelter deck. Passengers: 36 first, below the bridge.
B. Harland & Wolff Limited, Belfast.
4.3.1946      Launched as *Empire Mercia*, owned by the Admiralty, managed by the Ministry of Transport.
12.1946      Delivered as *Empire Star* to Frederick Leyland & Company Limited, Blue Star Line Limited as managers. She was fitted with thermometers in the holds that could be read on the bridge. Placed on the Glasgow–South Africa–Australia route.
1950      Owned by the Lamport & Holt Line but remained in the Blue Star Line fleet. Passengers: 12.
16.10.1971      Arrived at Kaohsiung to be broken up by Long Jong Industries.

*Empire Star* (3). (Wallace Trickett)

60. *Gothic Star* (2)/*Nelson Star* (1)/ *Patagonia Star* (2) (1943)

7,356 grt, 5,126 n., 448 x 57.3 x 33.6 feet, yard no. 1125.

Steel, single screw, oil, 6 cyls B&W type 2 stroke single acting, 2,650 BHP, 12 knots by Harland & Wolff, Govan. Two decks.

B. Harland & Wolff Limited, Belfast.

25.8.1942    Launched.

1.1943    Delivered as *Empire Castle* for the Ministry of War Transport, Blue Star Line Limited as managers.

1944    Managed by the Blue Star Line.

30.5.1946    Purchased by the Blue Star Line, renamed *Gothic Star*.

1947    Operating on the New Zealand service, becoming *Nelson Star* (1).

1958    Transferred to the South American service and renamed *Patagonia Star*.

5.1961    Sold to Gregory Maritime Limited, renamed *Birini* and managed by G. A. Theodorou & Sons (Shipping) Company, Cyprus.

9.1970    Bought by Angila Shipping Company, renamed *Byzantium*. Laid up at Gibraltar with engine problems. Following assessment she was found to be beyond economical repair.

17.8.1971    Arrived in tow at Puerto de Santa Maria, Cadiz, and broken up.

61. *Saxon Star* (2) (1942)

7,355 grt, 5,120 n., 450.4 x 57.3 x 33.6 feet, yard no. 1120, IMO 1168519.

Steel, single screw, oil, 6 cyls B&W type 2 stroke single acting, 2,650 BHP, 12 knots by Harland & Wolff, Govan. Two decks.

B. Harland & Wolff Limited, Belfast.

28.5.1942    Launched as *Empire Strength* for the Ministry of War Transport, managed by the Blue Star Line Limited.

12.1942    Delivered.

*Patagonia Star* (2).

15.3.1946    Purchased by Frederick Leyland & Company Limited and renamed *Saxon Star* (2), Blue Star Line Limited as managers.

1950    Transferred to the Lamport & Holt Line, same name.

1954    Transferred to the Booth Line.

1959    Owned by the Blue Star Line Limited.

8.1961    Sold to D. L. Street for £117,000, renamed *Redbrook*, employed on tramping duties.

1965    Purchased by Hegif Cia Nav. SA, Greece, renamed *Evangelia*.

15.10.1968    On a voyage from Rijeka to Constantia in ballast, she was driven ashore at Constantia and became a total loss.

62. *Ionic Star* (2)/*Napier Star* (2) (1942)

7,166 grt, 4,279 n., 431.3 x 57.4 x 34.2 feet, yard no. 690.

Steel, single screw, oil, 4 cyls, Doxford design, 2 stroke single acting, 10 knots. By builder. Two decks.

B. Barclay Curle & Company, Whiteinch.

26.8.1942     Launched as *Empire Highway* for the Ministry of War Transport with Blue Star Line Limited as managers.

27.7.1943     On a voyage from Avonmouth and Milford Haven to Buenos Aires, she was damaged following a bomb attack off Lisbon.

29.7.1943     She berthed at Gibraltar for repairs to be carried out.

16.4.1946     Owned by the Union Cold Storage Company Limited, renamed *Ionic Star* (2), Blue Star Line Limited as managers.

1.1947     Renamed *Napier Star* (2), taller funnel fitted.

1949     Owned by Frederick Leyland & Company Limited, same managers.

1950     Transferred to Lamport & Holt Line, same name, same managers.

1953     Transferred to Booth Line, same name.

1959     Owned by the Blue Star Line.

31.3.1963     Arrived at Timaru to celebrate the 100th call at the port by a Blue Star Line vessel.

20.7.1965     On a voyage from Rio Gallegos to London she grounded at Bahia Potrero, Punta del Este, Uruguay.

18.8.1965     Refloated.

21.8.1965     Moved to drydock at Montevideo.

10.1965     Declared at total loss.

16.2.1966     Sold to Urria & Cia to be broken up. Attempts had been made to sell her for further trading and it was two years before demolition commenced.

63. *Oregon Star* (2) (1944)

7,283 grt, 4,497 n., 441.7 x 57 x 34.8 feet, yard no. 2216.

Steel, single screw, triple expansion, 3 cyls, 2,500 IHP, steam pressure 240 lbs, 2 water tube boilers. 10½ knots. By Harrisburg Machinery Corporation, Harrisburg, Pa. Two decks, three masts.

B. New England Ship Building Company, Portland, Maine.

31.1.1944     Launched as *Samannan* for the American War Shipping Administration, on charter to the Ministry of War Transport, managed by the Blue Star Line Limited.

28.4.1947     Purchased by the Blue Star Line, renamed *Oregon Star* (2) and employed on the north Pacific service.

3.1952     Transferred to the Lamport & Holt Line, renamed *Laplace*.

4.1953     Sold to San Panteleimon Cia Nav. SA, Costa Rica, renamed *San Panteleimon*.

1959     Registered in Greece.

16.7.1963     On a voyage from Morocco to China she was beached near to Galle, Sri Lanka, when the engine room flooded.

28.7.1963     Re-floated, repaired and completed her voyage.

27.3.1967     Broke adrift in a gale at Kobe and collided with a stone wall.

20.4.1967     Arrived at Yokosuka to be broken up by Matsukura Kaiji.

64. *Pacific Star* (2) (1944)

7,259 grt, 4,486 n., 441.7 x 57 x 34.8 feet, yard no. 2309.

Steel, single screw, triple expansion, 3 cyls, 2,500 IHP, steam pressure 240 lbs, 2 water tube boilers. 10½ knots. By Worthington Pump & Machinery Company, Hamilton, Ontario. Two decks, 3 masts.

B. Bethlehem Fairfield Shipyard, Baltimore, Ohio.

15.1.1944     Launched as *Samnid* by Mary Pickford for the United States War Shipping Administration, chartered to the Ministry of War Transport, Blue Star line Limited as managers.

28.4.1947     Purchased by the Blue Star Line.

| 2.7.1947 | Renamed *Pacific Star* for the north Pacific service. |

10.1950           She was slightly damaged by a fire at Cardiff.

1951           Transferred to the Lamport & Holt Line, renamed *Lalande* then sold to SA Importazione Carboni e Nav. (SAICEN), becoming *Ninfea*.

1959           Sold to the People's Republic of China, Shanghai, renamed *Nan Hai 147*.

1973           Owners restyled as China Ocean Shipping Company (COSCO).

1979           Registered in Canton as *Hong Qi 147*, same owners.

### 65. *Royal Star* (2)/ *Caledonia Star* (1) (1942)

9,205 grt, 5,065 n., 487.6 x 63 x 38.1 feet, yard no. 451, IMO 5057802. Steel, single screw, triple expansion, 3 cyls and LP turbines, 10½ knots. By J. G. Kincaid Limited. Three decks.
B. Greenock Dockyard Company, Greenock.

29.7.1942       Launched as *Empire Wisdom* for the Ministry of War Transport, Clan Line, Cayzer, Irvine & Company Limited as managers.

11.1942         Delivered.

1944           Managed by the Blue Star Line Limited.

19.9.1946       Purchased by the Union Cold Storage Company Limited, renamed *Royal Star* (2), Blue star Line Limited as managers.

10.1961         Transferred to the Blue Star Line Limited, converted to a motor ship at Bremer Vulkan, Vegesack, 2 x 5 cyls, 9,000 BHP, 12½ knots, new larger funnel fitted.

1962           Came out of shipyard as *Caledonia Star* (1), owned by the Blue Star Line.

*Above: Caledonia Star.* (Chris Finney)

*Below: Royal Star* (2).

9.12.1971    Arrived at Kaohsiung from Osaka to be broken up by Dah Yung Steel Limited.

66. *Tuscan Star* (2)/*Timaru Star* (1)/ *California Star* (2) (1945)
7,930 grt, 4,686 n., 474.2 x 63.3 x 35 feet, yard no. 1231, IMO 5058002.
Steel, single screw, oil, 8 cyls Burmeister & Wain 2 stroke double acting, 14 knots. By builder. Two decks and part of third.
B. Harland & Wolff Limited, Belfast.

14.5.1945    Launched.
10.1945    Delivered as *Empire Clarendon* for the Ministry of War Transport, P&O as managers.
27.11.1946    Purchased by Frederick Leyland & Company Limited, Blue Star Line Limited as managers.
1947    Renamed *Tuscan Star*.
28.8.1948    Renamed *Timaru Star* for the New Zealand service.
1950    Transferred to Lamport & Holt Line.
10.1954    Assisted the *Trojan Star* (1) when she was on fire off Colombo.
1958    Renamed *California Star* (2) when she was transferred to the north Pacific service.
1959    Owned by the Blue Star Line Limited.
1967    Transferred to the New Zealand route.
3.1968    Laid up in the River Blackwater.
22.6.1968    Sailed from London on her final voyage to New Zealand.
21.4.1969    Arrived at Kaohsiung to be broken up by Tsuan Yan Steel.

67. *Celtic Star* (2) (1942)
7,046 grt, 4,906 n., 447.6 x 56.2 x 34.2 feet, yard no. 970.
Steel, single screw, triple expansion, 3 cyls, 549 NHP, 2 single ended boilers, 10½ knots. By J. G. Kincaid & Company Limited. Two decks.
B. Vickers Armstrong & Company Limited, Barrow.

*California Star* (2).

18.5.1942    Launched as *Empire Galahad* for the Ministry of War Transport, managed by the Blue Star Line Limited.
7.1942    Delivered.
1.4.1946    Purchased by the Blue Star Line, renamed *Celtic Star* (2).
1947    Transferred to the Lamport & Holt Line, renamed *Murillo*.
4.1952    Sold to Industriale Marittima S.p.A., renamed *Bogliasco*.
1954    Re-engined with 6 cyls, 2 Sc. sa oil engine by Cantieri Riuniti dell Adriatico, Trieste.
1963    Purchased by Ocean Shipping & Enterprises (Panama) SA, renamed *Ocean Peace*.
13.9.1967    Arrived at Kaohsiung to be broken up.

68. *Oregon Star* (3) (1942)
7,018 grt, 4,099 n., 446.3 x 56.2 x 34.2 feet, yard no. 439.

Steel, single screw, triple expansion, 3 cyls, 549 NHP, 2 single ended boilers, 10½ knots. By J. G. Kincaid & Company Limited. Two decks.
B. Charles Connell & Company Limited, Scotstoun.

1.9.1942    Launched as *Empire Geraint* for the Ministry of War Transport, Royal Mail Line as managers.

12.1942    Delivered.

7.3.1943    In collision with the Royal Mail Line's *Andes* at Southampton. Taken out of service for repairs.

1.1945    Managed by Lamport & Holt Line.

6.3.1945    On a voyage from New York to Liverpool she was hit by a torpedo from U-1302 off Milford Haven. She unloaded her cargo at Swansea and proceeded to Newport News to be repaired.

26.4.1945    Sailed to Newport for dry-docking.

16.1.1946    Purchased by the Lamport & Holt Line, renamed *Millais*.

1952    Transferred to the Blue Star Line Limited, renamed *Oregon Star* (3) for the north Pacific service.

5.1954    Sold to the Iris Shipping & Trading Corporation, renamed *Captayannis*.

1960    Purchased by the Paleocrassis Brothers, Piraeus, retained same name.

28.2.1962    She went aground near Goeree Lightship, Holland, and a voyage to Rotterdam.

1.3.1962    She was re-floated but suffered bottom damage and was broken up by Frank Rijsdijk at Hendrik ido Ambacht.

## 69. *Corrientes* (*Oakland Star*) (1945)

7,078 grt, 4,756 n., 446.5 x 56.2 x 34.2 feet, yard no. 480.
Steel, single screw, triple expansion, 3 cyls, 549 NHP, 2 single ended boilers, 10½ knots. By North East Marine Engineering Company Limited, Newcastle. Two decks.

B. Short Brothers, Sunderland.

24.12.1943    Launched as *Empire Cromer* for the Ministry of War Transport, Blue Star Line Limited as managers.

4.1944    Delivered.

20.3.1946    Purchased by Donaldson Brothers, renamed *Corrientes*.

3.1954    Donaldson's north Pacific services were taken over by the Blue Star Line and it was proposed to change her name to *Oakland Star*, but she was put up for sale. Consequently, she did not wear Blue Star colours or complete any voyages for the line.

1955    Owned by Williamson & Company, Hong Kong, renamed *Inchmay*.

1966    Purchased by the National Shipping Corporation of Pakistan, renamed *Kaukhali*.

2.4.1968    Arrived at Karachi with engine problems.

10.1968    Sold and broken up by Eastern Steel Limited at Gadani Beach the following year.

## 70. *Argentina Star* (1) (1947)

10,716 grt, 6,328 n., 502.8 x 68.3 x 35.9 feet, yard no. 1173, IMO 5023227.
Steel, single screw, 3 ahead and 2 astern double reduction geared Parson's steam turbines, 2 Babcock & Wilcox water tube boilers. Steam pressure 480 lb at 750° F. By builder.
Passengers: 60 in first class in single and double cabins on bridge deck.
B. Cammell Laird & Company Limited, Birkenhead.

26.9.1946    Launched.

6.1947    Delivered as replacements for the five 'A' class liners lost during the Second World War. Owned by Frederick Leyland & Company Limited, Blue Star Line Limited as managers.

14.6.1947    Maiden voyage from London to Lisbon, Tenerife, Rio de Janeiro, Santos, Montevideo and Buenos Aires.

1950        Owned by Union International Company Limited.

1972        Sold to Nissho-Iwai Company Limited, Japan, and resold to their Taiwan subsidiary.

19.10.1972   Arrived at Kaohsiung to be broken up by Yi Ho Steel & Iron Works.

### 71. *Brasil Star* (1) (1947)

10,716 grt, 6,342 n., 502.8 x 68.3 x 35.9 feet, yard no. 1174, IMO 5050581.

Steel, single screw, 3 ahead and 2 astern double reduction geared Parson's steam turbines, 2 Babcock & Wilcox water tube boilers. Steam pressure 480 lb at 750° F. By builder.

Passengers: 60 in first class in single and double cabins on bridge deck.

B. Cammell Laird & Company Limited, Birkenhead.

6.3.1947     Launched.

15.10.1947   Maiden voyage from London to Lisbon, Tenerife, Rio de Janeiro, Santos, Montevideo and Buenos Aires. Owned by Frederick Leyland & Company Limited, Blue Star Line Limited as managers.

1950        Owned by Union International Company Limited.

1972        Sold to Nissho-Iwai Company, Japan, resold to Tung Seng Steel & Iron Works, Taiwan, to be broken up.

10.10.1972   Arrived at Kaohsiung and broken up.

### 72. *Uruguay Star* (1) (1948)

10,723 grt, 6,330 n., 502.8 x 68.3 x 35.9 feet, yard no. 1180.

Steel, single screw, 3 ahead and 2 astern double reduction geared Parson's steam turbines, 2 Babcock & Wilcox water tube boilers. Steam pressure

*Above: Argentina Star.*

*Below: Argentina Star* (1). (Barry Eagles)

*Brasil Star.* (Barry Eagles)

*Uruguay Star.*

480 lb at 750° F. By builder.

Passengers: 60 in first class in single and double cabins on bridge deck.

B. Cammell Laird & Company Limited, Birkenhead.

| | |
|---|---|
| 15.10.1947 | Launched for the Blue Star line Limited. |
| 22.5.1948 | Maiden voyage from Liverpool to Lisbon, Tenerife, Rio de Janeiro, Santos, Montevideo and Buenos Aires, then from London. Owned by the Blue Star Line. |
| 1972 | Sold to be broken up. |
| 25.8.1972 | Arrived at Kaohsiung and broken up by Nan Feng Steel Enterprise Company Limited. |

### 73. *Paraguay Star* (1) (1947)

10,723 grt, 6,330 n., 502.8 x 68.3 x 35.9 feet, yard no. 1181, IMO 5270480.

Steel, single screw, 3 ahead and 2 astern double reduction geared Parson's steam turbines, 2 Babcock & Wilcox water tube boilers. Steam pressure 480 lb at 750° F. By builder.

Passengers: 60 in first class in single and double cabins on bridge deck.

B. Cammell Laird & Company Limited, Birkenhead.

| | |
|---|---|
| 23.4.1948 | Launched. |
| 12.8.1969 | While berthed at the Royal Albert Dock, London, she suffered a serious fire in her engine room which spread to the passenger accommodation. She was declared to be beyond economical repair and was sold to Eckhardt & Company of Hamburg. |
| 15.9.1969 | Left London in tow. |
| 19.9.1969 | Arrived in Hamburg to be broken up. |
| 3.1970 | Demolition commenced. |

*Paraguay Star.*

*Imperial Star* (2). (Chris Finney)

**74. *Imperial Star* (2) (1948)**
13,181 grt, 8,113 n., 572.3 x 70.3 x 40.7 feet, yard no. 1350, IMO 5159624.
Steel, twin screw, oil, 2 x 8 cyls, B&W type, 2 stroke double acting, 16,000 BHP, 17 knots. By builder. Three decks.
B. Harland & Wolff, Govan.

17.6.1947    Launched.
3.1948       Delivered to Union Cold Storage Company Limited, Blue Star Line Limited as managers.
1949         Owned by Union International Company Limited.
5.1970       Carried the first consignment of frozen meat from New Zealand to Gdynia.
17.9.1971    Arrived at Kaohsiung and broken up by Tung Ho Steel Enterprises.
10.12.1971   Demolition commenced.

**75. *Melbourne Star* (2) (1948)**
13,179 grt, 8,091 n., 572.3 x 70.3 x 40.7 feet, yard no. 1351, IMO 5231563.
Steel, twin screw, oil, 2x8 cyls, B&W type, 2 stroke double acting, 16,000 BHP, 17 knots. By builder. Three decks.
B. Harland & Wolff, Govan.

2.10.1947    Launched.
7.1948       Delivered to Union Cold Storage Company Limited, Blue Star Line Limited as managers.
27.7.1949    Owned by Union International Company Limited.
1972         Sold to Embajada Cia Nav. SA for her final voyage, renamed *Melbo*.
21.6.1972    Sailed from London to Hong Kong.
7.8.1972     Arrived Kaohsiung to be broken up by Tung Cheng Steel & Iron Works.

*Above Left: Melbourne Star* (2). (Chris Finney)

*Above Right: Melbourne Star* (2).

*Below: Melbourne Star* (2). (Chris Finney)

76. *Rhodesia Star* (1) (1943)

8,642 grt, 4,997 n., 492 x 69.5 x 29.3 feet, yard no. 37, IMO 6116420.

Steel, single screw, double reduction geared turbines, 2 water tube boilers, steam pressure 525 lb, 16 knots. By Allis-Chalmers Manufacturing Company, Milwaukee, Wisconsin. One deck and shelter deck.

B. Seattle Tacoma Ship Building Company, Tacoma.

1943        Laid down as a standard C2-S-A1 cargo vessel and purchased by the United States Navy and delivered as the Smiter class escort carrier *Estero*.

3.11.1943        Transferred to the British Navy on land-lease with eighteen similar vessels, renamed HMS *Premier*.

11.11.1943        Sent to Burrard Dry Dock Company, Vancouver, for modifications to be completed.

9.1.1944        Delivered.

12.4.1946        Returned to the United States Navy, laid up and converted back to a C2 type freight vessel by the Gulf Shipbuilding Corporation, Mobile, and laid up for two years.

1948        Purchased by the Blue Star Line Limited, renamed *Rhodesia Star* (1). Converted by the Gulf Shipbuilding Corporation Limited, Mobile, Alabama.

1948        Transferred to the Lamport & Holt Line, same name.

1959        Owned by the Blue Star Line Limited.

1967        Sold to the International Export Lines, C. Y. Tung Group, renamed *Hong Kong Knight*, registered in the Bahamas.

1971        Purchased by the United Overseas Marine Corporation SA, Panama, same name.

5.1.1974        Arrived at Kaohsiung.

10.2.1974        Demolition commenced by Yung Steel Corporation.

77. *South Africa Star* (1) (1943)

8,529 grt, 4,988 n., 492 x 69.5 x 29.3 feet, yard no. 49.

Steel, single screw, double reduction geared turbines, 2 water tube boilers, steam pressure 525 lb, 16 knots. By Allis-Chalmers Manufacturing Company, Milwaukee, Wisconsin. One deck and shelter deck.

B. Seattle Tacoma Ship Building Company, Tacoma.

2.1943        Laid down as a standard C2-S-A1 cargo vessel and purchased by the United States Navy and delivered as USS *Reaper*, a Smiter class carrier, transferred to the British Navy as HMS *Winjah*.

22.11.1943        Launched as escort carrier *Winjah*.

2.1944        Delivered.

18.2.1944        Transferred to Royal Navy and renamed HMS *Reaper*.

31.3.–24.5.1944        Modified at the Burrard Dry Dock Company, Vancouver.

20.5.1946        Returned to the United States Navy, laid up and converted back to a C2 type freight vessel by the Gulf Shipbuilding Corporation, Mobile, and laid up for two years.

1948        Sold to the Blue Star Line Limited, renamed *South Africa Star* (1). Converted by the Gulf Shipbuilding Corporation Limited, Mobile, Alabama.

8.1949        Transported 400 cars from the Tyne to Sydney.

1963        A 180-ton derrick was installed by Howaldtswerke Hamburg AG, Hamburg. It was originally planned to install one of 250 tons but it was felt that this would create stability problems. A new vessel with the larger derrick was ordered and *Australia Star* (2) was delivered with a 300-ton Stulcken derrick in 1965.

1967        Sold for £108,000 to ship-breakers.

25.5.1967        Sailed from Tokyo for Mithara, Japan, and broken up by Nichimen Jitsuggo KK.

**78.** *Tacoma Star* (2) (1944)

7,201 grt, 4,946 n., 447.8 x 56.2 x 34.4 feet, yard no. 997.

Steel, single screw, triple expansion, 3 cyls, 560 NHP, 2 single ended boilers, 10½ knots. By Harland & Wolff Limited, Glasgow. Two decks.

B. Lithgow's Limited, Port Glasgow.

20.4.1944    Launched as *Empire Talisman* for the Ministry of Transport, Blue Star Line Limited as managers.

6.1944    Delivered.

6.6.1946    On bare-boat charter to the Blue Star Line Limited for three years, delivered at Cardiff.

1949    Purchased by the Blue Star Line Limited and renamed *Tacoma Star*.

1957    Transferred to Lamport & Holt Line, renamed *Murillo*.

19.11.1959    Laid up at the Gareloch on the River Clyde.

16.3.1961    Arrived at Vigo to be broken up.

**79.** *Dunedin Star* (2) (1950)

7,322 grt, 4,203 n., 496.8 x 64.7 x 28.3 feet, yard no. 623, IMO 5094800.

Steel, single screw, 3 double reduction geared turbines, 2 water tube boilers. Steam pressure 570 lb, 14 knots. By builder. One deck plus shelter deck.

B. Alexander Stephen & Sons, Linthouse.

1949    Laid down as *Bolton Castle* for the Lancashire Shipping Company Limited, Moller's Trust Limited, and acquired by the Blue Star line on the stocks. Consequently, she was a one-off vessel in the fleet. She was a smaller sister of *Penrith Castle/Benmhor and Thurland Castle/*

*Above: South Africa Star.*

*Below: Dunedin Star* (2). (Chris Finney)

*Cuzco/Benattow*. The three were designed as general cargo carriers with a common six-hatch deck layout, including full fore and main masts, each equipped with a 50-ton 'jumbo' serving one each of their respective holds. *Cuzco* had no bridge cabs and a taller funnel than the Ben Line vessel. *Dunedin Star* was fitted with a 46 feet by 23 feet diameter funnel with no bridge cabs, and the passenger capacity was reduced from twelve to two, which enabled all officers and crew to be accommodated amidships. Four lifeboats were replaced by two slightly larger boats, one at each side of the funnel. The full foremast obviated the need for a topmast at the main and eliminated the afterdeck 'jumbo' derrick.

| | |
|---|---|
| 18.4.1950 | Launched as *Dunedin Star* (2). |
| 9.1950 | Delivered. |
| 1956 | Numbers 2 and 3 holds and 'tween decks converted for the carriage of refrigerated products. |
| 1968 | Transferred to the Lamport & Holt Line, renamed *Roland*. |
| 1975 | Purchased by the Pallas Maritime Company, Cyprus, renamed *Jessica*, then re-sold to the Alligator Shipping Company. |
| 17.7.1976 | Arrived at Karachi for a special survey, which she passed. |
| 15.5.1978 | Arrived at Djibouti and sold to Carstairs & Cummings Limited. |
| 10.6.1978 | Arrived at Gadani Beach and broken up. |

## 80. *Adelaide Star* (2) (1950)

12,964 grt, 7,358 n., 573.8 x 72.7 x 37.1 feet, yard no. 657, IMO 5002455. Steel, twin screw, oil, 2 x 6 cyls Brown-Doxford 2 stroke single acting, 18½ knots. By builder. One deck plus shelter deck plus part third and fourth decks.

Passengers: 12.

B. John Brown & Company Limited, Clydebank.

| | |
|---|---|
| 2.8.1950 | Launched as the largest refrigerated ship in the world. |

| | |
|---|---|
| 12.1950 | Delivered to the Blue Star Line Limited. |
| 1964 | Operated for the Lamport & Holt Line. |
| 1965 | Transferred back to the Blue Star Line Limited. |
| 8.3.1975 | On a voyage from Timaru to Liverpool she suffered severe damage to the engines and machinery. After examination it was decided that it was uneconomical to replace the damaged parts. |
| 25.4.1975 | Sailed from Liverpool for Masan, Korea with a reduced crew. |
| 12.6.1975 | Arrived at Masan and was broken up by Hankook Steel Limited. |

## 81. *Tasmania Star* (1) (1950)

12,605 grt, 7,131 n., 572.3 x 72.7 x 37.1 feet, yard no. 1207, IMO 5353268. Steel, single screw, 3 double reduction geared turbines, 2 water tube boilers, steam pressure 550 lb, 18½ knots. By builder. One deck plus shelter deck plus part third and fourth decks.

Passengers: 12.

B. Cammell Laird & Company Limited, Birkenhead.

| | |
|---|---|
| 31.5.1950 | Launched for the Blue Star Line Limited. |
| 11.1950 | Delivered. |
| 12. 1950 | Sailed on her maiden voyage from Liverpool with 18,000 tons of cargo, which was one of the largest to be shipped from the port. |
| 20.9.1975 | Arrived at Kaohsiung and broken up by G. Yuen Steel Enterprise Company. |

## 82. *Wellington Star* (2) (1952)

12,539 grt, 7,358 n., 573.8 x 72.7 x 37.1 feet, yard no. 670, IMO 5387439. Steel, twin screw, oil, 2 x 6 cyls Brown-Doxford 2 stroke single acting, 18½ knots. By builder. One deck plus shelter deck plus part third and fourth decks.

Passengers: 12.

B. John Brown & Company Limited, Clydebank.

7.5.1952     Launched for the Blue Star Line Limited.

8.1952     Delivered.

12.1975     At Sydney she was sold to Broad Bay Shipping Company Limited, renamed *Hawkes Bay*, operated by the Blue Star Ship Management and converted to a cattle carrier at Singapore.

9.8.1979     Arrived at Kaohsiung and broken up by Nan Kwang Steel & Iron Company.

## 83. *Auckland Star* (2) (1958)

11,799 grt, 7,013 n., 572.3 x 72.7 x 37.1 feet, yard no. 1270, IMO 5030361. Steel, single screw, steam turbines double reduction geared, 16,000 BHP, 18½ knots. By builder. One deck plus shelter deck plus part third and fourth decks.

Passengers: 12.

B. Cammell Laird & Company Limited.

2.5.1958     Launched.

10.1958     Delivered to the Salient Shipping Company (Bermuda) Limited, Hamilton, Bermuda, on bare-boat charter to the Blue Star Line.

1962     Transferred to the British flag.

11.1963     Arrived at the Port of London with the largest single cargo from New Zealand.

10.4.1978     Sailed from Liverpool for the last time.

20.5.1978     Left Durban for Gadani Beach.

9.6.1978     Arrived at Gadani Beach and broken up by Standard Rolling Mills Limited.

*Above: Adelaide Star* (2). (Wallace Trickett)

*Below: Adelaide Star* (2).

*Right: Wellington Star* (2). (Wallace Trickett)

*Left: Tasmania Star.* (Wallace Trickett)

*Auckland Star* (2). (Wallace Trickett)

84. *Fresno Star* (2) (1944)
7,053 grt, 4,107 n., 446.6 x 56.3 x 35.2 feet, yard no. 481.
Steel, single screw, triple expansion, 3 cyls, 2 single ended boilers, steam pressure 200 lb, 12 knots. By Harland & Wolff, Glasgow. Two decks.
B. Short Brothers Limited, Sunderland.

| | |
|---|---|
| 11.4.1944 | Launched. |
| 6.1944 | Delivered as *Empire Pendennis* for the Ministry of War Transport, Ellerman & Bucknall Lines Limited as managers. |
| 1.4.1946 | Purchased by the Cunard Line, renamed *Vasconia*. |
| 1951 | Sold to the Blue Star Line, renamed *Fresno Star* (2). |
| 1957 | On bare-boat charter to Lamport & Holt Line, renamed *Millais*. |
| 1957 | Transferred back to the Blue Star line Limited. |
| 1.1.1960 | Sold to Grosvenor Shipping Company, Hong Kong, renamed *Grosvenor Navigator*. |
| 9.9.1966 | Arrived at Kaohsiung and broken up by Sing Chien Yung Steel & Ironworks Company. |

85. *Victoria Star* (1) (1943)
7,048 grt, 4,881 n., 446.3 x 56.3 x 35.2 feet, yard no. 4.
Steel, single screw, triple expansion, 3 cyls, 2 single ended boilers, steam pressure 200 lb, 12 knots. By North East Marine Engineering Company Limited. Two decks.
B. Armstrong Whitworth & Company Limited, Walker-on-Tyne.

| | |
|---|---|
| 2.6.1943 | Launched. |
| 10.1943 | Delivered as *Empire Flag* to the Ministry of War Transport, New Zealand Shipping Company Limited as managers. |
| 16.4.1946 | Purchased by the Donaldson Line. |
| 1946 | Transferred to the Donaldson Atlantic Line Limited, renamed *Carmia*. |
| 1949 | Owned by Donaldson Line Limited. |
| 3.1954 | Purchased by Blue Star Line Limited, renamed *Victoria Star*. |
| 10.1955 | Sold to Williamson & Company, Hong Kong, renamed *Inchean*. Operated by the Douglas Steam Ship Company, Douglas, Lapraik & Company as managers. |
| 26.3.1966 | Arrived at Osaka and broken up. |

86. *Vancouver Star* (1) (1943)
7,063 grt, 4,241 n., 446.5 x 56.3 x 35.2 feet, yard no. 474.
Steel, single screw, triple expansion, 3 cyls, 2 single ended boilers, steam pressure 200 lb, 12 knots. By Harland & Wolff, Glasgow. Two decks.
B. Short Brothers Limited, Sunderland.

| | |
|---|---|
| 8.12.1942 | Launched as *Empire Bardolph* for the Ministry of War Transport. |
| 3.1943 | Delivered with Donaldson Line as managers. |
| 1945 | Managed and then sold to Lamport & Holt Line. |
| 1946 | Renamed *Memling*. |
| 1953 | Transferred to the Blue Star Line Limited, renamed *Vancouver Star*. |
| 1957 | Operating for Lamport & Holt as Memling. |
| 19.10.1959 | Arrived at Flushing to be broken up by N. V. Simon's Metaalhandel. |

87. *Fremantle Star* (1)/*Catalina Star* (1) (1944)
9,883 grt, 6,185 n., 497.4 x 64.3 x 40 feet, yard no. 995, IMO 5423685.
Steel, single screw, oil, 6 cyls, B&W type, 2 stroke double acting, 12½ knots. By J. G. Kincaid Limited. Two decks and part third deck.
B. Lithgow's Limited, Port Glasgow.

| | |
|---|---|
| 6.10.1944 | Launched. |
| 12.1944 | Delivered as *Empire Haig* to the Ministry of War Transport, Ellerman's Wilson Line as managers. |

*Victoria Star.*

8.7.1946    Purchased by Lamport & Holt Line, renamed *Dryden*.

1952    Transferred to the Blue Star Line Limited, renamed *Fremantle Star* (1).

1958    Renamed *Catalina Star* (1) for north Pacific coast service.

1963    Renamed *Devis*.

1969    Transferred to Lamport & Holt Line

1969    Converted by the Gulf Shipbuilding Corporation Limited, Mobile, Alabama.

4.1969    Sold to Bry Overseas Navigation Incorporated, Panama, renamed *Mondia*.

23.12.1969    Arrived at Kaohsiung to be broken up and delivered to the Han Tai Iron & Steel Company.

## 88. *Malay Star* (1) (1952)

4,300 grt, 2,419 n., 410.6 x 55.1 x 24 feet, yard no. 332, IMO 5218224. Steel, single screw, oil, 6 cyls, 4S SA, 12½ knots. By Harland & Wolff Limited, Govan. One deck and shelter deck and part third deck.

2.1952    Ordered as *Clement* for the Booth Line and transferred on the stocks to the Blue Star Line Limited.

4.10.1952    Launched as *Malay Star*.

2.1953    Entered the Austasia Line's service as *Malay*.

3.1953    Austasia Line's first sailing from Singapore .

1964    Renamed *Mahsuri*.

1966    Transferred to the Booth Line, renamed *Benedict*.

1967    Became *Renoir*.

1971    Sold to the Starlight Shipping Company SA, Panama, renamed *Diamond Star*.

1973    Purchased by the Minlex Navigation SA, same name with Starlight Shipping as managers.

12.10.1973    Sailed from Kaohsiung and arrived at Suao, Taiwan, and broken up following a short period being laid up.

## 89. *English Star* (1) (1950)

9,996 grt, 5,950 n., 505.5 x 70.2 x 35.9 feet, yard no. 746, IMO 5104394.
Steel, twin screw, oil, 2 x 5 cyls, 2 stroke double acting Doxford, 11,600 BHP, 15½ knots. By builder. Two decks and part third deck.
B. Fairfield Ship Building & Engineering Company, Govan.

6.12 1949    Launched.

10.1950    Delivered to the Blue Star Line Limited.

21.9.1973    Arrived at Kaohsiung and broken up by Chin Tai Steel Enterprise Company.

90. *Scottish Star* (2) (1950)

10,174 grt, 5,960 n., 505.5 x 70.2 x 35.9 feet, yard no. 747, IMO 5315890. Steel, twin screw, oil, 2 x 5 cyls, 2 stroke double acting Doxford, 11,600 BHP, 15½ knots. By builder. Two decks and part third deck.

B. Fairfield Ship Building & Engineering Company, Govan.

15.5.1950    Launched for the Blue Star Line Limited.

1964    Transferred to Lamport & Holt Line.

1965    Owned by the Blue Star Line Limited.

18.5.1967    Sailed from Fremantle to the United Kingdom and Continental ports with a cargo of fruit, wool and timber.

6.6.1967    In convoy for a northbound transit of the Suez Canal. Trapped in the Great Bitter Lake with fourteen other ships when the canal was blocked during the Arab-Israeli war.

1968    Egypt attempted to clear the canal but when Israeli troops fired upon them they withdrew from the territory. It was decided to close down her refrigeration unit when it was discovered that the fruit was rotting.

1969    Declared a constructive total loss and transferred to the underwriters.

1970    She was abandoned to the underwriters, Standard Steamship Owners Mutual War Risks Association, Scottish Star Limited. Sold to the Scottish Star Limited.

30.5.1975    The canal was finally opened and *Scottish Star* was towed to Piraeus under the name of *Kavo Yerakas*. A survey was undertaken and it was found that the rotting fruit had corroded her hull. The cargo of wool was salvaged by her owners, Defteron Corporation, Piraeus, and she was laid up.

*Above: Vancouver Star.*

*Below: English Star* (1).

| 6.9.1975 | Laid up at Piraeus until 25.6.1979. |
| 1979 | Broken up in Spain. |

## 91. *Albion Star* (2)/*Norman Star* (2) (1939)

3,022 grt, 1,785 n., 336.3 x 45.8 x 26.1 feet, yard no. 661.
Steel, single screw, oil, 2 stroke single acting, 9 cyls, 12 knots. By builder.
Two decks plus part of third.
B. Burmeister & Wain Limited, Copenhagen.

16.8.1939    Launched as *Mosdale*.

10.1939    Delivered to A/S Mosvold Shipping Company, Norway.

5.1954    Originally intended to be named *Trinidad Star* but became *Albion Star* (2) when she was purchased by the Blue Star Line Limited. However, she was soon transferred to Lamport & Holt Line and renamed *Balzac*.

1959    Renamed *Carroll*.

2.1960    Transferred to the Blue Star Line Limited, becoming *Norman Star* (2). Sent to Middle Docks, South Shields, and converted for the carriage of edible oils in tanks.

1961    Transferred to Booth Line, renamed *Basil*.

5.1964    Sold to H. & D. Kyriakos and owned by Eleni D. Kyprianou, renamed *Eleni K.*

1966    Purchased by the Helen Shipping Corporation (Panama) Limited, renamed *Eleni Kypriakou*.

1970    Renamed *Olga*. Purchased by the Kreta Shipping Company, SA, becoming *Georgios Markakis*.

1973    Sold to Amarinthis Shipping Company, renamed *Nikos*. Broken up later that year by Hierros Ardes, Bilbao.

## 92. *Roman Star* (2) (1938)

3,000 grt, 1,759 n., 326.4 x 45.8 x 26.1 feet, yard no. 635.
Steel, single screw, oil, 2 stroke single acting, 9 cyls, 12 knots. By builder.
Two decks plus part of third.
B. Burmeister & Wain Limited, Copenhagen.

2.6.1938    Launched.

9.1938    Delivered to Compagnie Generale d'Armements Maritimes, Paris, as *Barfleur* for the West Indies banana trade.

1947    Transferred to Cie Generale Transatlantique, operating on the same route.

1955    Purchased by the Blue Star Line Limited and transferred to Lamport & Holt Line, becoming *Boswell*.

1960    Renamed *Crome*.

3.1960    Transferred to the Blue Star Line Limited, renamed *Roman Star* (2). Sent to Middle Docks, South Shields, and converted for the carriage of edible oils in tanks.

5.1961    Transferred to the Booth Line, renamed *Bede*.

1964    Sold to Rahcassi Shipping Company, renamed *Victoria Elena*.

16.1.1967    While loading a cargo of cotton she suffered a serious fire at Thessalonika and was declared a total loss.

10.9.1967    Demolition commenced at La Spezia by Lotti S.p.A.

## 93. *Drover* (1) (1923)

1,497 grt, 584 n., 280.5 x 37.2 x 17.4 feet, yard no. 284.
Steel, single screw, triple expansion, 3 cyls, 2 single ended boilers, steam pressure 185 lb, 10 knots. By builder.

18.6.1923    Launched as *Copeland*.

8.1923    Delivered to the Clyde Steam Ship Company.

1946    Sold to G. Heyn & Sons, Head Line, renamed *North Down*, operating for the North Continental Shipping Company.

10.1954    Purchased by Union International Company, renamed *Drover*, Blue Star Line Limited as managers. She was almost immediately sold to the Belfast Steam Ship Company, becoming *Ulster Herdsman*.

5.10.1963    Arrived at Passage West, Cork, and broken up by Haulbowline Industries.

94. *Geelong Star* (1) (1945)

8,641 grt, 6,197 n., 456 x 62.3 x 33.9 feet, yard no. 1182, IMO 5087596.

Steel, single screw, oil, 6 cyls, 2 stroke double acting, 13 knots. By builder. Three decks.

B. Harland & Wolff Limited, Belfast.

28.2.1945    Launched as *Defoe*.

5.1945    Delivered to Lamport & Holt Line as the last of the 'D' class.

4.1954    Transferred to the Blue Star Line Limited, renamed *Geelong Star* (1). Refrigeration units fitted.

4.1958    Returned to Lamport & Holt Line as *Defoe*.

2.1966    Sold to Astrofeliz Cia Nav. SA for £135,000, renamed *Argolis Star*. Operated by the Argolis Shipping Company.

1967    Sold to the Argolis Shipping Company.

17.10.1969    Sold to China National Machinery Import & Export Corporation and sailed from Singapore.

29.10.1969    Arrived at Shanghai and broken up.

95. *Pacific Star* (3) (1954)

11,218 grt, 6,328 n., 546 x 69.3 x 38.6 feet, yard no. 492.

Steel, single screw, oil, 5 cyls, 2 stroke single acting, Doxford type, 13 knots. By D. Rowan & Company, Glasgow.

B. William Hamilton & Company Limited, Port Glasgow.

22.1.1954    Launched.

4.1954    Delivered as the Line's only oil tanker. Owned by the Booth Line and on bare-boat charter to Blue Star Line.

4.1961    Owned by the Blue Star Line Limited. Her size and the closure of the Suez Canal meant that she soon became uneconomical to operate.

9.1964    Sold to Atlantic Overseas Bulk Carriers Limited, renamed *Silver Bay*.

22.4.1973    Arrived at Kaohsiung and broken up by Jung Ho Steel Enterprises.

96. *Oregon Star* (4) (1943)

7,040 grt, 4,973 n., 447.6 x 56.2 x 34.2 feet, yard no. 977.

Steel, single screw, triple expansion, 3 cyls, 558 NHP. 2 single ended boilers, steam pressure 220 lb, 10½ knots. By J. G. Kincaid & Company Limited, Greenock.

B. Lithgow's Limited, Port Glasgow.

28.12.1942    Launched.

3.1943    Delivered as *Empire Treasure* to the Ministry of War Transport, Port Line as managers.

10.5.1946    Sold to Donaldson Line, renamed *Gracia* for the north Pacific coast routes. Some summer sailings to Hudson Bay.

3.1954    Donaldson Line assets were acquired by the Blue Star Line. This included the ships and the Pacific coast services. Renamed *Oregon Star* (4).

5.1955    Sold to Williamson & Company Limited, Hong Kong, renamed *Inchleana*.

3.1966    Purchased by the National Shipping Corporation of Pakistan, becoming *Tetulia*.

1969    Broken up at Gadani Beach by Mohamadi Iron Traders Limited.

97. *Portland Star* (1) (1937)

7,783 grt, 4,865 n., 456 x 62.3 x 25.4 feet, yard no. 980.

Steel, single screw, oil, 2 stroke double acting, 6 cyls, 12 knots. By builder. Three decks.

B. Harland & Wolff Limited, Belfast.

12.4.1937     Launched.

7.1937     Delivered to Lamport & Holt Line as *Delius*, the first of three vessels.

27.4.1940     Damaged by air attack during the Norwegian campaign at Romdalsfjord, Norway.

21.11.1943     She was attacked by aircraft off the south-west of Ireland but managed to return to port.

1954     Renamed *Portland Star* for the north Pacific coast services.

1955     Transferred to the Blue Star Line Limited.

1958     Operated by Lamport & Holt Line as *Delius*.

10.1961     Sold to Compagnie Metallurgique et Miniere SA, Casablanca, renamed *Kettara VII*, Panamanian flag.

28.10.1961     Sailed from Hull for Casablanca and loaded a cargo of scrap metal for Japan.

24.2.1962     Arrived at Tokyo. Following discharge she was broken up by Izumi Ohtsu Limited.

30.4.1962     Demolition commenced.

## 98. *Seattle Star* (1) (1938)

7,761 grt, 4,854 n., 456 x 62.3 x 25.4 feet, yard no. 1001.

Steel, single screw, oil, 2 stroke double acting, 6 cyls, 12 knots. By builder. Three decks.

B. Harland & Wolff Limited, Belfast.

21.10.1937     Launched.

1.1938     Delivered as *Delane* to Lamport & Holt Line

1954     Transferred to the Blue Star Line Limited, becoming *Seattle Star* (1) for the north Pacific services. Refrigeration plants were installed.

6.1961     Sold to Compagnie Metallurgique et Miniere SA, Casablanca, for £85,000 and renamed *Kettara VI*. Panamanian flag with delivery at Glasgow.

15.7.1961     Sailed from Casablanca with a cargo of scrap to Osaka.

13.10.1961     Arrived at Hong Kong to be broken up. Sold to Hong Kong Rolling Mills Limited for £90,000.

27.12.1961     Demolition commenced.

## 99. *Oakland Star* (1) (1944)

8,148 grt, 5,831 n., 456.3 x 62.3 x 25.4 feet, yard no. 1181.

Steel, single screw, oil, 2 stroke double acting, 6 cyls, 12 knots. By builder. Three decks.

Passengers: 12.

B. Harland & Wolff Limited, Belfast.

25.3.1944     Launched.

8.1944     Delivered to Lamport & Holt Line as *Devis*.

1955     Transferred to Blue Star Line Management, renamed *Oakland Star* (1) for the north Pacific coast service. Refrigeration plant installed.

1957     Operated by Lamport & Holt Line as *Devis*.

1962     Sold for £11 16s per ton light displacement for breaking up.

4.7.1962     Arrived at La Spezia and broken up by Cantieri Navali del Golfo, La Spezia.

## 100. *Washington Star* (1) (1940)

8,105 grt, 5,858 n., 456 x 62.3 x 33.9 feet, yard no. 1029.

Steel, single screw, oil, 6 cyls, 2 stroke double acting, 13 knots. By builder. Three decks plus part of fourth.

B. Harland & Wolff Limited, Belfast.

23.3.1940     Launched.

5.1940     Delivered to Lamport & Holt Line as *Debrett*.

7.1955    Transferred to the Blue Star Line Limited, becoming *Washington Star* (1) for the north Pacific coast services.

1956    Renamed *Debrett*.

16.4.1964    Arrived at Recife with a fire in her engine room. She was severely damaged on a voyage from Buenos Aires to Liverpool. Sold to Embajada Cia Nav. SA, renamed *Ambasciata*.

28.12.1964    Arrived at Osaka and broken up.

101. *Canberra Star* (1)/*Buenos Aires Star* (1) (1956)
8,257 grt, 4,966 n., 519.5 x 70.3 x 30 feet, yard no. 851, IMO 5059977.
Steel, single screw, oil, 10 cyls MAN, 2 stroke single acting, 11,250 BHP, 17½ knots. By builder. Two decks plus part of third.
B. Bremer Vulkan Schiffsbau und Maschinenfabrik, Bremen-Vegesack.

25.12.1955    Launched.

5.1956    Delivered to the Salient Shipping Company (Bermuda) Limited for the Australia and New Zealand service.

1962    Registered at London.

1972    Renamed *Buenos Aires Star* (1), replacing *Hobart Star* (1).

9.12.1979    Arrived at Kaohsiung and broken up by Lung Fa Steel & Iron Company Limited.

102. *Newcastle Star* (1)/*Montevideo Star* (1) (1956)
8,398 grt, 4,934 n., 519.5 x 70.3 x 30 feet, yard no. 854, IMO 5250351.
Steel, single screw, oil, 10 cyls MAN, 2 stroke single acting, 11,250 BHP, 17½ knots. By builder. Two decks plus part of third.
B. Bremer Vulkan Schiffsbau und Maschinenfabrik, Bremen-Vegesack.

28.5.1956    Launched.

10.1956    Delivered to the Blue Star Line Limited.

1973    Renamed *Montevideo Star* (1). *Canberra Star* (1), *Queensland Star* (1) and *Montevideo Star* (1) replaced the 'A' class ships which had been withdrawn and broken up.

1975    Laid up at Barry Docks under Blue Star Ship Management Company. Sold to Conquest Shipping Company, Limassol, renamed *Golden Madonna*.

1976    Purchased by Universe Sunset Marine Incorporated, Piraeus, same name.

5.2.1980    Arrived at Kaohsiung and broken up by Nan Yet Steel Enterprise Company Limited.

103. *Hobart Star* (1)/*Buenos Aires Star* (2)/*Hobart Star* (1956)
8,257 grt, 4,937 n., 519.5 x 70.3 x 30 feet, yard no. 853, IMO 5151866.
Steel, single screw, oil, 10 cyls MAN, 2 stroke single acting, 11,250 BHP, 17½ knots. By builder. Two decks plus part of third.
B. Bremer Vulkan Schiffsbau und Maschinenfabrik, Bremen-Vegesack.

10.4.1956    Launched.

7.1956    Delivered to the Salient Shipping Company (Bermuda) Limited, Bermuda flag.

1962    British registered.

1972    Renamed *Buenos Aires Star* (2) for the South American routes.

11.1972    After completing one voyage she was damaged in a collision and was replaced by *Canberra Star* (1). Renamed *Hobart Star*.

1978    Sold to Atacos Cia Nav. SA, Enais Shipping Company as managers, renamed *Aegean Prosperity*, operated by Fairmont Shipping Company SA, Panama.

10.3.1980    Arrived at Kaohsiung and broken up by An Hsiung Iron & Steel Company.

104. *Gladstone Star* (1) (1957)
10,635 grt, 6,432 n., 516.3 x 70.3 x 30.4 feet, yard no. 865, IMO 5131646.

Steel, single screw, oil, 10 cyls, 2 stroke single acting, 11,250 BHP, 17 knots. By builder. Two decks plus part of third.

B. Bremer Vulkan Schiffsbau und Maschinenfabrik, Bremen-Vegesack.

28.5.1957      Launched.

10.1957      Delivered to the Salient Shipping Company (Bermuda) Limited, Blue Star Line as managers. Placed on the Australian route.

1958      British registered.

1982      Sold to Kate Shipping Company, Intercon Transport Management Limited as managers, Malta, becoming *Gladys*.

16.10.1982      Arrived at Karachi and broken up by the United Steel Scrapping Mills Limited.

13.11.1982      Demolition commenced at Gadani Beach.

105. *Townsville Star* (1) (1957)

10,632 grt, 6,432 n., 516.3 x 70.3 x 30.4 feet, yard no. 866, IMO 5366435. Steel, single screw, oil, 10 cyls, 2 stroke single acting, 11,250 BHP, 17 knots. By builder. Two decks plus part of third.

B. Bremer Vulkan Schiffsbau und Maschinenfabrik, Bremen-Vegesack.

22.8.1957      Launched.

12.1957      Delivered to the Salient Shipping Company (Bermuda) Limited, Blue Star Line Limited as managers for the Australian service.

1958      British registered.

25.8.1962      Sailed from Brisbane on a new service to the east coast of the United States and Canada.

15.12.1978      During the Iraq-Iran war she became trapped for two months at Khorramshahr.

*Above: Canberra Star.* (Wallace Trickett)

*Below: Buenos Aires Star* (1).

*Above left: Hobart Star.*

*Above right: Hobart Star* in Compass Line Limited colours. (Chris Finney)

*Below: Hobart Star.* (Chris Finney)

1980        Sailed on her final voyage from Australia to Odessa with a cargo of frozen meat.
18.6.1980        Arrived at Kaohsiung and broken up by the Nan Long Steel & Iron Company.

### 106. *Queensland Star* (1)/*Brasilia Star* (1) (1957)

9,920 grt, 6,422 n., 511.5 x 68.3 x 30.1 feet, yard no. 779, IMO 5288126.
Steel, single screw, oil, 2 x 5 cyls Doxford ,2 stroke single acting, 11,600 BHP, 17 Knots. By builder. Two decks plus part of third and fourth decks.
B. Fairfield Ship Building & Engineering Company, Govan.
15.3.1957        Launched.
11.1957        Delivered to the Blue Star Line Limited.
1964        Transferred to Lamport & Holt Line, Blue Star Line Limited as managers.
1965        Owned by the Blue Star Line Limited.
8.1972        Renamed *Brasilia Star* (1) for use on the South American routes.
1975        Managed by Blue Star Ship Management Limited.
1977        Renamed *Queensland Star*.
1978        Became *Brasilia Star*.
16.11.1979        Sailed from Newhaven, where she had been laid up.
16.12.1979        Arrived at Kaohsiung and broken up by Lung Fa Steel & Iron Company.

### 107. *Rockhampton Star* (1) (1958)

10,619 grt, 6,407 n., 507.1 x 68.3 x 30.1 feet, yard no. 1277, IMO 5298250.
Steel, single screw, oil, 8 cyls 13,300 BHP Harland & Wolff-Burmeister & Wain type, 107 rpm, 17 knots. By builder. Two decks plus part of third and fourth decks.
B. Cammell Laird & Company Limited, Birkenhead.

24.9.1957        Launched.
1.1958        Delivered to the Blue Star Line Limited for the Australian routes.
1964        Transferred to Lamport & Holt Line, Blue Star Line Limited as managers.
1965        Owned by the Blue Star Line Limited.
1975        Managed by Blue Star Line Ship Management Limited.
1981        Laid up at Falmouth. Sold to Festasi Shipping Company SA, Panama, renamed *Golden Lady*.
1983        Sold to be broken up at Karachi and re-sold to Bangladesh interests.
20.6.1983        Arrived at Chittagong Roads and broken up.

### 108. *Canadian Star* (2) (1957)

6,291 grt, 3,639 n., 473.3 x 63.3 x 28 feet, yard no. 508, IMO 5059848.
Steel, single screw, oil, 6 cyls, 2 stroke single acting, Scott-Doxford type, 8,000 BHP, 16 knots. By Scott's Ship Building & Engineering Company, Greenock.
B. Caledon Ship Building & Engineering Company, Dundee.
5.10.1956        Launched.
2.1957        Delivered to the Blue Star Line Limited.
1967        Converted to carry containers and general cargo by Cammell Laird & Company Limited at Birkenhead.
1972        Transferred to Lamport & Holt on bare-boat charter, renamed *Raeburn*.
1975        Blue Star Ship Management Limited as managers. Transferred to Lamport & Holt Line.
1979        Sold to Vertigo Shipping Company Limited, Limassol, renamed *Braeburn* and then to Ahmed Shipping Lines, Panama.
1.3.1979        Sailed from Casablanca for Taiwan.

*Above: Gladstone Star.*

*Right: Gladstone Star* at Liverpool.

20.4.1979   Arrived at Kaohsiung and broken up by Keun Hwa Iron & Steel Works.

109. *Colorado Star* (1) (1952)
8,292 grt, 4,968 n., 466 x 63.4 x 28.8 feet, yard no. 1444, IMO 5077307.
Steel, single screw, oil, 7 cyls, 2 stroke single acting B&W type, 16 knots. By builder. Two decks plus part of third.
B. Harland & Wolff Limited, Belfast.
6.8.1952   Launched.
11.1952   Delivered to Lamport & Holt Line as *Raeburn*.
1958   Transferred to the Blue Star Line Limited, renamed *Colorado Star*.
1965   Blue Star Line Limited as managers.
1972   Transferred to Lamport & Holt Line, chartered to Austasia Line, becoming *Mahsuri*.
1977   Returned to Lamport & Holt Line, renamed *Roland*, Blue Star Line Ship Management Limited as managers.
5.10.1978   Arrived at Faslane and broken up by Shipbreaking Industries Limited.

110. *Siddons* (1959)
1,282 grt, 566 n., 265.3 x 41.9 x 15.1 feet, yard no. 271.
Steel, single screw, oil, 8 cyls, 4 stroke single acting, 2,000 BHP, 12 knots. By MAN, Hamburg. One deck and shelter deck.
B. George Brown & Company (Marine) Limited, Greenock.

*Above: Townsville Star.*

*Below: Brasilia Star.*

*Rockhampton Star.*

stern, single mast and oval-shaped funnel. She had two complete steel decks, lower and orlop decks forward and aft of machinery space, bridge deck, long forecastle, boat deck and bridge deck. The hull was divided into nine watertight compartments by eight watertight bulkheads. A double bottom, suitably divided, was fitted fore and aft, and arranged for the carriage of oil fuel, water ballast and lubricating oil. Fresh water was carried in tanks at the sides of the shaft tunnel aft. She was fitted with six main cargo holds, four forward and two aft of the machinery space, with corresponding forecastle, shelter, upper and lower 'tween decks. Number 1 forecastle and shelter 'tween decks were insulated for the carriage of fruit or bananas and No. 2 forecastle and Nos 2 and 3 shelter 'tween decks for the carriage of chilled meat or bananas. General cargo was carried in the 'tween deck hatch trunks. Accommodation was provided in a deckhouse on the boat deck for six passengers in two single-berth rooms and two two-berth rooms.

1964        Transferred to Lamport & Holt Line, Blue Star Line Limited as managers.

1965        Owned by the Blue Star Line Limited.

1972        Transferred to the South American services when the passenger vessels were withdrawn, name remained the same.

1975        Managed by Blue Star Ship Management Limited.

13.8.1979   Arrived at Kaohsiung and broken up by Nan Hor Steel Enterprises Company.

4.1959        Laid down for the Blue Star Line and completed as *Siddons* for the Lamport & Holt Line.

111. *Ulster Star* (1) (1959)
10,413 grt, 6,341 n., 519.3 x 70.4 x 27.6 feet, yard no. 1568, IMO 5372599.
Steel, single screw, oil, 6 cyls, 2 stroke single acting, 10,000 BHP, B&W type, 17 knots. By builder. Two decks and part of third.
Passengers: 6.
B. Harland & Wolff Limited, Belfast.
26.2.1959     Launched.
7.1959        Delivered to Blue Star Line Limited for the Australian services. She was designed with a curved raked rounded stem, cruiser

112. *Canterbury Star* (1) (1960)
7,539 grt, 4,140 n., 462.8 x 63.2 x 30.1 feet, yard no. 385, IMO 5060328.
Steel, single screw, oil, 2 stroke single acting, 8 cyls, Sulzer 8RD 76 type, 12,000 BHP, 17 knots. By G. Clark & Company Limited, Sunderland.
B. Bartram & Sons Limited, Sunderland.
9.6.1960      Launched by Mrs E. Vestey.

*Canadian Star* (2). (Wallace Trickett)

12.1960      Delivered to Union International Company Limited, Blue Star Line Limited as managers. She was built with her main propelling machinery aft of amidships and was subdivided by six main transverse watertight bulkheads, extending to the level of the upper deck, into three holds forward, and one hold aft of the machinery space, with the side bunkers extended to the second deck having settling tanks built. Two complete steel decks extended over the whole length of the vessel, while a third deck was arranged in Nos 2 and 3 holds. Each of the holds and 'tween decks were insulated and arranged for the carriage of frozen cargo, except the forecastle 'tween deck over No. 1 hold, where un-insulated cargo only was carried. Each weather deck hatchway was fitted with a MacGregor patent single pull watertight steel cover, and each lower deck hatchway fitted with a 'Greer' Hydro hatch cover.

1963      Owned by the Blue Star Line Limited.

1975      Managed by Blue Star Ship Management.

11.7.1980      Arrived at Bombay and broken up by Ghaziran Gokulchand & Company Limited.

*Colorado Star.*

### 113. *Montreal Star* (1) (1963)

7,365 grt, 4,186 n., 462.8 x 63.2 x 30.1 feet, yard no. 395, IMO 5241130. Steel, single screw, oil, 2 stroke single acting, 8 cyls, Sulzer 8RD 76 type, 12,000 BHP, 17 knots. By G. Clark & Company Limited, Sunderland. B. Bartram & Sons Limited, Sunderland.

14.12 1962      Launched by Mrs Ronald Vestey for the Blue Star Line Limited. With the main propelling machinery aft of amidships, she was subdivided by six main transverse watertight bulkheads, extending to the level of the upper deck into three holds forward, and one hold aft of the machinery space, with their associate 'tween decks. Accommodation for the crew was arranged in a long bridge deck house on the upper deck, surmounted by a three-tier deckhouse. Deck and engineer officers and petty officers each had a separate single berth cabin, while ratings were accommodated in two-berth cabins, also catering staff.

9.1963      Together with *Townsville Star* (1), she was employed on the service from Australia to the east coast of the United States and Canada.

1975      Managed by Blue Star Ship Management Limited.

1.8.1980      Arrived at Gadani Beach and broken up by the Noori Trading Corporation.

### 114. *America Star* (1) (1963)

7,365 grt, 4,186 n., 462.8 x 63.2 x 30.1 feet, yard no. 396, IMO 5418666. Steel, single screw, oil, 2 stroke single acting, 8 cyls, Sulzer 8RD 76 type, 12,000 BHP, 17 knots. By G. Clark & Company Limited, Sunderland.

*Ulster Star.*

B. Bartram & Sons Limited, Sunderland.

19.8.1963      Launched by Mrs J. G. Payne, wife of the assistant manager of the Blue Star Line Limited. *America Star* was subdivided by six main transverse watertight bulkheads, extending to the level of the upper deck, into three holds forward and one hold aft of the machinery space with their associated 'tween decks. Chilled meat lockers were provided port and starboard in Nos 2 and 3 upper 'tween decks, with general cargo at the centre. The deck beams in these compartments were especially strengthened for hanging cargoes. Cargo was handled by four 5-ton, two 10-ton, two 7-ton and eight 3-ton tubular steel derricks, each of sufficient length to reach 20 feet overside. In addition, a 30-ton derrick was arranged to serve No. 2 hatch. The accommodation for the ship's company

was arranged in a long bridge deckhouse on the upper deck, surmounted by a three-tier deckhouse. Deck and engineer officers and petty officers each had a separate single berth cabin while ratings were accommodated in two-berth cabins, as were the catering staff. Separate toilet facilities were provided in each department. A crew mess room and recreation room was provided together with a separate petty officers' mess room. En-suite accommodation comprising dayroom, bedroom and bathroom was provided for the captain and the chief engineer.

6.1964      Delivered for the Australia–United States–Canadian east coast service.

11.1972      Lengthened by 78 feet by Framnaes at Sandfjord, Norway (540.4 feet) and equipped for the carriage of bananas.

4.4.1973      Returned to service.

1975      Managed by Blue Star Ship Management Limited.

1982      Sold to Vermerar Cia Nav., Panama, renamed *Golden Princess*.

6.1984      Broken up at Shanghai.

115. *Quebec Star* (1)/*Halifax Star* (1) (1964)

7,327 grt, 4,199 n., 462.8 x 63.2 x 30.1 feet, yard no. 398, IMO 6405939. Steel, single screw, oil, 2 stroke single acting, 8 cyls, Sulzer 8RD 76 type, 12,000 BHP at 119 rpm, 17 knots. By G. Clark & Company Limited, Sunderland.

B. Bartram & Sons Limited, Sunderland.

29.1. 1964      It was intended to name her *Quebec Star* but she was launched by Pamela, Lady Vestey, mother of Lord Vestey, as *Halifax Star* for the Blue Star Line Limited.

6.1964      Delivered as the fourth of a series built by Bartram's that were especially designed for the carriage of refrigerated cargo, chilled meat and general cargo. The special features of the class included the provision of deck cranes for cargo operation, and a system of automatic machinery operation, which provided bridge control of the main machinery and also allowed a reduction in the number of engine room personnel. She was constructed with the use of 'Monopol' automatic plate cutting machinery. All steel plates and sections were shot-blasted and coated with Vedette zinc-rich paint. With the main propelling machinery aft of amidships, she was subdivided by six main transverse watertight bulkheads extending to the upper deck into three holds forward and one hold aft of the machinery space, with their associated 'tween decks. In the machinery space, side bunkers extended to the second deck, having settling tanks built in. Two complete steel decks extended over the whole length of the vessel, while a third deck was arranged in Nos 2 and 3 holds. Each of the holds and 'tween decks, including the long bridge, was insulated and arranged for the carriage of frozen cargo. Un-insulated cargo was carried in the long forecastle, at the centre portion of Nos 2 and 3 upper 'tween decks, and the long bridge hatch trunk. Chilled meat lockers were provided port and starboard in Nos 2 and 3 upper 'tween decks. The deck beams in these compartments were especially strengthened for hanging cargoes.

Accommodation for the crew was arranged in a long bridge deck house on the upper deck, surmounted by a three-tier deckhouse. Deck and engineer officers and petty officers were each provided with a separate single berth cabin while ratings and catering staff were accommodated in two-berth cabins. Separate toilet facilities were provided in each department. A crew mess room and recreation room were provided together with a separate petty officers' mess room. The public rooms comprised a spacious dining saloon to seat twenty persons, and a smoking room. The crew accommodation was mechanically heated and ventilated

*Above: Montreal Star.*

*Below: America Star.* (Barry Eagles)

by a combined plant incorporating heating units connected by trunking to directional louvres throughout, officers' accommodation being heated by convector heaters to each room.

The normal arrangement of masts, winches and derricks was supplemented by a number of fixed cranes for cargo handling purposes. From the foremast, two 7-ton derricks were arranged to serve No. 1 hold. Two 10-ton deck derricks and a 50-ton heavy derrick were fitted to No. 2 hold. Two 5-ton derricks were stepped on the midship house front at the after end of No. 3 hold, and two 5-ton derricks stepped upon derrick posts at the fore end of No. 4 hold. Four Clarke Chapman electrically driven level deck cranes of fixed type, each of 3-ton capacity, were arranged to serve No. 1 hold forward, No. 2 hold aft, No. 3 hold forward and No. 4 hold aft.

7.1972    Lengthened by 78 feet by Framnaes at Sandfjord, Norway, (540.4 feet) and equipped for the carriage of bananas.

1975    Managed by Blue Star Ship Management Limited.

1983    Laid up on the River Fal.

11.1983    Sold and broken up in China.

116. *New York Star* (1) (1965)
7,372 grt, 4,161 n., 462.8 x 63.2 x 30.1 feet, yard no. 405, IMO 6506989.
Steel, single screw, oil, 2 stroke single acting, 8 cyls, Sulzer 8RD 76 type, 12,000 BHP, 17 knots. By G. Clark & Company Limited, Sunderland & North East Marine Limited.
B. Bartram & Sons Limited, Sunderland.

3.2.1965    Launched by Mrs D. J. Wortley, wife of the manager of the Blue Star Line.

9.1965    Delivered to the Blue Star Line Limited as the fifth of the series. Constructed by means of Monopol automatic plate cutting machinery, as it was the builder's standard practice, all steel plates and

sections were shot-blasted and coated with Vedette zinc-rich paint. She was fitted with bridge control of the main engines, allowing for a reduction in engine room personnel. Two Clark-Chapman fixed deck cranes were fitted, and two of their traversing type. A 50-ton derrick was situated at No. 2 hatch, and the other derricks had a 20-foot reach overside. Two complete steel decks extended the length of the ship, while a third deck was arranged in Nos 2 and 3 holds. Each of the holds and 'tween decks was insulated for frozen cargo, while un-insulated cargo was carried in the long forecastle and the centre portions of Nos 2 and 3 upper 'tween decks; at the sides were chilled meat lockers. The vessel was built to comply with the St Lawrence Seaway requirements.

1973    Lengthened by 78 feet by Framnaes at Sandfjord, Norway, (540.4 feet) and equipped for the carriage of bananas.

1975    Managed by Blue Star Ship Management Limited.

1980    Operated by Calmedia S.p.A. di Nav., Panama, managed by Blue Star Ship Management and renamed *Liguria*.

1981    Sold to the Panama Shipping Company, managed by Blue Star Ship Management Limited.

1983    Purchased by Euroatlantic Shipping Corporation for one voyage to the ship-breakers.

22.12.1983    Arrived at Gadani Beach and broken up by Ahmed Mercantile Limited.

117. *Fremantle Star* (2) (1960)
8,403 grt, 4,949 n., 519 x 70.2 x 30 feet, yard no. 1290, IMO 5121055.
Steel, single screw, oil, 8 cyls, 2 stroke single acting, 13,300 BHP, 18 knots. By Harland & Wolff, Belfast. One deck and shelter deck plus part of third and fourth decks.
Passengers: 6, in two double berths and two single-berth staterooms on the boat deck.

B. Cammell Laird & Company Limited, Birkenhead.

30.12.1959    Launched by Mrs W. Vestey, sister-in-law of Mr Ronald Vestey, for the Blue Star Line Limited. The North West Tug Company's *Flying Cock* was launched twenty minutes prior to *Fremantle Star* by Cammell Laird at Birkenhead.

27.4.1960    Delivered for the service from the United Kingdom to Australia and New Zealand.

1964    Transferred to Lamport & Holt Line, Blue Star Line Limited as managers.

1965    Owned by the Blue Star Line Limited.

1975    Managed by Blue Star Ship Management Limited.

1979    Owned by Caxton Marine Enterprises Corporation, renamed *Catarina*.

30.11.1979    Arrived at Kaohsiung and broken up by Nan Long Steel & Iron Company.

## 118. *Santos Star* (1) (1959)

3,594 grt, 1,999 n., 338 x 47.1 x 20 feet, yard no. 264, IMO 5313359.
Steel, single screw, oil, 7 cyls, 2 stroke single acting, 4,600 BHP, 16 knots. By MAN, Hamburg. Two decks and part of third deck.
B. Brooke Marine Limited, Lowestoft.

26.6.1959    Launched.

12.1959    Delivered as *Constable* for Lamport & Holt Line.

1962    Transferred to Blue Star Line Limited, renamed *Santos Star* for a new service between South American ports and Italian and French Mediterranean destinations.

*Above: Halifax Star.*

*Below: Halifax Star.*

1964      Lengthened by Harland & Wolff at Belfast (391.5 feet/ 3,775 grt).

1966      Transferred to Calmedia S.p.A. di Nav. Cagliari, renamed *Calagaribaldi*.

1981      Owned by Nourfo Cia Naviera SA, Panama, renamed *Gafredo*.

29.4.1984      Arrived at Barcelona and broken up by Desguaces Maritimos SA.

### 119. *Mendoza Star* (1) (1960)

3,563 grt, 1,972 n., 338 x 47.1 x 20 feet, yard no. 662.

Steel, single screw, oil, 7 cyls, 2 stroke single acting, 5,000 BHP Sulzer design, 16 knots. By builder. Two decks and part of third deck.

B. Alexander Stephen & Sons Limited, Linthouse.

1.12.1959      Launched by Mrs Crebbin, wife of Captain F. E. Crebbin, principal marine superintendent of Lamport & Holt Line Limited.

2.1960      Delivered to Lamport & Holt Line as *Chatham* to carry bananas and other perishable goods between the United Kingdom and the West Indies. She was built to the special survey of Lloyd's Class +100 A 1 with refrigeration. She had six watertight bulkheads extending to the upper deck and forming the forepeak and aft peak tank, motor room and three insulated cargo holds forward and one aft. The double bottom was arranged for the carriage of oil fuel or water ballast and extended forward to the forepeak bulkhead. Two double-bottom deep tanks were arranged under No. 1 hold. Oil fuel settling and overflow tanks, also drinking water tanks, were situated at sides of the shaft tunnel. She had eleven insulated cargo spaces served from seven cooler rooms.

The installation of fans, coolers and refrigeration machinery was supplied by J. & E. Hall Limited of Dartford. To obtain the maximum air circulation, the 'tween deck in Nos 2 and 3 holds was arranged as a spar

*Fremantle Star* (2).

deck. Provision was made for the carriage of chilled meat in No. 3 hold and 'tween deck and No. 4 hold and 'tween deck and an arrangement of meat rails was installed to ensure that the maximum possible meat cargo could be carried. Six 5-ton derricks were fitted at Nos 1, 3 and 4 cargo hatches and two 10-ton derricks at No. 2 hatch. Each hatch was served by two 3-ton electric winches. Separate winch controls were arranged close to the hatch coamings. To facilitate the rapid discharge of cargo, hydraulically operated hatch covers were installed throughout.

The crew were accommodated entirely on the upper deck in cabins, none of which had more than two berths. Every cabin had natural lighting and was well fitted out. A large recreational room was fitted out for the crew in a deckhouse on the upper deck aft. Independent mess rooms for officers and ratings were also provided, as were stewards. A combined system of heating and ventilation was fitted to the officers' and crew accommodation and toilets, chart room, radio room, dining saloon and lounge. All lifeboats were built of African mahogany and the motor boat was provided with a Petter AVA 2 Diesel engine.

4.1962      Transferred to Blue Star Line Limited, renamed *Mendoza Star* (1) for the South America–Mediterranean service.

1963      Lengthened by SA Cockerill-Ougree at Hoboken (391.5 feet/3,666 grt).

1967      Transferred to Calmedia S.p.A. di Nav., Cagliari, renamed *Calavittoria.*

1979      Owned by Laguna Shipping Company, managed by Laskaridis Shipping Limited, Piraeus, renamed *Frio Aegean.*

1981      Sold to Enias Shipping Company, Piraeus, and then to Tobermory Shipping Company, same managers.

26.3.1984      Arrived at Gadani Beach and broken up by Habib Maritime Limited.


120. *Iberia Star* (1) (1950)
10,854 grt, 6,190 n., 505 x 64.8 x 27.5 feet, yard no. 720, IMO 5405322. Steel, single screw, oil, 8 cyls, 2 stroke double acting, 9,250 BHP, 16 knots. By builder at the Seraing Works. Two decks and part of third deck. B. John Cockerill SA, Hoboken.

4.3.1950      Launched as *Baudouinville* for Cie Maritime Belge.

9.1950      Delivered for the West Africa service.

1957      Renamed *Thysville* and name given to a new vessel in the fleet.

2.1961      Sold to the Booth Line, renamed *Anselm* for the Liverpool–Manaus service.

1963      Transferred to the Blue Star Line Limited, renamed *Iberia Star.* Sent to Bremer Vulkan at Vegesack, where she was converted to carry chilled meat.

Passengers: 248. She initially sailed from Liverpool but later out of London.

1965      Transferred to the Austasia Line, renamed *Australasia,* owned by the Blue Star Line.

1971      Registered at Singapore.

16.12.1972      Sold to Euroasia Carriers Limited and left Singapore in tow to be broken up.

3.1973      Broken up by Chou's Iron & Steel (Industrial) Company at Hualien.


121. *Genova Star* (1) (1956)
5,137 grt, 2,869 n., 396.5 x 54.1 x 23.5 feet, yard no. 474, IMO 5255911. Steel, single screw, oil, 8 cyls, 2 stroke single acting, 5,700 BHP, B&W type, 15 knots. By builder. Four decks. B. Eriksbergs M/V A/B, Gothenburg.

24.8.1956      Launched as *Norefjell* for Olsen & Ugelstad.

1964      Purchased by the Blue Star Line Limited, renamed *Genova Star* (1) for the South America–Mediterranean service.

1966      Transferred to Calmedia S.p.A. di Nav, Cagliari, renamed *Calabella.*

1974      Owned by Nouro Cia Nav. SA, Piraeus, renamed *Annaflora.*

1978      Sold to Samos Shipping Enterprises, Piraeus, managed by Fotis C. Georgopoulos, renamed *Nissos Samos.*

21.6.1981      Arrived at Gadani Beach and broken up by Paruma (Eastern) Limited.


122. *Padova Star* (1) (1956)
3,667 grt, 1,994 n., 391.1 x 49.1 x 20.1 feet, yard no. 689, IMO 5270985. Steel, single screw, oil, 7 cyls, 2 stroke single acting, 4,670 BHP, 16½ knots, By MAN, Augsburg. Two decks and part of third deck. B. Deutsches Werft, Hamburg.

24.2. 1956    Launched as *Parthenon* for Laiesz & Company, Africanische Frucht-Cie., and delivered as a fruit carrier for service between the Cameroons and Hamburg.

1962    Chartered to the Geest Line for their services from Barry and Preston to the West Indies.

8.1964    Purchased by the Blue Star Line Limited, renamed *Padova Star* (1) for the South America–Mediterranean service.

1966    Transferred to Calmedia S.p.A. di Nav., Cagliari, renamed *Calarossa*.

1974    Sold to Nogrou Navigation Company, Limassol, renamed *Imperia*. The company later became Gofrou Navigation Company.

22.10.1980    Arrived at Gadani Beach and broken up by Paruma International Limited.


123. *Barcelona Star* (1) (1955)

4,705 grt, 1,994 n., 393.3 x 49.1 x 20.1 feet, yard no. 682, IMO 5279216.

Steel, single screw, oil, 7 cyls, 2 stroke single acting, 4,670 BHP, 16½ knots. By MAN, Augsburg. Two decks and part of third deck.

B. Deutsches Werft Aktiengesellschaft, Hamburg.

8.12.1954    Launched.

1955    Delivered as *Piraeus* for Afrikanische Frucht Compagnie Laiesz & Company, F. Laeisz manager.

1.1965    Purchased by the Blue Star Line Limited, renamed *Barcelona Star* (1) for the South America–Mediterranean route.

1965    Transferred to Calmedia S.p.A. di Nav., Cagliari, renamed *Calasetta*.

1974    Sold to Nogrou Navigation Company, Limassol, renamed *Sanstefano*.

1976    The company later became Norfo Cia Nav. SA., Panama.

27.5.1981    Laid up at Bombay.

11.1981    Broken up by Gokalchand & Company at Darukhana.


124. *Avanti* (1964)

3,374 grt, 1,820 n., 443.8 x 55.3 x 21.6 feet.

Steel, 8 cyl 2 SCSA 9,600 BHP oil engine by Masch, Augsburg.

B. Lubecker Flender Werke AG, Lübeck, yard no. 542.

18.12.1963    Launched for W. Burns & Company, Hamburg, as *Brunskoog*.

1972    Sold to Soberanom Delmare SA, Piraeus, renamed *Rosaria*.

1977    Purchased by Taro Shipping & Enterprises SA, Piraeus, renamed *Taro*.

1979    Sold to Avanti Shipping Corporation Incorporated, Panama, managed by the Blue Star line Limited, renamed *Avanti*.

31.7.1980    Left Rio Grande, Brazil, for Buenos Aires. Fire broke out in engine room and crew abandoned the ship.

4.8.1980    Tow attached and she later sank. Broken up where she lay at Rio Grande.


125. *Waveney Star* (1)/*Waveney* (1956)

487 grt, 281 n., 169 x 27.5 x 11.2 feet, yard no. 140, IMO 5264807.

Steel, single screw, 6 cyls, 4 stroke single acting, 395 BHP, 9 knots. By Motorenwerke, Mannheim. One deck.

B. Schpsw, Bodewes Gruno, Foxhol.

25.6.1956    Launched.

9.1956    Delivered as Orient for *Rederij Vebo*, Groningen, managed by Kamps, Scheep & Handel NV.

196    Renamed *Zaandijk* on charter to Solleveld's S&A, Maats, managed by NV Solleveld's Scheepv & Agentuur Maats.

1962    Name changed to *Orient* when charter finished, Kamps, Scheepv & Handelmaats NV as managers.

1964          Purchased by the Blue Star Line Limited, renamed *Waveney Star* (1) for European–London feeder services.

1965          Renamed *Waveney*, operated by G. T. Gillie & Blair Limited, managed by the Blue Star Line Limited.

1969          Sold to D. P. Kalkassinas, Thessaloniki, renamed *Meropi*.

1975          Purchased by Zissis Triantafyllou & Company and G. Topalis.

12.1985       Renamed *Stelios A*, owned by Nikolas Kritsinaris, then Stelios Amorgianos.

1985          Renamed *Sandra*.

1996          Became *Saranta*.

1999          Renamed *Seda*.

2005          Renamed *Geneos*.

5.1.2012      Not on register.

## 126. *Orwell Star* (1)/*Orwell* (1956)

495 grt, 314 n., 173.2 x 28.6 x 10.4 feet, yard no. 555, IMO 5407655.
Steel, single screw, oil, 6 cyls, 4 stroke single acting, 395 BHP, 10 knots. By Motorenwerke, Mannhein. One deck.

22.12.1955    Launched.

2.1956        Delivered as *Julia-Anna* for E. Smid, NV, Carebeka as managers, later NV Gruno.

1961          NV Scheepvaartbedrijf Gruno as managers.

1963          Purchased by the Blue Star Line Limited, renamed *Orwell Star* for North Sea–London feeder services.

1965          Renamed *Orwell*, managed by G. T. Gillie Blair Limited in Blue Star Line colours.

1968          Purchased by S. W. Coe & Company Limited, Liverpool, renamed *Booker Trader*, operated by Booker Shipping (Demerara) Limited.

1975          Owned by Booker Line Limited.

1977          Sold to the Ministry of Works & Transport, Government of Guyana.

1979          Renamed *Guytrader*.

1981          Sold to Guyana National Shipping Corporation Limited, Georgetown.

2003          Renamed *Lady Chandra II*.

5.1.2012      Not on register.

## 127. *Crouch* (1) (1966)

500 grt, 289 n., 183.5 x 28.8 x 10.9 feet, yard no. 1024, IMO 6611447.
Steel, single screw, oil, 6 cyls, 4 stroke single acting, 530 BHP, $10\frac{1}{2}$ knots.
By Blackstone & Company, Stamford. One deck.
B. Boele's Schps & Mchf, Bolnes, Holland.

19.4.1966     Launched as *Crouch* for the Blue Star Line Limited, managed by G. T. Gillie & Blair Limited. Feeder services.

1971          Sold to Mardorf, Peach & Company Limited, renamed *Camilla Weston*, G. T. Gillie & Blair Limited as managers.

1976          Owned by Weston Shipping Limited.

1977          Transferred to Mardorf, Peach & Company Limited

15.2.1984     The German vessel *Larissasee* collided with her while she was at anchor off Happisburgh and she sank.

## 128. *Deben* (1) (1966)

500 grt, 289 n., 183.5 x 28.8 x 10.9 feet, yard no. 1023, IMO 6609078.
Steel, single screw, oil, 6 cyls, 4 stroke single acting, 530 BHP, $10\frac{1}{2}$ knots.
By Blackstone & Company, Stamford. One deck.
B. Boele's Schps & Mchf, Bolnes, Holland.

18.2.1966     Launched as *Deben* (1) for the Blue Star Line Limited, managed by G. T. Gillie & Blair Limited.

*Waveney.*

*Orwell Star.*

1971        Sold to Mardorf, Peach & Company Limited, renamed *Gretchen Weston*, G. T. Gillie & Blair Limited as managers.

1976        Sold to the Ramsey Steam Ship Company, renamed *Ben Ain*.

12.4.91     Renamed *Prince*.

3.6.99      Became *Abdoulah 1*.

13.11.2013  Not on register.

### 129. *Australia Star* (2) (1966)

10,025 grt, 5,842 n., 526.1 x 70.1 x 30 feet, yard no. 841, IMO 6513798. Steel, single screw, oil, 8 cyls, Sulzer, 17,600 BHP, 19 knots. By Vickers Armstrong (Engineering) Limited, Barrow. Two decks and part of third deck.

B. Austin & Pickersgill Limited, Sunderland.

11.5.1965   Launched by Mrs W. T. Rae for the Blue Star Line Limited.

12.1965     Towed to Hamburg for the 300-ton Stulcken derrick to be fitted. This was the largest to be fitted on a merchant ship.

1972        Chartered to Chr. Haaland, Norway, renamed *Concordia Star*.

1974        When charter was completed, she reverted to *Australia Star* (2).

4.1974      Sold to Costa Armatori S.p.A., Naples, renamed *Cortina*.

1984        Owned by the Jetset Shipping Corporation, Panama, renamed *Candy Ace*.

4.4.1985    Arrived at Shanghai and broken up.

**130. *Southland Star* (1) (1967)**
11,300 grt, 6,627 n., 552.3 x 73.3 x 29.3 feet, yard no. 929, IMO 6707909.
Steel, single screw, oil, 9 cyls, 2 stroke single acting, MAN type K9Z86/160E, 21 knots. By builder. Two decks and part of third and fourth decks.
B. Bremer Vulkan, Bremen-Vegesack.
10.1.1967   Launched for the Blue Star Line Limited.
6.1967   Delivered for the United Kingdom to Australia and New Zealand services.
1975   Managed by Blue Star Ship Management Limited.
1979   Converted to carry containers by builders.
25.7.1985   Took the yacht *Windwalker* in tow and passed her over to the United States Coastguard near Hawaii.
19.8.93   Arrived at Chittagong.
29.9.93   Beached and broken up.

**131. *New Zealand Star* (2)/*Wellington Star* (3) (1967)**
11,300 grt, 6,627 n., 552.3 x 73.3 x 29.3 feet, yard no. 930, IMO 6717320.
Steel, single screw, oil, 9 cyls, 2 stroke single acting, MAN type K9Z86/160E, 21 knots. By builder. Two decks and part of third and fourth decks.
B. Bremer Vulkan, Bremen-Vegesack.
11.5.1967   Launched for the Blue Star Line Limited.
9.1967   Delivered with space for ten containers as well as 566,000 cubic feet of chilled beef and refrigerated cargo. There was space for 2,000 tons of wool and mixed cargoes, and tank space for 400 tons of liquid such as tallow.
9.3.1970   The ship vibrated suddenly during the night and her speed began to drop. A dead 40-foot whale was found to be attached to her bow.
1975   Managed by Blue Star Ship Management Limited.
1977   Converted to container ship by builders, 11,393 grt, 6,503 net.

1979   Renamed *Wellington Star* (3) when the name was required for a new vessel.
1993   Broken up at Chittagong.

**132. *Timaru Star* (2) (1967)**
8,366 grt, 4,775 n., 496.9 x 65.2 x 29.8 feet, yard no. 408, IMO 6709945.
Steel, single screw, oil, 8 cyls, 2 stroke single acting Sulzer design, 12,000 BHP, 18 knots. By G. Clark & Company, Sunderland. Two decks and part of third deck.
B. Bartram & Sons Limited, Sunderland.
26.2.1967   Launched for the Blue Star Line Limited.
7.1967   Delivered for the Australia and New Zealand service.
1976   Managed by Blue Star Ship Management.
17.10.1978   A serious fire at Cardiff damaged her accommodation and two officers lost their lives.
1983   Transferred to Crest Shipping Limited, Hong Kong, renamed *Crest Hill*, Blue Star Ship Management as managers.
1.3.1985   Arrived at Huangpu, China, and broken up.

**133. *California Star* (3) (1971)**
19,095 grt, 10,730 n., 619.6 x 85 x 33 feet, yard no. 975, IMO 7045671.
Steel, single screw, oil, 9 cyls, MAN type K9SZ 90/160 low speed direct coupling, 26,100 BHP, 21½ knots. By builder.
B. Bremer Vulkan, Bremen-Vegesack.
12.1.1971   Launched for the Blue Star Line Limited to operate on the Scanstar joint service with the East Asiatic Company from Europe to the west coast of the United States. EAC vessels were *Flandria* and *Meonia*.
1975   Managed by Blue Star Ship Management.
1987   Transferred to the Austasia Line, renamed *Mulbera*.

*New Zealand Star* (2) and *Southland Star* in Gladstone Dock, Liverpool.

*New Zealand Star* (2).

| | |
|---|---|
| 1.3.93 | Transferred to the Blue Star Line, renamed *Fremantle Star* (3). |
| 1998 | Broken up at Alang. |

### 134. *Columbia Star* (2) (1971)

19,095 grt, 10,730 n., 619.6 x 85 x 33 feet, yard no. 976, IMO 7113301.
Steel, single screw, oil, 9 cyls, M.A.N. type K9SZ 90/160 low speed direct coupling, 26,100 BHP, 21½ knots. By builder.
B. Bremer Vulkan, Bremen-Vegesack.

| | |
|---|---|
| 26.6.1971 | Launched for the Blue Star Line Limited to operate on the Scanstar joint service with the East Asiatic Company from Europe to the west coast of the United States. EAC vessels were *Flandria* and *Meonia*. |
| 1975 | Managed by Blue Star Ship Management. |

| | |
|---|---|
| 1986 | Transferred to the Austasia Line, renamed *Mandama*. |
| 3.1992 | Transferred to the Blue Star Line, renamed *New Zealand Star* (4). |
| 14.2.98 | Beached at Chittagong and broken up. |

### 135. *Afric Star* (2) (1975)

9,784 grt, 5,428 n., 511.2 x 70.1 x 28.1 feet, yard no. 1328, IMO 7342964.
Steel, single screw, oil, 9 cyls, 2 stroke single acting Kincaid-B&W type 9K74EF turbo charged, 15,900 BHP at 120 rpm, 23 knots. By J. G. Kincaid & Company Limited. Three decks and part of fourth deck.
B. Smith's Dock & Company Limited, Middlesbrough.

| | |
|---|---|
| 3.9.1974 | Launched as the first of a class of six ships. |

*California Star* (3).

2.1975    Delivered to the Glencairn Shipping Company Limited on bare-boat charter to the Blue Star Line, managed by Blue Star Ship Management.

1987    Sold to High Herald Limited, Hong Kong, renamed *Lanark*, managed by Blue Star Ship Management.

18.9.2001    Beached at Alang and broken up.

136. *Avila Star* (2) (1975)

9,766 grt, 5,421 n., 511.2 x 70.1 x 28.1 feet, yard no. 208, IMO 7358810. Steel, single screw, oil, 9 cyls, 2 stroke single acting Kincaid-B&W type 9K74EF turbo charged, 15,900 BHP at 120 rpm, 23 knots. By Nylands M/V, Oslo. Three decks and part of fourth deck.

B. Akers Bergebs Mekaniske Verksteder and A/S Nakskov Skibs, Nakstov (hull).

20.11.1974    Launched.

6.1975    Delivered to the Blue Star Line Limited, Blue Star Ship Management. Completed by Akers Mekaniske Verksted A/S, Bergen (yard no. 711).

1979    Sold to Hidlefjord & Byfjord, Kornelius Olsen, Stavanger, renamed *Hidlefjord*.

1981    Transferred to PR Hidlefjord, Kornelius Olsen manager, same name.

1988    Renamed *Swan Lake*.

1.1992    Owned by Sunpor Reefer Schiffahrtsages GmbH, renamed *Sun Swan*.

1993    Renamed *Reefer Sun*.

12.1997    Sold to Reefer Sun Company.

10.1998    Purchased by Bright Sapphire Maritime Incorporated, Osterreichischer Lloyd Ship Management (Cyprus) Limited managers.

15.8.2007    Renamed *E. W. Jackson* at Piraeus, owned by E. W. Jackson, managed by Eastwind (Hellas) SA, Pireaus.

17.12.2009    Beached at Alang and broken up.

137. *Andalucia Star* (2) (1975)

9,784grt. 5,428 n., 511.2 x 70.1 x 28.1 feet, yard no. 1329, IMO 7342976. Steel, single screw, oil, 9 cyls, 2 stroke single acting Kincaid-B&W type 9K74EF turbo charged, 15,900 BHP at 120 rpm, 23 knots. By J. G. Kincaid & Company Ltd. Three decks and part of fourth deck.

B. Smith's Dock & Company Limited, Middlesbrough.

14.1.1975    She was named, but high winds delayed her launch until the following day. Delivered to Blue Star Ship Management. The largest ship to berth at the Pool of London.

*Afric Star* (2).

5.6.1977     Took part in the rescue of the crew of the *Ain Leuh*, which was on fire off South Korea, and took them to Las Palmas. Chartered to the Union Castle Line and painted in their colours.

1982     Chartered to the British Government and sent to the Falkland Islands as a supply ship. A helicopter pad was installed and the funnel was coloured white and black, with white bands and a black top.

1984     Sold to Highvale Limited, Wallem Ship Management Limited, Hong Kong; renamed *Fife*.

10.2010     Broken up in India.

138. *Almeria Star* (1) (1976)
9,781 grt, 5,416 n., 5,428 n., 511.2 x 70.1 x 28.1 feet, yard no. 1332, IMO 7402946.

Steel, single screw, oil, 9 cyls, 2 stroke single acting Kincaid-B&W type 9K74EF turbo charged, 15,900 BHP at 120 rpm, 23 knots. By J. G. Kincaid & Company Limited. Three decks and part of fourth deck.
B. Smith's Dock & Company Limited, Middlesbrough.

13.7.1976     Launched for Transport Exchange Company Limited on bare-boat charter to the Blue Star Line Limited.

11.1976     Delivered with Blue Star Ship Management as managers.

1977     Transferred to the Transport Commission-Tasmania, Blue Star Ship Management as managers.

14.6.1984     On a voyage from Antwerp to Sheerness she was in collision with Cunard Line's *Servia* off Zeebrugge. Sent to Flushing for repairs.

1984     Sold to New Prestige Limited, Wallem Ship Management Limited, Hong Kong; renamed *Perth*. On charter to Blue Star Line.

7.1985     Laid up in the River Blackwater, owned by High Herald Limited.

1986     Overhauled at Falmouth.

1987     Lion Shipping Limited as managers.

1988     Sold to Austasia Line; renamed *Almeria Star*.

1990     Renamed *Avila Star* (3).

1994     Transferred to Blue Star Reefers Limited.

1996 Owned by Tropic Marine SA, Target Marine SA, Piraeus, managers. Same name.

11.2002     Sold to Russian interests; renamed *Ice Bell*.

2006     Owned by Sanoma Enterprise Incorporated (Samskip Company Limited).

18.9.2009     Arrived at Alang and broken up.

139. *Almeda Star* (2) (1976)
9,781 grt, 5,416 n., 511.2 x 70.1 x 28.1 feet, yard no. 1331, IMO 7392737.
Steel, single screw, oil, 9 cyls, 2 stroke single acting Kincaid-B&W type

9K74EF turbo charged, 15,900 BHP at 120 rpm, 23 knots. By J. G. Kincaid & Company Limited. Three decks and part of fourth deck.

B. Smith's Dock & Company Limited, Middlesbrough.

2.11.1975      Launched for Airlease International and Vasivelt Limited.

4.1976      Delivered to Avelona Star Limited on bare-boat charter to Blue Star Limited. Managed by Blue Star Ship Management.

6.1984      Sold to Arran Shipping Limited, managed by Wallem Ship Management Limited, Hong Kong; renamed *Arran*. Chartered to Blue Star Line Limited.

7.1984      Final sailing for the Blue Star Line and then laid up in the River Blackwater.

1985      Renamed *Harlech*, managed by Wallem Ship Management Limited.

12.2001      Renamed *Baltic Wave*.

2009      Sold to Camden Limited, managed by Baltic Reefers, St Petersburg, Russia.

2010      Broken up.

140. *Avelona Star* (2) (1975)

9,784 grt, 5,428 n., 511.2 x 70.1 x 28.1 feet, yard no. 1330, IMO 7342988. Steel, single screw, oil, 9 cyls, 2 stroke single acting Kincaid-B&W type 9K74EF turbo charged, 15,900 BHP at 120 rpm, 23 knots. By J. G. Kincaid & Company Limited. Three decks and part of fourth deck.

B. Smith's Dock & Company Limited, Middlesbrough.

12.5.1975      Launched.

12.1975      Delivered to Avelona Star Limited, managed by Blue Star Ship Management.

1982      Chartered with *Andalucia Star* (2) for service in the Falkland Islands.

1984      Renamed *Castle Peak*, owned by Stirling Limited, Wallem

*Almeria Star.*

Ship Management Limited, Hong Kong. Chartered to the Blue Star Line.

12.2001      Renamed *Baltic Wind*.

20.9.2010      Sold and broken up at Sachana, India.

141. *Tuscan Star* (3) (1972)

6,671 grt, 3,641 n., 461.4 x 59.2 x 29.7 feet, yard no. 73, IMO 7217559. Steel, single screw, oil, 9 cyls, Sulzer type, 14,850 BHP, 23 knots. Four decks.

B. Drammen Slip & Verk, Drammen.

23.1. 1972      Launched.

5.1972      Delivered as *Labrador Clipper* to Maritime Fruit Carriers Limited, operated by Chichester Shipping Lines Limited, Glasgow.

27.7.1976      When the owners went into liquidation, she was purchased from Maritime Midland Bank Limited, renamed *Tuscan Star*, operated by Blue Star Ship Management, and registered in Glasgow.

1980      Owned by Sun Glory Compania Naviera SA, Piraeus, Diana

Shipping Agencies; renamed *Chios Pride*.

27.3.1993    Arrived at Bombay and broken up.

142. *Trojan Star* (2) (1972)

6,671 grt, 3,641 n., 461.4 x 59.2 x 29.7 feet, yard no. 1322, IMO 7233747. Steel, single screw, oil, 9 cyls, Sulzer type, 14,850 BHP, 23 knots. By Clark & N. E. M. Limited, Sunderland. Four decks. B. Smith's Dockyard Company, Middlesbrough.

20.11.1972    Launched as *Newcastle Clipper* for Maritime Fruit Carriers, Rockhampton Shipping Company.

3.1973    Delivered to Sovetur Shipping Company, managed by North West Shipping Company Limited, Glasgow.

27.7.1976    Purchased by the Blue Star Line Limited, managed by Blue Star Ship Management; renamed *Trojan Star*.

12.6.1980    Experienced rudder failure 800 miles from New Zealand during bad weather. Taken in tow by the tug *Raumanga* and towed 747 miles to Wellington.

24.6.1980    Arrived at Wellington.

10.1980    During the Iran-Iraq war she was unable to leave Bandar Khomeini for several weeks.

1981    Sold to Saful Navigation Company, Greece, Diana Shipping Agencies as managers; renamed *Chios Clipper*.

1992    Renamed *Frio Clipper*.

1994    Renamed *Roman Hurricane*.

12.4.1995    Arrived at Aliaga and broken up.

*Above: Avelona Star* (2).

*Below: Avelona Star* (2) aground off Ternuezen, Holland, on the morning of 15 March 1990. She was re-floated on the afternoon tide.

143. *Australia Star* (3) (1978)

17,082 grt, 8,930 n., 554 x 82.68 x 30.7 feet, yard no. 1340, IMO 7636676. Steel, single screw, oil, 6 cyls, Sulzer, 17,400 BHP, 18 knots. By Barclay Curle Limited, Glasgow. One deck.

B. Smith's Dockyard Company, Middlesbrough.

22.4.1978     Launched.

8.1978     Delivered to Brodies (London) Limited, Blue Star Ship Management.

27.9.1978     No. 4 Hatch Crane collapsed during loading at New Plymouth.

2.2.1989     Transferred to Austasia Line; renamed *Mahsuri* (4).

15.9.1990     On a voyage from Fremantle to the Middle East, she ran aground in the Straits of Malacca, damaging her hull. Refloated.

20.9.1990     Arrived at Singapore under tow for dry-docking.

12.1.1991     Repairs completed.

16.3.1992     Renamed *Australia Star*.

5.1994     Chartered by Pacific International Lines (Pte) Limited for the Australia–Malaysia service; renamed *Anro Fremantle*, registered in Nassau, Bahamas.

1995     Became *Sea Express*.

29.4.2001     Arrived at Chittagong and broken up.

144. *Brisbane Star* (2) (1978)

27,305 grt, 9,198 n., 203.85 x 30.99 x 18.8 metres, yard no. B456/01, IMO 7516371.

Steel, 1 x Sulzer 10RND90 slow speed direct drive, 29,000 BHP, 20½ k.

B. Stocznia Gdanska, Gdansk, Poland.

9.1978     Delivered as *La Fayette* to Compagnie Général Maritime, Le Havre.

*Tuscan Star* (3).

*Trojan Star* (2).

23.7.1993    Owned by Blue Star Limited, renamed *Brisbane Star* (2), registered in Nassau.

21.12.1997    To Blue Star Line, Marine Limited; renamed *Singapore Star*.

19.9.1998    To P&O Nedlloyd Limited; renamed *P&O Nedlloyd Lyttelton*.

2002    Sold and broken up in China.

145. *Choyang Sydney* (1981)

30,085 grt, 14,380 n., 200.26 x 31.73 x 9.5 metres, yard no. 324, IMO 7900065.

Steel, 10 cyls, 2 SCSA Sulzer 10RND90 type, 29,026 BHP. By H. Cegielski Zakłady Przemysłu Metalowego, Poznań, Poland.

B. Chantiers Navals de la Ciotat, France.

30.9.1980    Launched as *Tadeusz Kościuszko* for Francusko-Polskie Towarzystwo Zeglugowe, Gdynia.

5.1981    Delivered.

30.10.1992    Sold to Kingston Maritime Corporation, Egon Oldendorff KG, as managers; renamed *Gebe Oldendorff*.

3.3.1993    Chartered by Neptune Orient Line for four years. However, the charter only lasted for twelve months.

15.4.1993    Arrived at Jurong shipyard, and converted to a container vessel. Stern door, ramps and vehicle decks were removed, and bridge was raised by one deck.

2.6.1993    Work completed.

30.6.1993    Renamed *Neptune Lazuli*.

17.11.1994    Became *Singapore Express*. On charter to Hapag-Lloyd.

9.7.1996    To Blue Star Line Limited, Blue Star Ship Management Limited, Hong Kong as managers.

2.8.1996    Renamed *Choyang Sydney* (it was to have been *Tokyo Star*).

4.1998    To Blue Star Marine Limited, Hong Kong.

10.11.1998    On charter to A. P. Møller/Maersk Line, renamed *Maersk Hakata*.

1999    To P&O Nedlloyd Containers Limited.

2.6.1999    Became *Asia Star*.

25.11.1999    Renamed *P&O Nedlloyd Piraeus*.

1.2000    *P&O Nedlloyd Khaleej*.

18.5.2000    *P&O Nedlloyd Malacca*.

28.6.2002    *P&O Nedlloyd Nina*.

20.4.2006    Arrived at Zhenjiang, China and broken up by Jiagyin Changjiang shipbreaking factory.

146. *New Zealand Star* (3) (1979)

17,082 grt, 8,930 n., 554 x 82.68 x 30.7 feet, yard no. 1341, IMO 7636688.

Steel, single screw, oil, 6 cyls, Sulzer, 17,400 BHP, 18 knots. By Barclay Curle Limited, Glasgow. One deck.

B. Smith's Dockyard Company, Middlesbrough.

20.7. 1978    Launched with Blue Star Ship Management as managers.

1.1979    Delivered to Airlease International and New Zealand Star Limited.

1983    Transferred to New Zealand Star Limited, same managers.

5.1.1986    Arrived at Singapore and lengthened by a new centre section at the Jurong shipyard. Her capacity was raised to 1,151 TEUs and she was repainted in Lamport & Holt colours.

4.1986    Sailed to Montevideo for a homeward voyage to the United Kingdom.

12.5.1986    Renamed *Churchill* at Tilbury by Lady Soames, Sir Winston Churchill's daughter.

1991    Transferred to the Blue Star Line; renamed *Argentina Star* (2).

1993    Merchant Navy officers union, Numast, protested over Blue Star line's decision to flag out their last fully UK-manned ship. British junior officers and ratings were replaced by Filipinos when the ship was moved to the Bahamas register. British officers were retained in the rank of Master, Chief Engineer, Chief Officer, Refrigeration Engineer and Electrical Officer.

1998        Sold to P&O Nedlloyd.

14.1.2002    Arrived at Shanghai, discharged her cargo of empty containers.

22.2.2002    Arrived at Jiangyin and broken up.

**147. *Columbia Star* (3) (1980)**

19,636 grt, 9,280 n., yard no. 1002.
Steel, 9 cyls, 2 SCSA, MAN K9SZ70/125BL, 18,345 BHP.
B. Bremer Vulkan Schiffbau Maschinenfabrik, Vegesack.

24.9.1979    Launched as *New Zealand Caribbean* for Lloyd's Leasing Limited, the Shipping Corporation of New Zealand Limited, London as managers.

1.1980       Delivered.

1.9.1985     Operated by the New Zealand Line

9.9.1985     Registered in New Zealand.

1.1.1989     To Bass New World International Limited, Columbia Ship Management Limited, Nassau, as managers; renamed *Abacas*.

1.2.1989     Registry transferred to Nassau, Cunard Ellerman Shipping Limited; renamed *ACT 10*.

1991         To Claire Navigation SA, Blue Star Ship Management Limited as managers.

26.11.1991   Renamed *Columbia Star* (3).

5.1998       Sold to Capital Leasing Limited, P&O Nedlloyd Container Line Limited as managers.

15.2.2000    Transferred to P&O Nedlloyd Limited, P&O Nedlloyd BV as managers, operated by Oceanica AGW Com & Rep., Es Limited, Mercosul Line, Rio de Janeiro; renamed *Mercosul Argentina*.

6.2001       Renamed *P&O Nedlloyd Luanda*.

6.2002       Sold to Chinese ship-breakers.

17.6.2002    Arrived at Jiangyin and broken up.

**148. *Scottish Star* (3) (1985)**

10,291 grt, 5,398 n., 495.4 x 41.7 x 30.5 feet, yard no. 1722, IMO 8315994.
Steel, single screw, oil, 2S.SA, B&W type, 22,000 BHP, 20 knots.
B. Harland & Wolff Limited, Belfast.

23.9.1984    Named.

2.4.1985     Completed for Lombard Leasing Metropolitan Limited on bareboat charter to Blue Star Line, Blue Star Ship Management as managers.

2.1998       Transferred to Albion Reefers, Star Reefers as managers.

7.2001       Sold to Norwegian owners, operated by Star Reefers.

2011         Sold at Fujairah, UAE, to Indian ship-breakers.

23.7.2011    Sailed from Fujairah.

26.7.2011    Arrived at Alang and broken up.

**149. *English Star* (2) (1986)**

10,291 grt, 5,398 n., 495.4 x 41.7 x 30.5 feet, yard no. 1721, IMO 8315982.
Steel, single screw, oil, 2S.SA, B&W type, 22,000 BHP, 20 knots.
B. Harland & Wolff Limited, Belfast.

23.9.1984    Named.

16.12.1984   Over £1 million damage was caused when a fire broke out on the ship and delayed her completion for over six months. The engine room was completely replaced and the main engine was rebuilt.

19.11.1985   Delivered to Lombard Leasing Metropolitan Limited, Blue Star Ship Management Limited as managers.

15.1.1986    Sailed from Belfast for Saint-Nazaire.

1987         Chartered to Horn Linie, Hamburg; renamed *Hornsea*.

2.1998       Transferred to Albion Reefers, Star Reefers managers.

*Above left: Churchill.*

*Above right: Argentina Star* (2).

*Left: Auckland Star* (3).

| 7.2001 | Transferred to Norwegian owners. |
|---|---|
| 2001 | Owned by Star Reefers. |
| 7.2011 | Laid up at Gdynia, Poland. |
| 2011 | Broken up at Alang. |

### 150. *Auckland Star* (3) (1986)

10,291 grt, 5,398 n., 495.4 x 41.7 x 30.5 feet, yard no. 1723, IMO 8316003.
Steel, single screw, oil, 2S.SA, B&W type, 22,000 BHP, 20 knots.
B. Harland & Wolff Limited, Belfast.

| 4.3.1985 | Launched for Investors in Industry PLC, on bare-boat charter, Blue Star Ship Management as managers. |
|---|---|
| 1987 | Chartered to Horn Linie, Hamburg; renamed *Horncliff* for two years. |
| 2.1998 | Transferred to Albion Reefers, Star Reefers managers. |
| 7.2001 | To Norwegian owners, operated by Star Reefers. |
| 2002 | Owned by Star Reefers. |
| 31.8.2011 | Laid up at Gdynia. |
| 30.10.2011 | Delivered at Fujairah; renamed *Auckland* and broken up at Alang. |

### 151. *Canterbury Star* (2) (1986)

10,291 grt, 5,398 n., 495.4 x 41.7 x 30.5 feet, yard no. 1724, IMO 8316015.
Steel, single screw, oil, 2S.SA, B&W type, 22,000 BHP, 20 knots. By builder.
B. Harland & Wolff Limited, Belfast.

| 5.11.1985 | Launched as owned by Investors in Industry PLC. |
|---|---|
| 2.1998 | Transferred to Albion Reefers, Star Reefers as managers. |
| 7.2001 | Transferred to Norwegian owners, operated by Star Reefers. |
| 2002 | Owned by Star Reefers. |
| 3.6.2011 | Sold by Star Reefers to be broken up at Alang. Delivery took place at Fujairah, UAE. |

### 152. *Australia Star* (4) (1981)

29,259 grt, 8,778 n., 199.7 x 31.7 x 9.5 metres, yard no. M27, IMO 7900041.
Steel, 10 cyls, 2 SCSA Sulzer 10RND90 type engine, 28,977 BHP by Zakłady Przemysłu Metalowego H. Cegielski SA, Poznań, Poland.
B. Chantiers de L'Atlantique, (Penhoet-Loire), Saint-Nazaire, France.

| 27.8.1980 | Laid down. |
|---|---|
| 10.4.1981 | Launched for Francusko-Polskie Towarzystwo Zeglugowe (Polish Ocean Lines, as managers), Gdynia as *Kazimierz Pulaski*. |
| 1.1993 | Chartered to the Bridge Line Limited. |
| 18.2.1993 | Renamed *Pyrmont Bridge*. |
| 1.1996 | Sold to Blue Star Line Limited (Blue Star Ship Management Limited, as managers), renamed *Australia Star* (4). |
| 1999 | Transferred to P&O Nedlloyd Limited (P&O Nedlloyd BV, as managers); renamed *P&O Nedlloyd Taranaki*. |
| 24.2.2006 | Arrived at Jiangyin and broken up. |

### 153. *Saxon Star* (4)/*Tudor Star* (3) (1988)

9,417 grt, 5,590 n., 145.50 x 21.54 x 9.45 metres, yard no. 633, IMO 8222989.
Steel, 6 cyls, 2SCSA 13,000 BHP B&W oil engine by Mitsui Engineering & Shipbuilding Company Limited, Tamano.
B. Flender Werft AG, Lübeck.

| 19.8.1983 | Launched as *Helene Jacob* for Partenreederei MS, Ernst Jacob as manager. |
|---|---|
| 16.12.1983 | Delivered as *Blumenthal*. |
| 1988 | Renamed *Helene Jacob*. |
| 3.1993 | Chartered to the Blue Star Line Limited; renamed *Saxon Star* (4). |
| 1.1994 | Renamed *Helene Jacob* on completion of charter. |

*English Star* (2). (Chris Brooks/ShipFoto)

| | |
|---|---|
| 1.1996 | Sold to Scott Shipping Limited, Panama; renamed *Tudor Star* (3). |
| 7.1996 | Sold to Blue Star Reefers Limited, Blue Star Ship Management Limited as managers. |
| 1998 | Sold to Albion Reefers Limited, Norbulk Shipping (UK) Limited as managers. |
| 2002 | Sold to Swan Reefer IV A/S, Star Reefers A/S as managers. |
| 2003 | Managed by Teekay Marine Services Limited. |
| 2004 | Sold to Star Reefers Shipowning Incorporated. |
| 2.2006 | Managed by Star Reefers (UK) Limited. |
| 8.2006 | Star Reefers, Poland, as managers. |
| 7.2007 | Renamed *Sun Genius*, same owners. |
| 2008 | Sold to Blazoon Shipping Corporation, Virgin Islands. |
| 1.2010 | Purchased by Star Shipholding 1 Incorporated, St Petersburg; renamed *Sky Glider*. |
| 22.6.2011 | Arrived at Alang and broken up. |

## Chartered Vessels Operated in Blue Star Livery

### 154. *Yakima Star* (1929)

6,660 grt, 4,164 n., 461.3 x 60.6 x 27.3 feet.
Steel, twin screw, oil, 12 cyls, 2 stroke double acting, 16 knots. One deck, shelter deck and part of third deck.
B. Deutsches Werke, Kiel.

| | |
|---|---|
| 18.2.1928 | Launched. |
| 18.6.1928 | Trials. |
| 24.6.1928 | Delivered to Linea Sud Americano, Invar An Christensen, Oslo, as *Sud Americano*. |
| 1930 | Returned to builders as there was a dispute over her loaded speed specifications. The builders disputed this as she had met the desired speed on her trials. Renamed *Schleswig* and laid up at Kiel. |
| 1931 | Chartered to the Blue Star Line; renamed *Yakima Star*. Returned to builder and laid up at Kiel again. |
| 1934 | Sold to Hanseatische Schifffahrts- und Betriebs-GmbH (Norddeutscher Lloyd); renamed *Weser*. Rebuilt with a single funnel and new M. A. N. diesels installed. |
| 1937 | Transferred to Norddeutscher Lloyd, same name. |
| 25.9.1940 | While off the Pacific coast of Mexico, she was captured by HMCS *Prince Robert*; renamed *Vancouver Island*, operated by the Canadian Government Merchant Marine. |
| 15.10 1941 | On a voyage from Quebec to Belfast, she was torpedoed and sunk by U-558. |

### 155. *Wenatchee Star* (1929)

6,607 grt, 4,158 n., 461.3 x 60.6 x 27.3 feet.
Steel, twin screw, oil, 12 cyls, 2 stroke double acting, 16 knots. One deck, shelter deck and part of third deck.
B. Deutsches Werke, Kiel.

| | |
|---|---|
| 1929 | Delivered as *Sud Expresso*. |
| 1930 | Renamed *Holstein*, laid up at Kiel. |
| 1931 | Chartered to the Blue Star Line, renamed *Wenatchee Star*. |
| 1934 | Owned by Hanseatische S.u.B. Rebuilt with a single funnel, and new M. A. N. diesels installed. |
| 1937 | Transferred to Norddeutscher Lloyd, same name. |
| 6.6.1941 | Sunk off the Azores by aircraft from HMS *Eagle*. |

### 156. *Sherborne* (1950)

475 grt, 243 n., 143.4 x 27.2 x 10.1 feet, yard no. 166.
Steel, 6 cyls, 4SCSA, 375 BHP oil engine by Appingedammer Brons Motorfabriek NV, Appingedammer.

B. NV Schpsw 'Vooruitgang' Gebr., Suurmeijer, Foxhol.

| | |
|---|---|
| 10.10.1949 | Launched as *Ransel* for Jannes Teerling. |
| 11.1954 | Sold to John Carter (Poole) Limited, renamed *Sherborne*. |
| 1962 | Chartered to the Blue Star Line Limited. |
| 1966 | Purchased by Marine Enterprise (Malta) Limited, renamed *Tita*. |
| 1967 | Renamed *Rachel Pace*, same owners. |
| 1968 | Became *Ian Pace*, Maltese National Line Limited as managers, Bahamas registry. |
| 1969 | Owned by Marsa Industrial Limited, Malta. |
| 16.7.1970 | On a voyage from Bizerta to Malta with a cargo of cement she sank off Cape Bon. All on board survived. |

### 157. *Oakland Star* (2) (1966)

9,854 grt, 5,513 n., 510.9 x 67.8 x 40.3 feet, IMO 6700872.
Steel, single screw, oil, 6 cyls, single acting, 11,600 BHP, B&W type, 18¾ knots. By Bryansk Engine Works, Bryansk. Two decks, container ship.
B. Kherson Shipyard, Kherson.

| | |
|---|---|
| 1966 | Delivered as *Klavdia* to Klavdia Cia Nav, Piraeus. |
| 1969 | Chartered to the Blue Star Line, renamed *Oakland Star*. |
| 1971 | At the end of the charter, she reverted to *Klavdia*. |
| 2.8.1973 | On a voyage from Chicago, she grounded at Chittagong. |
| 10.8.1973 | Refloated. |
| 1981 | Sold to the New Delta Maritime Company, Panama; renamed *Union Hamburg and Hotagen*. |
| 1983 | Sold to the Pasture Navigation Corporation, Panama, and renamed *Balstad*. |
| 21.10.1984 | Arrived at Kaohsiung and broken up by Keun Hwa Iron Works & Enterprise Company. |

### 158. *Albion Star* (3) (1972)

8,329 grt, 5,696 n., 471.8 x 70.7 x 23.2 feet, IMO 7221457.
Steel, single screw, oil, 18 cyls, 4 stroke Pielstick single acting with reduction gearing, 9,630 BHP, 18 knots. By Blohm & Voss, Hamburg.

| | |
|---|---|
| 1972 | Delivered as *Rheingold* to Cosima Reederei KG, Poseidon Schifffahrt GmbH as managers. |
| 1973 | Renamed *Columbus California*. |
| 1979 | Reverted to Rheingold, Ernst Willner GmbH as managers. |
| 10.1.1982 | Chartered to the Blue Star line; renamed *Albion Star*. |
| 1984 | Renamed *Marina Sea*. |
| 1985 | Became *Adelaide Express*. |
| 1990 | Reverted to *Marina Sea*. Sold to Milky Way Shipping Incorporated, Lorenzo Shipping Corporation as managers; renamed *Lorcon Mindanao*. |
| 2.2008 | Sold and broken up. |

### 159. *Saxon Star* (3) (1976)

11,800 grt, 7,064 n., 531.5 x 72.9 x 33.2 feet, IMO 7427697.
Steel, single screw, oil, 6 cyls, single acting, 11,600 BHP, Burmeister & Wain type, 18¾ knots. By Bryansk Engine Works, Bryansk. Two-deck container ship.

| | |
|---|---|
| 1976 | Delivered as *Santa Rita*, a Russian 'Dnepr' class for Hamburg Sudamerikanische D.G., Eggert & Amsinck for the South America route. |
| 1979 | Renamed *Columbus Taranaki*, same owners, converted to full container ship. |
| 1980 | Renamed *Monte Olivia*, same owners. |
| 1982 | Became *Columbus California*. |
| 1983 | Chartered to the Blue Star Line, renamed *Saxon Star*. Operated on the Blue Star, Houlder, Lamport & Holt and Royal Mail joint service. |

*Albion Star* (3).

1986        Renamed *Columbus California*.

1988        Became *ACT 12*.

1991        Renamed *Kota Sabas*.

27.8.2003   Arrived at Alang and broken up.

160. *Napier Star* (3) (1979)

12,214 grt, 7,865 n., 530.94 x 75.36 x 32.64 metres, yard no. 906, IMO 7710800.

Steel, 4 cyls, 2 SCSA Doxford 76J4, 12,000 BHP. By Doxford Engines Limited, Sunderland.

B. Sunderland Ship Builders Limited, Sunderland.

13.6.1979   Delivered as Ruddbank to the Bank Line Limited for the United States–South Africa route.

10.1983     To Lamport & Holt Line Limited; renamed *Romney* (3).

7.1986      To Highvale Limited, Lion Shipping Company, Hong Kong, as managers; renamed *Lairg*.

3.3.1989    Blue Star Ship Management; renamed *Napier Star* (3).

18.11.1991  Sold to the Tamapatcharee Shipping Company, Hong Kong, renamed *Tamapatcharee*. Andrew Weir Shipping Limited, Hong Kong, as managers.

1995        To South Asia Shipping Limited, John McRick & Company, Hong Kong, as managers; renamed *Lady Rebecca*.

3.1998      Sold to the International Transport Workers Federation, Acomarit Services Maritime SA as managers; renamed *Global Mariner*.

2.2000      Completed a round-the-world voyage as an exhibition ship, visiting eighty-six ports and fifty-one countries.

2000        Became a cadet ship on charter to Guernsey Ship Management Limited, managed by Northern Marine and AST Seascot, Glasgow.

2.8.2000    In collision with the *Atlantic Crusader* near the Sidor Terminal, Matanzas, on the Orinoco River. Nos 2 and 3 holds flooded, and she sank.

6.2001      Moved from the shipping lane, beached and sold for scrap.

161. *Tuscan Star* (4) (1973)

9,609 grt, 3,911 n., 154.46 x 21.57 x 8.71 metres, yard no. 602, IMO 7229679.

Steel, 9 cyls, 2SCSA, 17,100 BHP, M. A. N. oil engine by Maschinenfabrik Augsburg.

B. Lübecker Flenderwerke AG, Lübeck.

12.10.1972  Launched as *Wild Cormorant* for the Federal Steam Navigation Company, P&O General Cargo Division as managers.

15.10.1981  Sold to Leslie Shipping Corporation, Piraeus; renamed *Attica Reefer*.

1984        Purchased by National Precedence Cia. Nav., Limassol.

12.1985     Sold to Embira Navigation Company Limited, Limassol; renamed *Silver Reefer*.

2.1988      Renamed Bassro Nordic on charter to Bassro A/S, Oslo.

1988        Sold to the Norton Shipping Company Limited, Limassol; renamed *Flamingo Reefer* and later sold to Number Shipping Company Limited, Limassol.

12.1988     Renamed *Horncliff*, on charter to Horn Linie.

5.1990      *Flamingo Reefer*.

21.1.1991   Chartered to the Blue Star Line as *Tuscan Star* (4).

6.1992      Sold to Ocean Shield SA, International Reefer Services as managers; renamed *Flamingo Reefer*.

1996        *Marathon Breeze*, same owners.

8.8.1998    Arrived at Alang and broken up.

162. *Oregon Star* (5) (1979)

24,081 grt, 10,081 n., 183.70 x 28.10 x 16.11 metres, yard no. 1023, IMO 7800150.

Steel, 6 cyls, 2SCSA, 14,400 BHP Sulzer oil engine by Sulzer Limited, Winterthur.

B. AG Weser Seebeckwerft, Bremerhaven.

4.11.1978     Launched as *Columbus Louisiana* for Hamburg Sudamerikanische Dampfschifffahrts, Hamburg.

28.10.1991     Renamed *Oregon Star* (5) on charter to the Blue Star Line.

20.1.1994     On completion of the charter, she was renamed *Columbus Victoria*.

17.11.1996     In collision with the *Sampet Hope* in Port Philip Bay, slightly damaged.

8.1997     Sold to Strait Navigation Limited, Columbus Ship Management GmbH as managers.

5.2000     Purchased by Labano Marine Company Limited, Kotani Ship Management Limited as managers.

11.2001     Owners became Zodiac Maritime Agencies Limited.

6.5.2002     Aground at Kingston, Jamaica.

3.1.2007     Arrived at Chittagong and broken up.

163. *Washington Star* (1979)

12,214 grt, 7,730 n., 161.83 x 22.97 x 9.95 metres, yard no. 11, IMO 7710836.

Steel, 4 cyls, 2SCSA, 12,000 BHP oil engine by Doxford Engines Limited, Sunderland.

B. Sunderland Shipbuilders Limited, Sunderland.

23.5.1979     Launched as *Dacebank* for Royal Bank Leasing, Bank Line Limited as managers.

1987     Sold to Navigator Maritime Incorporated, Leond Maritime Inc., Greece; renamed *Anna L.*

1992     Renamed *Washington Star* (2), when chartered to the Blue Star Line Limited.

1994     On completion of the charter, she reverted back to *Anna L.*

1996     Sold to Erling Shipping Company Limited, Leond Maritime Inc., Cyprus, as managers.

1997     Purchased by Lorena Shipping Company Limited, Square Limited as managers; renamed *Aris K.*

1999     Owned by the Amalfi Shipping Company Limited, Square Limited as managers; renamed *Paradise*.

9.2000     Sold to Beijing Star Enterprises Limited, Hong Kong.

2.2001     Renamed *Bute*, same owners.

7.10.2002     Arrived at Alang and broken up.

164. *Roman Star* (3) (1992)

10,381 grt, 5,253 n., 150.01 x 22.80 x 9.06 metres, yard no. 864, IMO 9016674.

Steel, 6 cyls, 2SCSA, 13,769 BHP Burmeister & Wain oil engine by Mitsui Engine & Shipbuilding Company Limited, Tamano.

B. Shikoku Dockyard Company Limited, Takamatsu.

19.3.1992     Launched as *Roman Star* (3) for Glasson Investments Incorporated, Panama.

8.7.1992     Delivered as *Chiquita Sulu*, chartered to the Great White Fleet Limited.

12.1994     Chartered to the Blue Star Line Limited; renamed *Roman Star* (3).

1998     Sold to P&O Nedlloyd Limited.

12.1999     Renamed *Roman Bay*.

2000     Managed by Unique Shipping (Canada) Incorporated.

6.2004     Sold to Hawk Bay Shipping Company, Seatrade Groningen as managers; renamed *Hawk Bay*.

5.2006    Owned by Hawk Bay Schifffahrts GmbH.

2013    Sold to Roycan Overseas Corporation, Bremen, Ost West Handel und Schifffahrt, Bremen as managers; renamed *Baltic Performer*.

### 165. *Royal Star* (3) (1992)

10,381 grt, 5,253 n., 150.01 x 22.80 x 9.06 metres, yard no. 863, IMO 9016662.

Steel, 6 cyls, 2SCSA, 13,770 BHP Burmeister & Wain oil engine by Mitsui Engine & Shipbuilding Company Limited, Tamano.

B. Shikoku Dockyard Company Limited, Takamatsu.

22.11.1991    Launched as *Royal Star* (3) for Gladman Investments Incorporated, Panama.

31.3.1992    Delivered as *Chiquita Honshu* for the Great White Fleet.

1994    Chartered to the Blue Star Line Limited as *Royal Star*, Unique Shipping Agencies (HK) Limited as managers.

5.1998    Sold to Gallant Maritime Corporation

1998    Sold to P&O Nedlloyd Limited.

12.1999    Renamed *French Bay*, same owners.

2000    Managed by Unique Shipping (Canada) Incorporated.

7.2004    Owned by Buzzard Bay Shipping, Holland, Seatrade Groningen as managers; renamed *Buzzard Bay*.

5.2006    Owned by Buzzard Bay Schifffahrts GmbH, Triton Schifffahrts GmbH as managers.

2013    Owned by Vistra Business Corporation, Bremen, Ost West Handel und Schifffahrt, Bremen, as managers; renamed *Baltic Pilgrim*.

### 166. *Baltic Star* (1983)

9,628 grt, 4,045 n., 460.9 x 72.8 x 33 feet, yard no. 322, IMO 88221832.

Steel, single screw, oil, direct drive, 20,000 BHP, 22½ knots. By builder. Two decks.

B. Sasebo Heavy Industries, Sasebo.

26.5.1983    Launched for Tokumaru Kaium Kaisha, chartered to the Blue Star Line for five years as *Baltic Star*. Managed and crewed by Tokumaru Kaium Kaisha, corn yellow hull.

2002    Renamed *Baltic Start*, Baltic Start Shipping Limited, Holy House Shipping AB (Sweden) as managers.

2010    Renamed *Laura*, registered in the Cook Islands.

2011    Broken up.

### 167. *Tasman Star* (1983)

9,628 grt, 4,045 n., 460.9 x 72.8 x 33 feet, yard no. 323, IMO 8221844.

Steel, single screw, oil, direct drive, 20,000 BHP, 22½ knots. By builder. Two decks.

B. Sasebo Heavy Industries, Sasebo.

27.7.1983    Launched for Tokumaru Kaium Kaisha, chartered to the Blue Star Line for five years as *Tasman Star*. Managed and crewed by Tokumaru Kaium Kaisha, corn yellow hull.

2001    Renamed *Tasman Start*.

4.8.2011    Arrived at Alang.

11.8.2011    Beached and broken up.

### 168. *Atlantic Star* (1983)

9,628 grt, 4,045 n., 460.9 x 72.8 x 33 feet, yard no. 324, IMO 8221856.

Steel, single screw, oil, direct drive, 20,000 BHP, 22½ knots. By builder. Two decks.

B. Sasebo Heavy Industries, Sasebo.

28.7.1983    Launched for Tokumaru Kaium Kaisha, chartered to the Blue Star Line for five years as *Atlantic Star*. Managed and crewed by Tokumaru Kaium Kaisha, corn yellow hull.

2002    Renamed *Atlantic Start*.

2003        Owned by Stina Shipping Limited, Holy House Shipping AB, Sweden; renamed *Stina*.

9.6.2014     Arrived Alang and broken up.

### 169. *Pacific Star* (4) (1983)

9,628 grt, 4,045 n., 460.9 x 72.8 x 33 feet, yard no. 325, IMO 8221868.
Steel, single screw, oil, direct drive, 20,000 BHP, 22½ knots. By builder. Two decks.
B. Sasebo Heavy Industries, Sasebo.

31.8.1983    Launched for Tokumaru Kaium Kaisha, chartered to the Blue Star Line for five years as *Pacific Star*. Managed and crewed by Tokumaru Kaium Kaisha, corn yellow hull.

2002        Renamed *Pacific Start*.

1.12.2002    Owned by Holy House Shipping AB, Stockholm; renamed *Amalia*.

2014        Still in service.

### 170. *Santos Star* (2) (1972)

11,422 grt, 5,052 n., 568.5 x 81 x 31.4 feet, IMO 7117319.
Steel, single screw, oil, 2S.SA, 8 cyls, Sulzer, 8RND90 type, 23,200 BHP at 122 rpm, 22¾ knots. By Cie de Const. Mécaniquue Procedes Sulzer, Nantes.
B. Chantiers Navals de la Ciotat.

3.1972      Delivered to Saleninvest A/B as *Snow Flake*, managed by Salen Reefer Services A/B, Stockholm. Soon after delivery, it was found that she was uneconomic to operate, as the market could not sustain a ship of her size.

1984        Sold to South View Shipping, Hong Kong; renamed *South View*, Panamanian flag.

1985        Operated by Cool Ship Management, Hong Kong; renamed *Blue Sea*.

1986        On charter to the Blue Star Line; renamed *Santos Star*, Minolta Corporation, Hong Kong. Blue Star funnel, white livery, yellow cranes. Transferred to Lion Shipping Limited, Hong Kong, management; renamed *Limari*.

1986        Owned by Lion Shipping Limited, Hong Kong; renamed *Limari*.

1990s       Sold to Target Marine Limited, Piraeus, becoming *Santos Star*.

1996        Renamed *Snow Delta*.

2000        Became *Santos Star*.

29.7.2002    Arrived at the River Fal and laid up.

8.2006      Sold and broken up at Chittagong.

### 171. *Savona Star* (1) (1973)

11,422 grt, 5,052 n., 568.5 x 81 x 31.4 feet, IMO 7301013.
Steel, single screw, oil, 2S.SA, 8 cyls, Sulzer, 8RND90 type, 23,200 BHP at 122 rpm, 22¾ knots. By Cie de Const. Mécaniquue Procedes Sulzer, Nantes.
B. Chantiers Navals de la Ciotat.

8.1973      Delivered to Saleninvest A/B as *Snow Ball*, managed by Salen Reefer Services A/B, Stockholm. Soon after delivery it was found that she was uneconomic to operate, as the market could not sustain a ship of her size.

1981        Owned by Trans Malayan Shipping Incorporated, Manila; renamed *Malayan Queen*, managed by Salen Reefer Services A/B, Stockholm.

1985        Owned by South Joy Shipping Incorporated, Panama; renamed *South Joy*.

1986        On charter to the Blue Star Line; renamed *Savona Star*, Minolta Corporation, Hong Kong. Blue Star funnel, white livery, yellow cranes.

*Left: Santos Star* (2).

*Right: Regal Star.* (Chris Brooks/ShipFoto)

| | |
|---|---|
| 1986 | Managed by Lion Shipping Limited, Hong Kong. |
| 27.12.1988 | Chartered to CSAV, Valparaiso; renamed *Santiago Star*. |
| 11.1998 | Transferred to Albion Reefers Limited, Nassau. |
| 30.11.1998 | Sold to Ginetta Shipping SA, Target Marine SA as managers. |
| 12.8.2002 | Arrived at the River Fal and laid up. |
| 8.2006 | Sold and broken up at Chittagong. |

**172. *Napier Star* (4) (1977)**

10,828 grt, 6,349 n., 151.24 x 21.24 x 9.47 metres, yard no. 284, IMO 7610232.

Steel, 5 cyls, 2SCSA, 7,500 BHP Sulzer oil engine by Mitsubishi Heavy Industries Limited, Kobe, Japan.

B. Mitsubishi Heavy Industries Limited, Hiroshima, Japan.

| | |
|---|---|
| 24.2.1977 | Laid down as *Silverness* for Silverness Shipping Limited (Silver Line Limited as managers). |
| 8.1977 | Entered service. |
| 1978 | Renamed *Taabo*. |
| 1979 | Sold to Société Ivoirienne de Navigation Maritime, Adibjan, Ivory Coast (Silver Line Limited, London, as managers). |
| 1983 | Purchased by Ruby Compania Naviera SA, Panama (Mycali Maritime Corporation SA, Greece, as managers). |
| 1985 | Renamed *Agios Andreas*. |
| 1989 | Owned by K/S Mostween 5 (Mosvold Shipping Company A/S as managers); renamed *Mostween 5*. |
| 1991 | Managed by the Hudson Steamship Company Limited, Norway. |
| 8.1993 | Renamed *Napier Star* (4), chartered to the Blue Star Line Limited. |
| 8.1994 | Renamed *Mostween 5*. |

| | |
|---|---|
| 11.1994 | Purchased by the Rallia Shipping Company Limited, Cyprus; renamed *Rallia*. |
| 30.1.1999 | On a voyage from Zeebrugge to Iran with a cargo of sugar, she suffered a serious engine room fire off west Crete. The fire was brought under control and she was towed to Souda Bay, Crete. |
| 1.2.1999 | Arrived at Souda port. |
| 4.2.1999 | Berthed at Piraeus following a tow from Souda. |
| 22.9.2000 | Returned to service. |
| 15.10.2004 | Arrived at Alang and broken up. |

**173. *Norman Star* (3) (1979)**

10,153 grt, 4,618 n., 168.05 x 22.64 x 8.65 metres, yard no. 815, IMO 7809314.

Steel, 6 cyls, 2SCSA 14,400 BHP Sulzer oil engine by Ishikawjima Harima Industries, Aioi, Japan.

B. Koyo Dockyard Company Limited, Mihara, Japan.

| | |
|---|---|
| 10.8.1978 | Launched as *Humboldt Rex* for Hoko Senpaku KK (Reefer Express Lines Limited as managers). |
| 9.1989 | Renamed *Humboldt Rex No. 2*, same owners. |
| 10.1989 | Sold to Estelargo Maritime Company Limited (Norbulk Shipping Agencies Limited as managers); renamed *E. W. Andes*. |
| 10.1994 | Purchased by the Andes Shipping Corporation (Dobson Fleet Management as managers). Chartered to the Blue Star Line Limited; renamed *Norman Star*. |
| 1998 | Owned by P&O Nedlloyd Limited. |
| 2000 | Managed by Chartworld Shipping Corporation, Athens. |
| 18.7.2000 | Laid up until 25.11.2000. |
| 7.2004 | Sold to Baltic Reefers Limited (Ost. West Handel as managers). |
| 9.2004 | Renamed *Pietari Glory*. |
| 2005 | Owned by Samskip Company Limited. |

| | |
|---|---|
| 12.2008 | Managed by Polaris Maritime Limited. |
| 20.5.2009 | Arrived at Gadani Beach as *Glory*, and broken up. |

### 174. *Saxon Star* (5) (1979)

10,153 grt, 4,618 n., 168.05 x 22.64 x 8.65 metres, yard no. 816, IMO 7808906.

Steel, 6 cyls, 2SCSA, 14,400 BHP Sulzer oil engine by Ishikawjima Harima Industries Limited, Aioi.

B. Koyo Dockyard Company Limited, Mihara.

| | |
|---|---|
| 10.10.1978 | Launched as Tasman Rex for Hoko Senpaku KK, Reefer Express Lines Limited as managers. |
| 8.1989 | Sold to Estecasa Maritime Company Limited, Dobson Fleet Management as managers; renamed *E. W. Eiger*. |
| 9.1994 | Purchased by Eiger Shipping Corporation, chartered to the Blue Star Line Limited; renamed *Saxon Star* (5). |
| 6.1995 | Sold to Kappa Maritime Limited. |
| 1998 | Sold to P&O Nedlloyd Limited. |
| 6.2000 | Chartworld Shipping Corporation, Greece, as managers. |
| 7.2004 | Sold to Haslam Holdings Limited, St Vincent and the Grenadines (Samskip Company Limited); renamed *Pietari Great*. |
| 10.2008 | Owned by Glenstone Incorporated, Estonia, Marine Shipping as managers; renamed *Varadero*. |
| 7.9.2010 | Arrived at Alang and broken up. |

### 175. *Regal Star* (1) (1993)

10,375 grt, 5,253 n., 150.01 x 22.50 x 9.06 metres, yard no. 866, IMO 9053658.

Steel, 6 cyls, 2SCSA, 15,300 BHP Burmeister & Wain oil engine by Mitsui Engine & Shipbuilding Company Limited, Tamano.

B. Shikoku Dockyard Company Limited, Takamatsu.

| | |
|---|---|
| 11.11.1992 | Launched as *Chiquita Tauu* for Paulownia Maritime SA, Panama. |
| 2.1995 | Renamed *Hornstrait*, same owners. |
| 31.10.1995 | Became *Tauu*, same owners. |
| 12.1996 | Chartered to the Blue Star Line Limited; renamed *Regal Star*. |
| 1998 | Sold to P&O Nedlloyd Limited. |
| 1999 | Owned by Southern Route Maritime SA. |
| 6.2003 | Purchased by the Santa Rosa Navigation Limited. |
| 6.2003 | Sold to Regal Island Holdings (Star Reefers A/S), Fleet Management Limited as managers. |
| 12.2004 | Owned by Star Reefers Shipowning, Cayman Islands. |
| 6.2008 | Purchased by ONS Shipholding 111 AS, Norway, Star Reefers Poland Sp. z. o. o. as managers. |

### 176. *Brasil Star* (2) (1997)

25,608 grt, 208 m x 30 m, IMO 9149304

B. Kvaerner Warnow Werft, Nordic Yards, Warnemünde, Rostock.

| | |
|---|---|
| 1997 | Built as *Impala* for Hammonia Reederei, Hamburg. |
| 1997 | Renamed *Brasil Star* (2). Chartered to the Blue Star Line. |
| 1998 | Renamed *Impala*. |
| 1998 | Renamed *Cap Norte*. |
| 1999 | Renamed *Transroll Argentina*. |
| 2000 | Renamed *Sea Ocelot*. |
| 2002 | Renamed *Santos Express*. |
| 2003 | Renamed *Cap Norte*. |
| 2006 | Renamed *Cap Egmont*. |
| 2008 | Renamed *Belgica*. |
| 2010 | Renamed *Emirates Rafiki*. |
| 2011 | Renamed *Belgica*. |

*Brasil Star* (2). (Chris Brooks/ShipFoto)

**177.** *Oregon Star* (6) (1978)

28,060 grt, 13,193 n., 203.99 x 30.99 x 11.02 metres, yard no. B463/04, IMO 7711567.

Steel, 10 cyls, 2SA, 29,000 BHP Sulzer oil engine by H. Cegielski Zakłady Przemysłu Metalowego, Poznań.

B. Stocznia Gdanska im Lenina, Gdansk.

| | |
|---|---|
| 30.3.1978 | Launched as *Alemania Express* for Hapag Lloyd International SA. Hapag Lloyd AG as managers. |
| 5.1992 | Sold to Montemar SA; renamed *Uruguay Express*. |
| 12.1996 | Owned by Samos Shipping SA; renamed *Angela*. |
| 1997 | Sold to Kai Navigation Company Limited, Midocean Shipmanagement Limited as managers. |
| 11.1997 | Renamed *Oregon Star* (6) when chartered to the Blue Star Line Limited. |
| 1998 | At the end of the charter, she reverted to *Angela*. |
| 1999 | Renamed *Zim Beijing*, same owners. |
| 3.2001 | Managed by Peter Dohle Schifffahrts KG GmbH, Hamburg. |
| 5.2001 | Renamed *Angela*. |
| 7.2001 | *Indfex SCI*, same owners. |
| 11.2001 | Owned by the Fertroy Corporation, Pacific Marine Services Limited as managers; renamed MSC *Alpana*. |
| 2002 | Managed by MSC Shipmanagement (Hong Kong) Limited. |
| 12.4.2011 | Arrived at Chittagong and broken up. |

**178.** *Caribbean Star* (1997)

11,435 grt, 5,901 n., 154 x 24 x 13.30 metres, yard no. 884, IMO 9150810.

Steel, 6 cyls, 14,040 BHP Burmeister & Wain oil engine by Mitsui Engine & Shipbuilding Company Limited, Tamano.

B. Shikoku Dockyard Company Limited, Takamatsu.

| | |
|---|---|
| 3.7.1997 | Launched for Apsides Shipping Corporation SA, Panama, Unique Shipping (Canada) Inc. as managers. |
| 12.1998 | Renamed *Hornsea*, same owners. |
| 1998 | P&O Nedlloyd Limited as owners. |
| 1.2000 | *Caribbean Star*, same owners. |
| 7.2001 | Star Reefers sold to Norwegian owners. |
| 8.2003 | Owners Caribbean Shipping Limited, Fleet Management Limited Hong Kong as managers. |
| 3.2004 | Owned by Star Reefer Shipping Incorporated (Star Reefers A/S). |
| 5.2008 | Managed by Norbulk Shipping (UK) Limited. |
| 1.2012 | Managed by Star Reefers (UK) Limited. |
| 4.2013 | Managed by Star Reefers Poland Sp. z. o. o., Gdynia. |

**179.** *Cote d'Ivoirian Star* (1998)

11,733 grt, 5,899 n., 144.90x24 x 9.06 metres, yard no. 887, IMO 9172478.

Steel, 6 cyls, 2SCSA, 15,600 BHP Burmeister & Wain oil engine by Mitsui Engine & Shipbuilding Company Limited, Tamano.

B. Shikoku Dockyard Company Limited, Takamatsu.

| | |
|---|---|
| 28.1.1998 | Launched for Green Spanker Shipping SA, Panama, Kyowa Kisen Company Limited as manager, and chartered to the Blue Star Line Limited. |
| 7.2001 | Star Reefers sold to Norwegian owners. |
| 2.4.2009 | Owners Star Reefers Shipowning Inc., Cayman Islands, Norbulk Shipping (UK) Limited as managers. |
| 18.1.2012 | Managed by Star Reefers Poland Sp. z. o. o., Gdynia. |

**180.** *Colombian Star* (1998)

11,733 grt, 5,899 n., 144.90 x 24 x 9.06 metres, yard no. 888, IMO 9172480.

Steel, 6 cyls, 2SCSA, 15,600 BHP Burmeister & Wain oil engine by Mitsui

*Cote D'Ivoirian Star.* (Chris Brooks/ShipFoto)

Engine & Shipbuilding Company Limited, Tamano.

B. Shikoku Dockyard Company Limited, Takamatsu.

11.5.1998    Launched for Southern Route Maritime SA, Panama, Nissen Kaiun, Japan as managers.

7.2001    Star Reefers sold to Norwegian owners.

3.2009    Owners Star Reefers Shipowning Inc., Cayman Islands, Norbulk Shipping (UK) Limited as managers.

16.2.2012    Managed by Star Reefers Poland Sp. z. o. o., Gdynia.

181. *Costa Rican Star* (1998)

11,435 grt, 5,901 n., 154.90 x 24 x 9.01 metres, yard no. 885, IMO 9150822. Steel, 6 cyls, 2SCSA, 15,600 BHP Burmeister & Wain oil engine by Mitsui Engine & Shipbuilding Company Limited, Tamano.

B. Shikoku Dockyard Company Limited, Takamatsu.

17.10.1997    Launched.

1998    Chartered to the Blue Star Line Limited.

1998    Renamed *Hornwind*, same owners.

7.2001    Star Reefers sold to Norwegian owners.

8.2003    Owners Caribbean Shipping Limited, Fleet Management Limited Hong Kong as managers; renamed *Costa Rican Star*.

3.2004    Owned by Star Reefers Shipowning Inc., Cayman Islands.

5.2008    Norbulk Shipping (UK) Limited as managers.

3.2.2012    Managed by Star Reefers (UK) Limited.

During the Falkland Islands conflict the Blue Star Line acted as managers for the following ships:

182. *Rangatira* (1971)

9,387 grt, 4.031 n., 152.63 x 22.08 x 5.28 metres, yard no. 33. Two steam turbines driving two generators connected to two electric motors and single reduction geared to twin screws. By Associated Electrical Industries Limited, Manchester.

B. Swan Hunter Shipbuilders Limited, Walker on Tyne.

15.5.1982    Chartered by the Ministry of Defence from the Union Steam Ship Company of New Zealand and used as an accommodation ship off Port Stanley. Blue Star Ship Management as managers.

10.1983    Returned to the United Kingdom, refit to return to commercial traffic.

31.3.1984    Laid up on the River Fal.

183. *Keren* ex *St Edmund* (1974)

8,987 grt, 4,697 n., 130.08 x 22.64 x 5.2 metres, yard no. 1361. Four 8 cyls, 4 SCSA oil engines, single reduction geared to two screw shafts.

B. Cammell Laird & Company Limited, Birkenhead.

14.11.1973    Launched as *St Edmund* for Passtruck Shipping Company Limited, British Railways Board, London.

12.1974    Delivered for the Harwich–Hook of Holland route.

1.1.1979    Owned by Sealink UK Limited.

12.5.1982    Left Harwich for Devonport on charter, then purchased by the Ministry of Defence. Fitted with a helicopter pad.

14.7.1982    Transported Argentinian prisoners of war, including General Menendez from Port Stanley to Puerto Madryn

1.1983    Purchased from Sealink UK Limited for £7,750,000. Blue Star Ship Management as managers.

28.2.1983    Arrived in the Tyne and converted as a troop carrier by Tyne Ship Repair Limited.

4.4.1983    Because of industrial action she was commissioned as HMS *Keren*, with a naval crew.

8.4.1983    Reverted to the Red Ensign and managed by Blue Star Ship

Management. *Keren* acted as mother ship to HM Submarine *Opportune* and carried out trooping voyages between Ascension Island and Port Stanley.

5.1984          Returned to the Smith's Ship Repairers Limited on the Tyne for a refit.

20.6.1985    Arrived at Portsmouth and decommissioned. She had carried out twenty-seven round voyages and carried 18,000 people.

4.7.1984      Laid up in the River Stour.

1985            Sold to Cenargo Limited, renamed *Scirocco*.

11.6.1986    Chartered to Tirrenia di Navegazione for the Genoa–Sardinia route.

1989            Operated on the Poole–Channel Islands service for British Channel Islands Ferries as *Rozel*.

2004            Became *Santa Catherine 1*.

2006            Renamed *Sara 3* for the Jeddah–Sawakin pilgrimage service.

2009            Broken up in India.

### 184. *Hoegh Duke* (1984)

30,061 grt, 15,237 n., 198.03 x 32.28 x 12 metres, yard no. 118.
Single screw, 5 cyls, 2 SCSA Burmeister & Wain oil engine. By J. G. Kincaid & Company Limited, Greenock.
B. Swan Hunter Shipbuilders Limited, Wallsend on Tyne.

6.9.1983      Launched for Lombard Maritime Limited, London, and leased to Leif Hoegh & Company A/S, Oslo, Blue Star Ship Management as managers.

6.1984          Delivered.

1999            Sold and renamed *Edward Oldendorf*.

2004            Owned by the China Navigation Company Limited; renamed *Indotrans Makassar*.

2006            Became *Pacific Makassar*.

12.2011        Renamed *Hangchow*, same owners.

3.7.2012      Arrived at Jiangyin, China, and broken up.

## Compagnie Générale Frigorifique

At Majunga in Madagascar, a cold store was set up in 1915 and acted as a collecting centre for frozen meat prior to it being loaded onto a Blue Star Line vessel.

### 185. *General Pau* (1915)

254 grt, 120 n., 126 x 25.2 x 5 feet.
Steel, single screw, triple expansion, 3 cyls, 9 knots. By William Beardmore & Company, Glasgow. One deck.
B. The Montrose Shipbuilding Company, Montrose.

1914            Ordered by the Blue Star line.

29.6.1915    Launched.

6.1915          Transferred to CGF before completion.

1920            Transferred to Compagnie de Transportes et Remorquages de Madagascar (Transport & Towage Company of Madagascar), same name.

1958            Sold to Société Industrielle de la Côte Ouest de Madagascar.

1969            Owned by Monsieur M. Verdier.

### 186. *General Foch* (1916)

248 grt, 120 n., 126 x 25.2 x 5 feet.
Steel, single screw, triple expansion, 3 cyls, 9 knots. By William Beardmore & Company, Glasgow. One deck.
B. W. Beardmore & Company Limited, Glasgow.

15.6.1916    Launched for the Blue Star Line Limited and sold to Compagnie Générale Frigorifique.

1920    Owned by Transportes et Remorquages de Majunga.

1928    Owners restyled Cie de Transports et Remorquages à Majunga, France.

1957    Owned by J. Verdavainne et Cie Majunga; renamed *Djema*.

8.12.1959    Wrecked off Moroni, Madagascar.


187. *General Jarvoni* (1916)

233grt.

B. Methil.

16.9.1916    Sailed from Methil in tow for Majunga.

8.11.1916    Arrived in Marjunga, and used to carry live cattle to the abattoirs at Majunga, towed by a local tug.

1920    Owned by Transportes et Remorquages de Majunga.


188. *General Marcus* (1916)

233grt.

B. Methil.

16.9.1916    Sailed from Methil in tow for Majunga.

8.11.1916    Arrived in Marjunga, and used to carry live cattle to the abattoirs at Majunga, towed by a local tug.

1920    Owned by Transportes et Remorquages de Majunga.


## Sociedad Anonima Frigorifico 'Anglo', Buenos Aires

This subsidiary of the Blue Star Line operated the following two ships to collect frozen meat from ports in the River Plate.

189. *Zarate/Kingswood/Anglo No. 1* (1921)

1,354 grt, 795 n., 220.5 x 44.1 x 9.3 feet.

Steel, twin screw, 2 x 2 cyls compound inverted, 50 NHP, 9 knots. By builder. One deck.

B. Cammell Laird & Company Limited, Birkenhead.

1921    Delivered to the Union Cold Storage Company Limited as *Zarate*, managed by Frigorifico.

1922    Renamed *Shirley* and later *Kingswood*.

1923    Became *Anglo No. 1*.

1938    Frigorifico as owners.

1960    Sold to Naviero Panamericano SA; renamed *Santa Teresa*.

1966    Owned by Intervariou SA Cia, Buenos Aires, same name.

1966    Broken up at Buenos Aires.


190. *Anglo No. 2* (1901)

1,206 grt, 729 n., 230.2x42 x 11.5 feet.

Steel, twin screw, triple expansion, 3 cyls, 130 NHP, 9 knots. By Ross & Duncan Limited, Glasgow. One deck.

B. A. Rodger & Company Limited, Port Glasgow.

1901    Delivered to the River Plate Fresh Meat Company as *Reformer*.

1914    Purchased by the Las Palmas Produce Company.

1923    Transferred to the Union Cold Storage Company Limited. Renamed *Anglo No. 2*, managed by Soc. Anon. Frigorifico.

1935    Chartered to Cranston, Woodhead & Company; renamed *General Flores*.

1936    Became *Anglo No. 2* again, owned by Frigorifico.

1942    Renamed *Americano*.

1952    Sold to Sociedad Anonima Import y Export de la Patagonia, and later to Pedro G. Yachelini & Cia.

1957        Owned by Polar SRL.
1966        Broken up.

## Austasia Line

191. *Australasia* – see *Iberia Star*.

192. *Malay/Mahsuri* (1) – see *Malay Star*.

193. *Cuthbert/Mandama* (1) (1946)
4,249 grt, 2,292 n., 401.2 x 53.8 x 23 feet.
Steel, single screw, triple expansion, 3 cyls, 378 NHP, 2 single boilers, 220 psi, 11 knots. By John Brown & Company Limited, Clydebank. Two decks plus part of third in holds.
B. W. Pickersgill and Sons Limited, Sunderland.
5.3.1946    Launched as *Hubert* for the Booth Steam Ship Company Limited. Laid down for Ministry of War Transport
6.1946      Delivered.
1951        Renamed *Cuthbert*.
1953        Transferred to Austasia Line.
1954        Renamed *Mandama*.
1965        Sold to Mouzakies Ltda SA, Greece; renamed *Loucia N.*
26.11.1970  Arrived at Shanghai and broken up.

194. *Mandowi* (1) (1951)
4,472 grt, 2,559 n., 410.6 x 55.2 x 24 feet, IMO 5219216.
Steel, single screw, 3 cyls, triple expansion, 3 single boilers, 220 psi, 12½ knots. By North Eastern Marine Engineering Company (1938) Limited, Sunderland.
B. W. Pickersgill & Sons Limited, Sunderland.

23.5.1951   Launched as *Crispin* for the Booth Steam Ship Company.
8.1953      Transferred to Austasia Line; renamed *Mandowi*.
1966        Transferred to the Booth Steam Ship Company; renamed *Dunstan*.
1967        Renamed *Rubens*.
1973        Sold to George Kalogeras, Greece; renamed *Irini K.*
24.4.1974   Arrived at Istanbul and broken up.

195. *Malacca* (1945)
3,844 grt, 2,192 n., 103.25 x 15.25 x 7.2 feet.
Steel, single screw, 6 cyls, 2 SCSA oil, 1,750 BHP, 11 knots. By Nordberg Manufacturing Company, Milwaukee, USA. Two decks.
B. Leathem D. Smith Shipbuilding Company, Sturgeon Bay, Wisconsin, USA.
1945        Launched as *Tulare* for the United States Navy.
5.1945      Delivered as *Coastal Challenger* for the United States War Shipping Administration.
1946        Sold to Panama Shipping Company Limited, Booth Steam Ship Company as managers; renamed *Pachitea*.
1954        Transferred to the Booth Steam Ship Company; renamed *Dunstan*.
1958        Transferred to Lamport & Holt Line; renamed *Sallust* for the New York–South American service.
1959        Transferred to the Austasia Line; renamed *Malacca*.
1962        Sold to Kie Hock Shipping (HK) Company Limited, Hong Kong.
1963        Renamed *Tong Hong*.
25.10.1967  Left Kawasaki on a voyage to Singapore and Colombo with a cargo of ammonium sulphate and was lost. She had thirty-eight crew on board.

196. *Matupi* (1) (1945)

3,827grt 2,238 n., 338.5 x 50.1 x 26.5 feet.

Steel, single screw, oil, 6 cyls, 2SSA, 1,750 BHP, 11 knots. By General Machinery Corporation, Hamilton, Ohio. Two decks.

B. Consolidated Steel Corporation, Wilmington, California.

7.1945    Delivered as *Hickory Glen*, Type C1-M-A1. To the Maritime Commission/War Shipping Administration, chartered to Ministry of War Transport, China Navigation Company as managers.

1947    Purchased by Lamport & Hole Line; renamed *Sheridan*, for the New York–Brazil service.

1960    Transferred to the Austasia Line; renamed *Matupi*.

1964    Sold to Kie Hock Shipping (Hong Kong) Limited, Hong Kong; renamed *Tong Lam*.

1968    Purchased by Asia Selatan Enterprises Limited, same name.

27.10.1970    On a voyage from Korea to Chittagong with a cargo of pig iron, she went aground on Scarborough Reef, 420 miles from Manila. She broke into three pieces and was declared a total loss.


197. *Makati* (1953)

3,324 grt, 1,894 n., 303.4 x 46.3 x 21.3 feet.

Steel, single screw, oil, 6 cyls, 2SSA, 2,025 BHP, 12½ knots. By Burmeister & Wain Limited, Copenhagen. Two decks.

B. Aalborg Vaerft A/S, Aalborg.

30.6.1953    Launched as *Jonna Dan* for J. Lauritzen & Company Limited, Copenhagen.

11.11.1953    In service with Rederiet Ocean A/S.

27.4.1964    Renamed *Makita* for the Austasia Line.

1967    Transferred to the Booth Steam Ship Company Limited; renamed *Dominic*. Lengthened to 420 feet by Société Anonyme Cockerill-

Ougree, Hoboke 4,584 grt, 1,754 n.

1975    Transferred to the Blue Star Line management. Sold through Sinergasia Shipbrokers Limited, Cyprus, to Ring Shipping Company Limited, Limassol; renamed *Dominica*.

1976    Owned by the Carl Shipping Enterprises Corporation Limited, Piraeus; renamed *Trojan*.

1981    Purchased by Nikki Maritime Limited, Panama; renamed *Ragnar*.

18.9.1982    On a voyage from Cuba to Libya with a cargo of cement, her engine room flooded and she was abandoned in the Atlantic. Her crew of nineteen were rescued by the *Lima II*.


198. *Malaysia* (1955)

8,062 grt, 6,342 n., 438.95 x 18.38 x 7.71 feet.

Steel, single screw, 2 steam turbine, 5,800 BHP, 2 wetboilers, 495 psi, 14 knots. By builder. Two decks plus third deck. Passengers: seventy-four first, ninety-six tourist.

B. Cammell Laird & Company Limited, Birkenhead.

31.8.1954    Launched as *Hubert* for the Booth Line, a sister-ship to *Hildebrand*. Her first-class accommodation was on the upper promenade, boat and main decks, in single and double state rooms, with large windows as a feature. Tourist-class passengers were accommodated in two- and four-berth rooms on the main upper deck aft and in the poop. There were five holds for the carriage of general cargo. No. 4 hold was fitted with deep tanks for liquid cargoes, and No. 2 hold was served with a 50-ton derrick. The double bottom was subdivided into seven tanks fore and aft, four which were for oil fuel, one for feed water and two for domestic fresh water. A deep tank for oil fuel was arranged forward of the machinery compartment, and the fore and after peaks were fitted as ballast tanks.

11.2.1955     Maiden voyage from Liverpool to Leixoes, Lisbon, Madeira, Barbados, Para and Manaus.

1964     Transferred to the Blue Star Line and chartered to the Austasia Line; renamed *Malaysia*.

1976     Sold to the Atlas Shipping Agency (UK) Limited, Singapore, and converted to a cattle carrier; renamed *Khalij Express*, Gulfeast Ship Management Limited as managers. Sold to the Halena Shipping Company, Singapore, same managers.

1984     Broken up at Alang by N. C. K. Exports & Sons PVT Limited.

199. *Mahsuri* (2) – see *Colorado Star*.

200. *Matupi* (2) (1965)
4,478 grt, 2,289 n., 111.82 x 16.06 x 6.47 metres, IMO 6515447.
Steel, single screw, 6 cyls, 2SSA, Sulzer oil engine. By Compagnie de Constructions Mécaniques, Nantes, France.
B. Chantiers Navals de la Ciotat, La Ciotat, France.

22.4.1965     Launched as *Oyonnax* for Compagnie des Messageries Maritimes, France.

1966     Delivered.

1971     Sold to Transfruta Companhia Nacional de Navios Frigorificos Sàrl, Portugal; renamed *Frigomar*.

1975     Sold to Harvest Gold Shipping (Private) Limited, Singapore; renamed *Harvest Gold*.

1977     Purchased by Caxton Maritime Enterprises Corporation, Greece; renamed *Cavalaire*.

1978     Sold to Austasia Line; renamed *Matupi*.

1979     Owned by Phoenix Oceanic Limited, Enias Shipping Company SA, Greece, as managers; renamed *Aegean Destiny*.

1980     Sold to Remjay Limited, London; renamed *Renjay*.

22.11.1980     Laid up at Rotterdam.

1981     Sold to Nautilus Maritime Incorporated, Panama; renamed *Polar BV*.

1982     Purchased by Panamanian interests, becoming *Laric*. Resold to the Akola Shipping Corporation, Link Line Limited, Panama, as managers; renamed *Alka*.

1987     Renamed *Fairmay*.

1989     Became *Mahe Reefer*.

2001     Broken up in India.

201. *Mandowi* (2) (1965)
3,512 grt, 1,728 n., 111.82 x 16.03 x 6.50 metres.
Steel, single screw, 6 cyls, 2 SCSA, Sulzer oil engine. By Compagnie de Constructions Mécaniques,Nantes, France.
B. Société Anonyme des Ateliers et Chantiers de La Seine-Maritime, Le Trait, France.

10.12.1966     Launched as *Ivolina* for Nouvelle Compagnie Havraise Peninsulaire de Navigation, France.

1966     Delivered.

1969     Owner's name became Compagnie Havraise et Nantaise Peninsulaire (CHNP).

1972     Sold to Société Française de Transports Maritimes (SFTM).

1973     Purchased by Inanna Shipping Company Incorporated, Liberia; renamed *Inanna*.

1978     Sold to Monterone Maritime Corporation, Meridian Shipping Enterprises Limited, Greece, as managers; renamed *Couronne*.

1978     Purchased by Austasia Limited; renamed *Mandowi*.

1980     Sold to the Strategic Shipping Corporation, Enias Shipping Company SA, Greece, as managers; renamed *Aegean Island*.

1981        Owned by Seabow Maritime Incorporated, Panama; renamed *Meridian Paa*.
1982        Sold to Aquila Navigation Company, Petrozam Marine Enterprises SA, Panama, as managers; renamed *Aquila*.
18.6.1992    Arrived at Alang and broken up.

202. *Mandowi* (3) (1980)
18,236 grt, 9,428 n., 171.13 x 26.55 x 9.36 metres, yard no. 1345, IMO 7817103.
Steel, 6 cyls, Burmeister & Wain. By J. G. Kincaid & Company Limited, Glasgow.
B. Smith's Dock Company Limited, Middlesbrough.
25.6. 1980    Launched as *Willowbank* for the Bank Line Limited services from the United States Gulf ports to Australia and New Zealand.
1985        Owned by the Royal Bank Leasing Company Limited, London.
5.7.1988    Sold to Austasia Line; renamed *Mandowi* (3).
4.2.1989    Renamed *California Star* (4), managed by Blue Star Ship Management.
12.7.1990    To Pacific Coast Shipping Company (Bermuda) Limited, same managers.
20.7.1990    Transferred to Bermuda registry.
1993        To Star International Shipping Incorporated, Nassau.
1.1996      To Pacific International Lines (Private) Limited, Singapore; renamed *Sea Elegance*.
12.10.2003   Suffered a fire off South Africa; one crew member lost their life.
12.2003     Sold to Four Seasons Maritime Limited; renamed *Golden Gate*.
23.1.2009    Arrived at Alang and broken up.

203. *Mandama* (2) (1966)
10,983 grt, 6,126 n., 527.6 x 71.6 x 44.5 feet, IMO 6521410.
Steel, single screw, oil, Sulzer turbocharged type 8RD90, 17,600 BHP at 119 rpm, 20 knots. By G. Clark & North Eastern Marine Engineering Company Limited, Sunderland. Two decks and part of third deck.
B. Lithgows Limited, Port Glasgow.
27.8.1965    Launched as *Taupo* for the Federal Steam Navigation Company, the first British ship to have Hallen crane derricks, 1 x 30 ton, 2 x 25 tons and 4 x 10 tons. First Federal vessel to adopt the new grey-green hull colours.
3.1966      Delivered.
1971        Transferred to P&O Steam Navigation Company – General Cargo Division.
19.4.1973    Owned by P&O Line.
1979        Owned by the Strick Line, P&O as managers.
1980        Sold to Austasia Line; renamed *Mandama*.
28.5.1984    Anchored off Chittagong and broken up.

204. *Mandama* (3) – see *Columbia Star* (2).

205. *Mahsuri* (3) (1966)
10,975 grt, 6,151 n., 527.6 x 71.6 x 44.5 feet, IMO 6608878.
Steel, single screw, oil, Sulzer turbocharged type 8RD90, 17,600 BHP at 119 rpm, 20 knots. By G. Clark & North Eastern Marine Engineering Company Limited, Sunderland. Two decks and part of third deck.
B. Bartram & Sons Limited, Sunderland.
8.3.1966    Launched as *Tekoa* for the Federal Steam Navigation Company.
10.1966     Delivered to the New Zealand Shipping Company Limited.
1969        Transferred to the Federal Steam Navigation Company, New Zealand Shipping Company as managers.

*Taupo.*

| | |
|---|---|
| 1971 | Owned by P&O Line – General Cargo Division. |
| 19.4.1973 | Registered under Peninsular and Oriental Steam Navigation Company. |
| 1977 | Registered under the Strick Line Limited. |
| 7.1980 | Purchased by the Austasia Line; renamed *Mahsuri*. |
| 27.1.1984 | Arrived at Kaohsiung and broken up. |

206. *Mahsuri* (4) – see *Australia Star* (3).

207. *Mulbera* – see *California Star* (3).

## Crest Hill Shipping Limited

208. *Crest Hill* – see *Timaru Star* (2).

## Dunston Shipping Company Limited

209. *Westmorland* (1966)
8,231 grt, 4,468 n., 527.6 x 71 x 34.4 feet.
Steel, single screw, oil, 2 stroke single acting, Sulzer turbocharged, 8 cyls, 17,600 BHP at 119 rpm, 20 knots. By Sulzer, Winterthur, installed by builder. Two decks and part of third deck.
B. Bartram & Sons Limited, Sunderland.
9.9.1965    Launched as *Westmorland* by Mrs Beazley for the Federal Steam Navigation Company.

*Westmorland.*

2.1966       Delivered to the Federal Steam Navigation Company. She was built in the fastest time ever achieved by the builders for cargo liners. It was five months from the keel laying to her launching, and delivery was another three months. She was built as the second of a series of four, three of which were built at Bartram's, Sunderland, for the New Zealand Shipping Company. The class was specifically designed for the carriage of refrigerated cargo, general cargo and special liquid cargoes. Special features of *Westmorland* included a complete outfit of Hallen-type swinging derricks, which, in conjunction with hydraulically operated steel hatches, were designed to improve cargo handling efficiency.

21.2.1966    Maiden voyage.
10.1971      Registered under P&O Line – General Cargo Division.
19.4.1973    Owned by P&O Steam Navigation Company.
1978         Registered under the Strick Line Limited.
1980         Sold to Oceanic Shipping Sàrl, Rachid Fares Enterprises of Australia Pty Limited, Lebanon, as managers; renamed *Fares Reefer*.
1981         Sold to Dunston Shipping Company Limited, Blue Star Line Management as managers; renamed *Beacon Hill*.
6.3.1985     Arrived at Huangpu from Jebel Ali, where she had been laid up from 5.7.1984 to 14.2.1985, and broken up. ACTA Lines Limited.

210. *Dilkara* (1971)
13,151 grt, 6,875 n., 199.02 x 28.71 x 10.14 metres.
Steel, 18 cyls Pielstick engine.
B. Eriksbergs Mekaniska Verkstad AB, Gothenburg
10.1971      Delivered to ACTA Line Limited (Blue Star Line, Port Line and Ellerman Lines Limited).
29.12.1971   Arrived at Sydney from the United States on her maiden voyage.

2.12.1986    Arrived at Kaohsiung and broken up by Ankom Chin Tai Steel and Iron Limited.

# Starman Limited

211. *Starman/Starman America* (1973)
2,516 grt, 1,247 n., 93.63 x 15.27 x 4.13 metres, IMO 7330026.
Steel, twin screw, 12 cyls, 4 SCSA, oil. By W. H. Allen, Sons & Company Limited, Bedford.
B. Brooke Marine Limited, Lowestoft.
17.9.1973    Launched as *Starman* for Starman Limited, Cyprus.
5.1974       Delivered.
1975         Transferred to Starman Compania Naviera SA, Panama.
1977         Transferred to Starman Limited, London; renamed *Starman America*.
1982         Sold to Caribbean Heavy Lift NV, Netherlands, Antilles, Superpesa Industrial of Brazil.
1986         Sold to Petromac Offshore International Company Inc.; renamed *Star of America*.
24.12.1990   Laid up until 1.9.1991.
9.1.1992     Laid up until 13.7.1994.
1996         Operated by Supersesa Transportes Maritimos Ltda, Rio de Janeiro.
2002         Chartered to Kaiser Brewery as *Star of America*.
2009         Broken up.

212. *Starman Anglia* (1977)
2,776 grt, 1,013 n., 93.86 x 16.03 x 4.50 metres.
Steel, twin screw, 8 cyls, 4 SCSA, oil, single reduction geared, 3,520 BHP.

By Klockner-Humboldt-Deutz, Cologne, West Germany. Heavy lift ship with 300-tonne capacity.

B. Swan Hunter Shipbuilders Limited, Wallsend-on-Tyne.

| | |
|---|---|
| 21.7.1977 | Launched as *Starman Anglia* for Ship Mortgage Finance Company Limited, Blue Star Line Management as managers. |
| 1.1978 | Delivered. |
| 1984 | Owned by Investors in Industry PLC, managed by Blue Star Ship Management. |
| 1984 | Sold to Atlanska Plovidba, Yugoslavia; renamed *Lapad*. |
| 6.2006 | Broken up at Aliaga. |

### 213. *Starman Africa* (1977)

2,934 grt, 93.53 x 16.13 x 4.64 metres, IMO 7607649.

Steel, twin screw, 8 cyls, 4 SCSA, oil, single reduction geared, 3,520 BHP.

By Klockner-Humboldt-Deutz, Cologne, West Germany. Heavy lift ship with 300-tonne capacity.

| | |
|---|---|
| 2.3.1977 | Launched. |
| 6.1977 | Delivered. |
| 1984 | Blue Star line withdrew from the Starman consortium. Managed by Mammoet Shipping Company, Amsterdam. |
| 2.1986 | Sold and renamed *Storm*. |
| 1994 | Purchased by Finaval Offshore SRL, Italy, owned and operated by the Fagioli Group. |
| 2003 | Purchased by S. Marco Shipping, Venice. |
| 2005 | Sold to Ocean SRL, Trieste. |
| 5.2011 | Owned by S. Marco Shipping, Venice. |
| 2014 | Sold to Strategic Sea Lift Transporter, Abu Dhabi, UAE; renamed *African Storm*. |

## Associated Container Transportation Limited

### 214. *ACT 1* (1969)

24,821 grt, 14,771 n., 712.9 x 95.4x 34.6 feet

Two Stal Laval steam turbines by shipbuilder, 2 x Foster Wheeler ESD III boilers, reduction geared to single shaft. Refrigerated Container Ship 1,334 TEUs.

B. Bremer Vulkan Schiffbau & Maschinenfabrik, Vegesack, Germany

| | |
|---|---|
| 18.10.1968 | Launched. |
| 3.1969 | Delivered. |
| 9.2.1998 | Sold to P&O Nedlloyd; renamed *Discovery Bay*, St Vincent & Grenadines flag. |
| 9.1998 | Sold to Indian ship-breakers and broken up at Alang. |

### 215. *ACT 2* (1969)

24,821 grt, 14,771 n., 712.9 x 95.4 x 34.6 feet

Two Stal Laval steam turbines by shipbuilder, 2 x Foster Wheeler ESD III boilers, reduction geared to single shaft. 2 x Brotherhood Turbo-Alternators of 1360 kW at 12,000 rpm and 2 x Rolls-Royce D Range V8 of 440 kW at 1800 rpm. Refrigerated Modular Containership 1,334 TEUs

B. Bremer Vulkan Schiffbau & Maschinenfabrik, Vegesack, Germany

| | |
|---|---|
| 5.1969 | Delivered. |
| 9.2.1998 | Sold to P&O Nedlloyd; renamed *Moreton Bay*. |
| 5.1998 | Sold and broken up. |

### 216. *Australian Endeavour* (1969)

25,144 grt, 14,403 n., 712.9 x 95.4 x 34.6 metres, yard no. 941.

Steel, two steam turbines, 30,000 SHP, DR geared to one screw shaft by builder.

*Right: ACT 2.*

*Left: ACT3.* (Barry Eagles)

B. Bremer Vulkan Schiffbau & Maschinenfabrik, Vegesack, Germany.

16.4.1969     Launched for Blue Star Line Limited, Port Line Limited, Ellerman Lines Limited as *ACT 3*. Purchased by the Australian Coastal Shipping Commission during fitting out; renamed *Australian Endeavour*.

1974          Owners became the Australian Shipping Commission, Australian National Line Limited as managers.

10.6.1985     Arrived at Kaohsiung and broken up by the Ton Tai Steel Works Company Limited.

### 217. *ACT 3* (1971)

24,821 grt, 14,771 n., 712.9 x 95.4x 34.6 feet, IMO 7052909.

Two Stal Laval steam turbines by shipbuilder, 2 x Foster Wheeler ESD III boilers, reduction geared to single shaft. Refrigerated Container Ship 1,334 TEUs.

B. Bremer Vulkan Schiffbau & Maschinenfabrik, Vegesack, Germany.

1971          Delivered.

1987          Re-engined with the steam plant being removed and an IHI-Sulzer 8RTA68 (Yokohama) diesel engine, of 17,100 BHP, installed.

11.1991       Transferred to the Blue Star line; renamed *America Star* (2).

9.2.1998      Sold to P&O Nedlloyd, same name.

16.2.2003     Arrived at Shanghai and broken up.

### 218. *ACT 4* (1971)

24,821 grt, 14,771 n., 712.9 x 95.4 x 34.6 feet, IMO 7108162.

Two Stal Laval steam turbines by shipbuilder, 2 x Foster Wheeler ESD III boilers, reduction geared to single shaft. Refrigerated Container Ship 1,334 TEUs.

B. Bremer Vulkan Schiffbau & Maschinenfabrik, Vegesack, Germany.

11.5.1971     Launched.

9.1971        Delivered.

1.1992        Transferred to Blue Star Line; renamed *Melbourne Star*.

9.2.1998      Sold to P&O Nedlloyd, same name.

2003          Broken up at Shanghai.

### 219. *Australian Exporter* (1972)

23,486 grt, 15,326 n., 712.9 x 95.3 x 34.6 feet, yard no. 973.

Steel, two steam turbines, 32,000 SHP, DR geared to one screw shaft by builder.

B. Bremer Vulkan Schiffbau & Maschinenfabrik, Vegesack, Germany.

29.3.1972     Launched for the Australian Coastal Shipping Commission, Melbourne.

1974          Owners became the Australian Shipping Commission, Australian National Line.

1987          Withdrew from the ACTA/ANL services.

10.10.1990    Arrived at Hong Kong.

1.12.1990     Sold to the Red Riband Corporation, Monrovia, later sold to ship-breakers in India and renamed *Ali*.

1991          Sold to the Mediterranean Shipping Company SA, Geneva; renamed MSC *Mirella*.

9.1991        Owned by Raisun Investments Incorporated SA, Panama.

17.4.1999     Arrived at Alang and broken up.

### 220. *ACT 5* (1971)

24,821 grt, 14,771 n., 712.9 x 95.4 x 34.6 feet, IMO 7123382.

Two Stal Laval steam turbines by shipbuilder, 2 x Foster Wheeler ESD III boilers, reduction geared to single shaft. Refrigerated Container Ship 1,334 TEUs.

B. Bremer Vulkan Schiffbau & Maschinenfabrik, Vegesack, Germany.

3.11.1971     Launched.

| | |
|---|---|
| 2.1972 | Delivered. |
| 3.1987 | Re-engined by IHI, Yokohama, Japan. |
| 13.12.1991 | Transferred to the Blue Star Line; renamed *Sydney Star* (2). |
| 1998 | Sold to P&O Nedlloyd, same name. |
| 24.1.2003 | Arrived at Jiangyin and broken up. |

## 221. *ACT 6* (1972)

24,907 grt, 10,707 n., 712.9 x 95.4 x 34.6 feet, IMO 7226275.
Two Stal Laval steam turbines by shipbuilder, 2 x Foster Wheeler ESD III boilers, reduction geared to single shaft. Refrigerated Container Ship 1,334 TEUs.
B. Bremer Vulkan Schiffbau & Maschinenfabrik, Vegesack, Germany.

| | |
|---|---|
| 5.9.1972 | Launched. |
| 12.1972 | Delivered. |
| 1987 | Re-engined as a motorship by IHI, Yokohama, Japan. |
| 10.10.1991 | Transferred to the Blue Star Line; renamed *Queensland Star*. |
| 1998 | Owned by Blue Star, managed by P&O Nedlloyd. |
| 10.2.2003 | Arrived at Shanghai and broken up. |

## 222. *Remuera* (1973)

42,007 grt, 24,806 n., 826.10 x 105.5 x 36.2 feet, yard no. 40.
Four steam turbines, 48,660 SHP, DR geared to 2 screws by English Electric AEI, Manchester.
B. Swan Hunter Shipbuilders Limited, Walker.

| | |
|---|---|
| 12.6.1972 | Launched for the P&O Steam Navigation Company Limited. |
| 1973 | Chartered to Associated Container Transport. |
| 1977 | Renamed *Remuera Bay* for P&O Containers Limited. |

| | |
|---|---|
| 1983 | Purchased by Headwest Limited, and later went to Lombard Charter Hire Limited. |
| 1983 | Re-engined. |
| 1985 | Sold to Overseas Containers Limited. |
| 1987 | Owned by P&O Containers Limited. |
| 1991 | Sold to Abbey National March Leasing Limited. |
| 12.1993 | Renamed *Berlin Express*. |
| 1997 | Sold to P&O Nedlloyd Limited. |
| 3.2002 | Renamed *Press*. |
| 3.6.2002 | Left Hong Kong for Shanghai and broken up by Jiangyin Shipbreaking Company. |

## 223. *Australian Venture* (1977)

43,878 grt, 32,011 n., 248.60 x 32.24 x 21.62, yard no. 1004.
Steel, two 2SA 8 cyls, 53,360 BHP M. A. N. oil engine by builder.
B. Bremer Vulkan Schiffbau & Maschinenfabrik, Vegesack, Germany.

| | |
|---|---|
| 22.10.1976 | Launched for the Australian Shipping Commission (Australian National Line). |
| 28.2.1977 | Delivered. |
| 1985 | Owned by Lombard Leasing Company and HBZ Finance AG, Melbourne. |
| 1987 | Taken out of ACT service. |
| 6.1996 | Purchased by Lavicer Investment Corporation, Panama (Mediterranean Shipping Company SA, Geneva as managers); renamed *MSC Nuria*. |
| 11.2006 | Renamed *Ria*. |
| 21.12.2006 | Arrived at Chittagong and broken up. |

## 224. *ACT 7* (1977)

43,992 grt, 31,962 n., 248.60 x 32.31 x 12.027 metres, IMO 7416923.

*Left: Sydney Star* (2).

*Right: ACT 6.* (Barry Eagles)

Two 8-cyl SCSA M.A.N. oil engine by shipbuilder. Refrigerated Cellular Containership 2,485 TEUs.
B. Bremer Vulkan Schiffbau & Maschinenfabrik, Vegesack, Germany.

| | |
|---|---|
| 22.3.1977 | Launched. |
| 6.1977 | Delivered. |
| 29.11.1991 | Renamed *Pallister Bay*. |
| 24.4.2002 | Sailed from New Zealand for Lisbon. |
| 8.2002 | Arrived at China and broken up. |

### 225. *ACT 8* (1978)

52,055 grt, 21,263 n., 258.55 x 32.26 x 20.65 metres, yard no. 1401.
Steel, two 8-cyl 2SA 51,360 BHP M. A. N. oil engines by Masch Augsburg, Nuremberg.
B. A. G. Weser, Bremen, West Germany.

| | |
|---|---|
| 16.9.1977 | Launched as *City of Durban* for Ellerman Lines Limited and the Charente Steamship Company Limited, Ellerman Lines Limited as managers. |
| 2.6.1978 | Delivered. |
| 1983 | Renamed *Portland Bay*. |
| 1984 | Renamed *City of Durban*. |
| 1985 | Renamed *ACT 8*. |
| 1990 | Renamed *City of Durban*. |
| 1991 | Ellerman Lines purchased by P&O Containers Limited. |
| 7.1996 | Renamed *Pegasus Bay*. |
| 1997 | Owned by P&O Nedlloyd Limited and the Charente Steamship Company Limited. |
| 1999 | Transferred to P&O Nedlloyd Limited. |
| 14.11.2002 | Arrived at Jiangyin and broken up. |

### 226. *ACT 9* (1984)

9,764 grt, 5,509 n., 148.55 x 21.71 x 11.26 metres, yard no. 946, IMO 8403595
Steel, two 4SA 8 cyls, 9,514 BHP oil engine by Kloeckner Humboldt Deutz, Voerde.
B. J. J. Sietas KG Schiffswerft GmbH & Company, Hamburg.

| | |
|---|---|
| 5.11.1984 | Launched as *Hannoverland* for Bugsier, Reederei und Bergungs GmbH, Hamburg. |
| 9.12.1984 | Delivered. |
| 1985 | Renamed *Lloyd Londres*. |
| 1986 | *Hannoverland* and later *ACT 9*. |
| 1990 | *Columbus Oregon*. |
| 1991 | *Hannoverland*. |
| 2.1991 | *Sea Beach*. |
| 3.1993 | *Hannoverland*. |
| 8.1994 | *Maersk La Plata*. |
| 1997 | Purchased by Reederei 'Christine Eberhardt' GmbH & Company, Carl F. Peters & Company, Hamburg, as managers; renamed *Christine Eberhardt*, later *GCM de Lesseps*. |
| 4.1998 | Renamed *Melbridge Christine*. |
| 1999 | *Christine Eberhardt*, later *Horizon*. |
| 1.2000 | *Christine Eberhardt*. |
| 9.2000 | *Coral Christine*. |
| 5.2001 | *MSC Christine*. |
| 11.2001 | *Christine Eberhardt*. |
| 12.2003 | *P&O Nedlloyd Christine*. |
| 11.2004 | Sold to Feeder Associate Systems Sàrl, Malta, CMA CGM as managers; renamed *CMA CGM North Africa 2*. |
| 10.2007 | Purchased by CMA CGM, France. |
| 12.2009 | Sold to Alessia Navigation Limited, Transyug Shipping Company as managers; renamed *Alessia*. |

*Pegasus Bay.*

BLUE STAR LINE: FLEET LIST & HISTORY   151

227. *ACT 10* (1986)

8,106 grt, 4,088 n., 132.7 x 22.7 x 10.8 metres, yard no. 200, IMO 8516603.

Steel, 7 cyls, 4SA, 4,622 BHP M. A. N. oil engine by M. A. N. B&W Diesel GmbH, Augsburg.

B. Martin Jansen GmbH & Company KG, Schiffsw U. Masch, Leer.

16.4.1986       Launched as *Maria Sibum* for Reederei Hermann Sibum GmbH & Company.

8.10.1986       Delivered as *ACT 10*.

1988            Renamed *Karaman*.

5.1993          *Independent Concept*.

12.1993         *Kent Trader*.

12.1997         *Maria Sibum*.

6.2000          Sold to Nimmrich & Prahn Reed GmbH & Company, renamed *APL Belem*.

6.2001          Renamed *Maria*, same owners.

4.2002          *Tiger Sun*, same owners, later *Maria*, when transferred to Cirksena Shipping Company Limited, Antigua & Barbuda, Nimmrich & Prahn Reed GmbH & Company as managers.

12.2004         Purchased by Compania Naviera Shirley SA, MSC Ship Management HK Limited, Hong Kong, as managers; renamed *MSC Shirley*.

28.8.2012       Arrived at Alang and broken up by Bansal Infracon Limited.


228. *ACT 10* (2) – see *Columbia Star* (3).


229. *ACT 11* (1986)

8,641 grt, 4,079 n., 133.38 x 21.71 x 11.31 metres, yard no. 979, IMO 8603559.
Steel, 9 cyls, 4SA, 4,044 BHP M. A. N. oil engine by M. A. N. B&W Diesel GmbH, Augsburg.

B. J. J. Sietas KG Schiffswerft GmbH & Company, Hamburg.

28.9.1986       Launched as *Jan Ritscher* for Partenreederims 'Jan Ritscher' GmbH & Company, Hamburg. Delivered as *ACT 11*.

1988            Renamed *Jan Ritscher*, later *Independent Pursuit*.

4.1993          *Jan Ritscher*.

4.1996          Sold to Mild Lin Shipping Corporation, Panama, Moon Keung Shipping & Transportation Limited, Hong Kong, as managers; renamed *Mild Lin*.

1997            Sunscot & Company Limited, Hong Kong, as managers.

2006            Shanghai Jinjiang Shipping Corporation as managers.

31.12.2009      Arrived in China and broken up.


230. *ACT 12* – see *Saxon Star* (3).


231. *Tarihiko* (1984)

2,169 grt, 650 n., 81.11 x 13.81 x 6.91 metres, yard no. 559, IMO 8203232.

Steel, two 6-cyl 4SA, 2,692 BHP oil engines by Krupp Mak Maschinenbau GmbH, Kiel.

B. Ferguson Ailsa Limited, Troon.

29.3.1983       Launched for Ship Leasing (1982) Limited, Wellington, The Shipping Corporation of New Zealand Limited, Wellington, as managers.

24.2.1984       Delivered.

1989            Managed by Blueport ACT (NZ) Limited, Wellington, later by New Zealand Line Limited.

1991            Managed by P&O Containers Limited, Wellington.

7.1999          Purchased by Kil Shipping Pte Limited, Singapore; renamed *Kilgas Centurion*.

15.2.2001       Aground on Horsey Beach in thick fog.

16.2.2001       Re-floated, towed to Lowestoft.

17.2.2001      Left Lowestoft.

3.2001      Tschudi & Eitzen A/S Lysaker as managers; renamed *Sigas Centurion*.

12.2002      Purchased by Sigas Singapore, Camillo Eitzen & Company A/S as managers.

3.2006      Eitzen Gas A/S, Copenhagen, as managers.

3.2010      Sold to Starway Management Property, Anship LLC, Moscow, as managers; renamed *Angas*.

## 232. *New Zealand Pacific* (1978)

43,704 grt, 21,228 n., 248.60 x 32.31 x 12.02 metres, yard no. 1008.
Steel, two 8 cyls, 2SA, 53,279 BHP M. A. N. oil engines by builder.
B. Bremer Vulkan Schiffbau & Maschinenfabrik, Vegesack, Germany.

23.5.1978      Launched for The Shipping Corporation of New Zealand, Wellington.

1989      Sold to Fuday Limited, Hong Kong, Denholm Ship Management Limited as managers; renamed *Tui*.

4.1989      Purchased by Blue Star Line Limited, Port Line Limited and Ellerman Lines Limited.

9.1989      Transferred to Associated Container Transportation (Aust) Limited; renamed *New Zealand Pacific*.

1991      Owned by P&O Containers Limited, P&O Limited as managers.

1996      Sold to Capital Bank Leasing Limited, P&O Nedlloyd Limited as managers.

1998      Purchased by P&O Nedlloyd Limited.

11.11.2002      Arrived at Jiangyin and broken up.

## 233. *New Zealand Mariner* (1977)

11,217 grt, 4,908 n., 144.86 x 22.01 x 11.03 metres, yard no. 101.

Steel, 12 cyls, 4SA, 9,300 BHP M. A. N. oil engine SR geared to screw shaft by Maschinenbau Augsburg.
B. Howaldtswerke Deutsche Werft AG, Hamburg.

1.4.1977      Launched as *Ulanga* for Willner Oltanker GmbH & Cosima Reederei KG, Hamburg, Poseidon Schifffahrt GmbH as managers.

30.6.1977      Entered service as *Gulf Clipper*.

1978      Sold to K. G. Nordest Container Linien GmbH, Hamburg; renamed *Ulanga*, Transocean Liners Reederei GmbH, Hamburg, as managers.

1985      Purchased by The Shipping Corporation of New Zealand, Wellington; renamed *New Zealand Mariner*.

4.1989      Sold to the Blue Star Line Limited, Port Line Limited, Ellerman Lines Limited.

9.1989      Owned by NWS9 Limited, Chester, Associated Container Transportation (Aust.) Limited as managers.

1.1991      Renamed *Marin*.

1991      Sold to P&O Containers limited, P&O Limited as managers.

1996      Owned by Capital Bank Leasing Limited, P&O Nedlloyd Limited as managers.

1998      Sold to P&O Nedlloyd Limited.

28.2.2002      Arrived at China and broken up.

# Ships Managed on Behalf of the Ministry of War Transport

## 234. *Empire Glade* (1941)

7,006 grt, 4,209 n., 418 x 57.4 x 34.2 feet.
Steel, single screw, 4 cyls, 2 SCSA, Doxford oil engine by builder.
B. Barclay Curle & Company Limited, Glasgow.

12.6.1941    Launched for the Ministry of War Transport, Blue Star Line as managers.

9.1941    Delivered.

28.11.1942    Attacked by U-67 in the North Atlantic on a voyage from Alexandria to Charleston, New York and the United Kingdom. One crew member lost his life.

7.12.1942    Arrived at Charleston for repairs to be completed.

1943    G. Heyn & Sons Limited, Belfast, as managers.

11.1945    Sold to the Ulster Steam Ship Company Limited, G. Heyn & Sons Limited as managers; renamed *Inishowen Head*.

1962    Sold to Platsani Ltda, SA, Greece; renamed *Maria N.*

10.7.1972    Arrived at Istanbul and broken up by Yeni Dogu Ticaret Limited.

235. *Empire Galahad* – see *Celtic Star* (2).

236. *Empire Might* (1942)

9,209 grt, 4,922 n., 463.8 x 63 x 29.9 feet.

Steel, single screw, 6 cyls. By J. G. Kincaid & Company Limited, Greenock.

B. Greenock Dockyard Company Limited, Greenock.

17.4.1942    Launched for the Ministry of War Transport, Blue Star Line as managers, as *Empire Might*.

8.1942    Delivered.

17.4.1946    Sold to the Clan Line, Cayzer Irvine & Company Limited as managers; renamed *Clan Macrae*.

1959    Transferred to Bullard, King & Company Limited, London; renamed *Umgeni*.

1960    Sold to Springbok Shipping Company Limited, South Africa; renamed *Gemsbok*.

1961    Renamed *South African Financier*.

10.2.1962    Arrived at Spanish ship-breakers under the name of *Santa Maria de Ordaz*, and broken up.

237. *Empire Highway* – see *Ionic Star* (2).

238. *Empire Lakeland* (1942)

7,015 grt, 4,757 n., 430.9 x 56.2 x 35.2 feet.

Steel, single screw, 3 cyls. By builder.

B. J Redhead & Sons Limited, South Shields.

14.9.1942    Launched as *Empire Lakeland* for the Ministry of War Transport, Blue Star Line as managers,

11.1942    Delivered.

23.2.1943    Sailed from New York to Glasgow in Convoy SC 121.

8.3.1943    Torpedoed by U-190 in the North Atlantic.

11.3.1943    Reported to have sunk. Her crew of fifty-seven and eight gunners were lost.

239. *Empire Strength* – see (2).

240. *Empire Camp* (1943)

7,052 grt, 4,760 n., 431 x 56.3 x 35.2 feet.

Steel, single screw, 3 cyls. By North Eastern Marine Engineering Company Limited, Sunderland.

B. Short Brothers Limited, Sunderland.

17.6.1943    Launched as *Empire Camp* for the Ministry of War Transport, Blue Star Line as managers.

10.1943    Delivered.

28.3.1946    Sold to the Cunard Steamship Company Limited; renamed *Valacia*.

1951        Purchased by the Bristol City Line, Charles Hill and Sons Limited; renamed *New York City*.

1955        Sold to S. S. Induna Company Limited, Maclay and McIntyre Limited, Glasgow, as managers; renamed *Loch Morar*.

1959        Owned by Lutfi Yelkenci Eviatiari Donatma Istiraki, Turkey; renamed *Yelkenci*.

20.2.1971    Arrived at Istanbul and broken up.

### 241. *Empire Anvil* (1944)

7,177 grt, 4,823 n., 396.5 x 60.1 x 35 feet.

Steel, single screw, two steam turbines, double reduction geared to one screw shaft. By Joshua Hendy Iron Works, Sunnyvale, California.

B. Consolidated Steel Corporation Limited, Wilmington, California.

14.10.1943    Launched as *Cape Argos* for the United States War Shipping Administration.

1.1944      Delivered as *Empire Anvil*, chartered to the Ministry of War Transport, Blue Star Line as managers.

1.11.1944    Transferred to the Royal Navy as a Landing Ship Infantry, renamed *Rocksand*.

21.6.1946    Returned to the Ministry of Transport, Furness Withy & Company Limited as managers; renamed *Empire Anvil*.

26.8.1947    Returned to the United States Maritime Commission.

1948        Renamed *Cape Argos*.

1948        Reported that she was to be sold to the Republic of China and renamed *Hai Ya*. However, the sale did not materialise, and she reverted to *Empire Anvil*.

1960        Sold to China Merchants Steam Navigation Company Limited, Taiwan; renamed *Hai Ya*.

1973        Purchased by the Yangming Marine Transport Corporation, Taiwan; renamed *Fu Ming*.

1974        Broken up at Taiwan.

### 242. *Empire Javelin* (1944)

7,177 grt, 4,823 n., 396.5 x 60.1 x 35 feet.

Steel, single screw, two steam turbines, double reduction geared to one screw shaft. By Westinghouse Electric and Manufacturing Company Limited, Essington, Pennsylvania.

B. Consolidated Steel Corporation Limited, Wilmington, California.

25.10.1943    Launched as *Cape Lobos* for the United States War Shipping Administration.

1.1944      Delivered as *Empire Javelin*, chartered to the Ministry of War Transport, Blue Star Line as managers.

28.12.1944    On a voyage from the Solent to Le Havre, carrying 1,448 American troops and 115 crew and gunners, she was torpedoed and sunk by U-772, 40 miles south of St Catherine's Point, Isle of Wight. Seven of her crew lost their lives. The ship sank three hours after she was torpedoed.

### 243. *Samtay* (1944)

7,219 grt, 4,380 n., 422.8 x 57 x 34.8 feet.

Steel, single screw, 3 cyls. By General Machinery Corporation Limited, Hamilton, Ohio.

B. Bethlehem-Fairfield Shipyard Incorporated, Baltimore, Maryland.

10.1.1944    Launched as *Samtay* for the United States War Shipping Administration, chartered to the Ministry of War Transport, Blue Star Line as managers.

1947        Sold to the Ropner Shipping Company Limited; renamed *Rudby*.

1952        Purchased by Transmarina Compania Naviera SA, Panama; renamed *Thekla*.

1954         Owned by Esperanza Compania Naviera SA, Panama; renamed *Adamas*.

10.9.1968      Arrived at Sakaide, Japan, and broken up by the Miyaji Salvage Company.

244. *Samannan* – see *Oregon Star* (2).

245. *Saminver* (1944)

7,210 grt, 4,395 n., 423.1 x 57.1 x 34.8 feet.

Steel single screw, 3 cyls. By Ellicott Machinery Corporation Limited, Baltimore, Maryland.

B. Bethlehem-Fairfield Shipyard Incorporated, Baltimore, Maryland.

8.2.1944      Launched as *Saminver* for the United States War Shipping Administration, chartered to the Ministry of War Transport, Blue Star Line as managers.

2.1944        Delivered.

1948          Returned to the United States Maritime Commission.

26.12.1963    Sold to the Southern Scrap Material Company Limited.

27.3.1964     Arrived at New Orleans and broken up.

246. *Empire Cromer* – see *Corrientes*.

247. *Empire Talisman* – see *Tacoma Star* (2).

248. *Empire Wisdom* – see *Royal Star* (2).

249. *Empire Castle* – see *Gothic Star* (2).

250. *Empire Falkland* (1945)

7,006 grt, 4,030 n., 432.9 x 56.3 x 34.3 feet.

Steel, single screw, 6 cyls, 4 SCSA Burmeister & Wain oil engine. By Harland & Wolff Limited, Belfast.

B. Harland & Wolff Limited, Belfast.

2.9.1944      Launched as *Empire Falkland* for the Ministry of War Transport, Blue Star Line as managers.

2.1945        Delivered.

15.5.1946     Sold to the Scottish Shire Line Limited, Turnbull Martin & Company Limited as managers; renamed *Stirlingshire*.

1960          Owned by the Houston Line Limited, Cayzer Irvine & Company Limited, Glasgow, as managers.

1963          Owned by Huntley, Cook and Company Limited, Huntley Cook South Africa Pty Limited, South Africa.

2.9.1966      Arrived at Ghent and broken up by Van Heyghen Frères Limited.

## Crusader Shipping Company (Jointly Owned by the Blue Star Line, New Zealand Shipping Company, Port Line and Shaw, Savill & Albion Line)

251. *Crusader* (1957)

3,461 grt, 1,237 n., 406.1 x 53.61 x 20.8 feet.

B. Valmet O/Y, Helsinki.

1957          Laid down as *Edith Thorden* for Thorden Lines.

1957          Delivered as *Crusader* for Crusader Shipping Limited.

1972          Sold to Everett Orient Line, Monrovia; renamed *Rentoneverett*.

19.10.1983    Arrived Kaohsiung and broken up.

**252. *Saracen* (1958)**
3,441 grt, 1,237 n., 406.1 x 53.61 x 20.8 feet, IMO 5313919.
B. Valmet O/Y, Helsinki.

| | |
|---|---|
| 1958 | Delivered to Crusader Shipping Company. |
| 1971 | Sold to Shaw, Savill & Albion Line; renamed *Langstone*. |
| 1975 | Sold to Petries Cia Nav. SA, Piraeus; renamed *Dimitrios K.* |
| 14.3.1981 | Left Cochin and broken up at Bombay. |

**253. *Knight Templar* (1948)**
3,971grt.
B. Eriksbergs, Gothenburg.

| | |
|---|---|
| 1948 | Delivered as *Arctic Ocean* to Ocean-kompaniet A/S. |
| 1963 | Sold to Crusader Shipping Limited; renamed *Knight Templar*. |
| 1968 | Owned by Litton & Company, Manila; renamed *Mindanao Sea*. |
| 26.1.1973 | Suffered a serious fire at Bislig and declared a constructive total loss. |
| 1973 | Broken up at Cebu. |

## Vessels Time-Chartered to the Crusader Shipping Company Limited

**254. *Norman* (1) (1959)**
5,957 grt, 3,245 n., 422.1 x 55.9 x 33.6 feet, yard no. 428.
Steel, 4 cyls, 2SCSA, 4,450 BHP Doxford oil engine by builder.
B. Taikoo Dockyard & Engineering Company Limited, Hong Kong.

| | |
|---|---|
| 13.10.1958 | Launched as *Kwangtung* for the China Navigation Company Limited, J. Swire & Sons Limited as managers. |

| | |
|---|---|
| 10.3.1965 | Chartered to the Crusader Shipping Company Limited; renamed *Norman* (1). |
| 30.10.1966 | Charter completed, reverted to *Kwangtung*. |
| 1977 | Operated by Taikoo Navigation Company Limited, J. Swire & Sons Limited as managers. |
| 1979 | Sold to Gordon Navigation Company SA, Johnson Company (Asia) Limited, Hong Kong as managers; renamed *California*. |
| 1983 | Operated by Juniper Shipping Company SA, Panama; renamed *Wayful*. |
| 1984/85 | Broken up at Shanghai. |

**255. *Norman* (2) (1959)**
5,957 grt, 3,245 n., 422.1 x 55.9 x 33.6 feet, yard no. 435.
Steel, 4 cyls, 2SCSA 4,450 BHP Doxford oil engine by builder.
B. Taikoo Dockyard & Engineering Company Limited, Hong Kong.

| | |
|---|---|
| 5.1.1959 | Launched as *Kweichow* for the China Navigation Company Limited, J. Swire & Sons Limited as managers. |
| 4.11.1966 | Chartered to the Crusader Shipping Company Limited; renamed *Norman* (2). |
| 20.5.1968 | Charter completed, reverted to *Kweichow*. |
| 1974 | Sold to Compania de Navegacion 'Orient Victory' SA, Phoenix Enterprises Company Limited as managers; renamed *Orient Victory*. |
| 1977 | Operated by Phoenix Enterprises SA, Panama; renamed *Fortune Victory*. |
| 1982 | Transferred to Compania de Navegacion 'Orient Victory' SA, Panama. |
| 1984 | Broken up at Shanghai. |

# FLEETLIST 2000–2001

In 2000–01, Star Reefers' parent company was Rudolf A. Oetker and the Vestey Group. The company was sold to Swan Reefers ASA.
   The fleet consisted of the following ships:

| Ship | Year | dwt | grt | Dimensions | Speed |
|---|---|---|---|---|---|
| *Afric Star* | 1975 | 11,093 dwt | 10,012 grt | 155.8 x 21.3 x 9.2 | 18 k |
| *Almeda Star* | 1976 | 11,093 dwt | 10,012 grt | 155.8 x 21.3 x 9.2 | 18 k |
| *Auckland Star* | 1985 | 11,434 dwt | 10,291 grt | 151 x 22 x 8.7 | 18 k |
| *Avelona Star* | 1975 | 11,093 dwt | 10,012 grt | 155.8 x 21.3 x 9.2 | 18 k |
| *Avila Star* | 1976 | 11,093 dwt | 10,012 grt | 155.8 x 21.3 x 9.2 | 18 k |
| *Canterbury Star* | 1986 | 11,434 dwt | 10,291 grt | 150.7 x 22 x 8.7 | 18 k |
| *Cap Triunfo* | 1988 | 9,734 dwt | 8,487 grt | 141 x 20.6 x 8.5 | 18 k |
| *Colombian Star* | 1998 | 10,350 dwt | 11,733 grt | 154 x 24 x 9 | 21.4 k |
| *Cote d'Ivoirian Star* | 1998 | 10,350 dwt | 11,733 grt | 154 x 24 x 9.1 | 21 k |
| *English Star* | 1986 | 11,434 dwt | 10,291 grt | 150.7 x 22 x 8.7 | 18 k |
| *French Bay* | 1992 | 10,621 dwt | 10,381 grt | 150 x 22.5 x 9.1 | 18 k |
| *Hornsea* | 1997 | 10,362 dwt | 11,435 grt | 154 x 24 x 9 | 20.3 k |
| *Hornwind* | 1998 | 10,350 dwt | 11,435 grt | 154 x 24 x 9 | 20.5 k |
| *Nauru* | 1993 | 10,621 dwt | 10,374 grt | 150 x 22.5 x 9.1 | 18 k |
| *Norman Star* | 1979 | 9,984 dwt | 10,153 grt | 168 x 22.6 x 8.7 | 18 k |
| *Roman Bay* | 1992 | 10,603 dwt | 10,381 grt | 150 x 22.5 x 9.1 | 18 k |
| *Saxon Star* | 1979 | 9,996 dwt | 10,153 grt | 168 x 22.6 x 8.7 | 18 k |
| *Scottish Star* | 1985 | 11,434 dwt | 10,291 grt | 151 x 22 x 8.7 | 18 k |
| *Snowcape* | 1973 | 15,710 dwt | 14,512 grt | 173.3 x 24.6 x 10.3 | 18 k |
| *Snowdelta* | 1972 | 15,710 dwt | 14,512 grt | 173.3 x 24.6 x 10.3 | 18 k |
| *Trojan Star* | 1984 | 11,756 dwt | 9,417 grt | 146.1 x 21.5 x 9.5 | 18 k |
| *Tudor Star* | 1983 | 11,806 dwt | 9,417 grt | 146.1 x 21.5 x 9.5 | 18 k |

*Canterbury Star* (1).

*Colombian Star.* (Chris Brooks/ShipFoto)

# ACKNOWLEDGEMENTS AND BIBLIOGRAPHY

Cary, Alan L., *Liners of the Ocean Highway* (Sampson, Low, Marston & Co., 1938).

Gibbs, Commander C. R. Vernon, Royal Navy, *British Passenger Liners of the Five Oceans* (Putnam, 1963).

Haws, Duncan, *Merchant Fleets 14: Blue Star Line* (TCL Publications, 1988).

Haws, Duncan, *Merchant Fleets 34: Lamport & Holt and Booth* (TCL Publications, 1998).

Jordan, Roger, *The World's Merchant Fleets 1939 – The Particulars and Wartime Fates of 6,000 Ships* (Chatham, 1999).

Kaplan, Philip and Jack Currie, *Convoy: Merchant Sailors at War 1939–45* (Aurum, 1998).

*Marine News* (World Ship Society).

*Sea Breezes.*

*Shipping & Transport.*

*Shipping Today & Yesterday.*

Taffrail (Captain Taprell Dorling, DSO, FRHistS, Royal Navy), *Blue Star Line: A Record of Service 1939–45* (Blue Star, 1948).

*The Journal of Commerce.*

The Komrowski Shipping Group.

*The Motor Ship.*

*The Syren & Shipping Illustrated.*

Watson, Milton H., *Disasters at Sea* (Harpercollins, 1987).

All images are by the author or from his collection, unless otherwise credited.